The Texas Experience

FRIENDSHIP & FOOD
TEXAS STYLE

Introduction by Frank X. Tolbert

A Cookbook from The Richardson Woman's Club

Proceeds from the sale of **THE TEXAS EXPERIENCE** *will be used for community service projects and philanthropies sponsored by the Richardson Woman's Club, Inc.*

*Our sincere appreciation and
a round of applause to those who helped with this
"Special Edition" of* **THE TEXAS EXPERIENCE.**

*George Palacios and
The Grand Kempinski Hotel
The Martinez Cafe
McDonalds
Pop Corn Papa
Memories Antique Mall*

Creative Writer
Jackie Johnson

Graphics
Janet Harvey

Editor
Ivanette Dennis

ISBN 0-9609416-0-6
Richardson Woman's Club, Inc.
Library of Congress Catalog Card Number 82-83061

First Printing, November 1982, 10,000 copies
Second Printing, June 1983, 10,000 copies
Third Printing, July 1984, 10,000 copies
Fourth Printing, November 1985, 10,000 copies
Fifth Printing, November 1986, 10,000 copies
Sixth Printing, February 1989, 10,000 copies
Seventh Printing, November 1990, 20,000 copies
Eighth Printing*, November 1993, 20,000 copies

(***Southern Living**® **Hall of Fame** edition)

Thank You!

COOKBOOK COMMITTEE

CHAIRMAN
Paula Harkey

SECRETARY
Virginia Thompson

TREASURER
Gayle Wisman

COOKBOOK BOOSTERS
Norman Bishop

MARKETING
Jean Beler
Jean Bragg
Carolyn Georges
Nancy Hicks
Peggy Jones
Bonita Kennedy
Judy Mays
Joanne Richardson
Sue Smith
Lyn Tragesser

PAST CHAIRMEN
Linda Juba
Betty Stripling
Pat Reinhart
Zoe Brewer
Pat Cutler
Martha Crowley
Danna Almon
Doris Abernathy
Courtenay Tanner

ORIGINAL COMMITTEE
Chairman, Linda Juba; Co-Chairman, Ivanette Dennis; Tura Bethune, Martha Crowley, Martha Clem, Danna Almon, Novella Bailey, Dot McCalpin, Lois Williams, Eileen MacWithey, Pat Horton, Pattie Baily, Jean Zinzer, Judy West, Shirley Rind, Mary Lassiter, Pat Brott, Peggy Jones, Pat Woodard, Pat Williams, Betty Stripling, N.J. Metcalf, Carol Garrigues, Yvonne Prevo, Cathy Hill, Charlotte Clark, Mary Drake, Marge Alesh, Cindy Levi, Ruth Quance, and Hat Madsen.

T is to Tolbert as T is to Texas for he probably knew more about our state than any other person. He'd traveled and written about it all and was a fifth generation Texan. In 1967 he co-founded the Annual World Championship Chili Cook-off at Terlingua and the rest is history. He was the author of **A Bowl of Red**, **"Natural History of Chili Con Carne"**, **The Day of San Jacinto**, **Tolbert's Texas**, and countless articles.

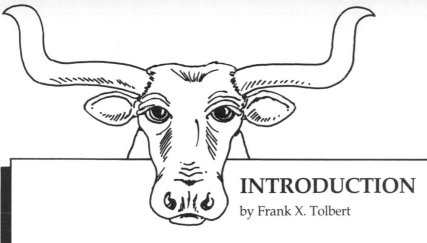

INTRODUCTION
by Frank X. Tolbert

The girls of the Richardson Woman's Club gave me a preview of the recipes in this wonderful collection. And I was inspired to go to the kitchens at Tolbert's on McKinney and try several of them, such as the formula for "avocado margarita appetizer."

You peel the avocados, cut them in half, remove the seed. You douse them generously with lime juice and sprinkle a little salt and pepper. Then you fill the twin cavities with tequila and let it soak for a spell before savoring.

The girls have imagination And many of the recipes, such as the avocado margarita appetizer, will give your taste buds fresh and pleasant memories.

The Richardson Woman's Club comes out stoutly for Texas cooking.

Now old time Texas cooking is rated poorly by some newcomers to Dallas, especially the hordes from the eastern reaches of the U.S. They speak as if the many French chefs who have migrated to the big Texas cities arrived just in time.

Truth is that French cuisine was introduced in Dallas in 1885 when the La Reunion colonists from France settled on bluffs over the west fork of the Trinity River and a few miles west of the village of Dallas.

Just for another example, there was so-called continental cooking in the village of Pampa, near my Grandfather Tolbert's ranch in the Texas Panhandle in the early 1900's. (Some of the biggest ranches in the Panhandle were owned by British noblemen in the old days but I'm glad they didn't force English cooking on us. In fact, they soon became converts to chuck wagon style fare.)

My father, who went to the University of Texas in the early 1900's, said there was never a better restaurant than the one in San Antonio owned by two chefs from France, Paul Bergeron and John Loustanau. But they had the good sense to pick up some Texas culinary accents.

Some Texas writers have bad-mouthed Texas food – after they moved into Yankee land. For example, after the Texas novelist, George Sessions Perry, moved to Connecticut, he claimed that the only tasty entrée on most Texas café menus referred to the "pot of chili con carne simmering on the back of the stove."

Paul Bergeron of San Antonio said that Texas offered more materials to inspire a cook (outside of truffles) than did his native France. A native of Nova Scotia, James Pearson Newcomb, complained that there was too much inexpensive food in 1874 Texas. Newcomb was then editor of the Republican Party-financed State Journal in Austin. And he wrote in January, 1874:

"Cheap land and great herds of cattle make the living easier in Texas while citizens in the northern U.S. suffer from the financial panic of 1873. Foodstuffs are so inexpensive here that idleness is encouraged.

"Our gardens are running over with roses and vegetables in January. Cabbages and collards bloom. Beans are bursting. Even red-nosed loafers bloom in the open air on the corners of Commerce and Main Plaza rather than in the back rooms of saloons as they would in cities of the north at this time of the year.

"Fishing is too easy in the pure streams. Good cuts of beef are 4¢ a pound, and wild game such as prairie chicken, quail, ducks, geese, dove, cottontail rabbit, pronghorn antelope and venison are sold in the markets at about the same price as beef. It's even easier to be well-fed with little effort on the Texas seacoasts. Our correspondent from the middle coast reports that the waters of Matagorda Bay cover one vast oyster bed. All you have to do is wade out into the bay with a bottle of pepper sauce. And oysters by the bushels can be harvested by waders."

Foodstuffs continued to be inexpensive as long as Texas was sparsely settled. At Paul Bergeron's and John Loustanau's restaurant in San Antonio in the second decade of this century you could have dinner for $2.00 and sherry went with game, port with the nuts, liquers with the cigars and coffee.

Now, sadly, with thousands of new settlers coming into our borders, foodstuffs are no longer inexpensive in Texas. But you can have some that are delicious and imaginative if you will follow the recipes in this collection.

Chili was proclaimed the state dish of Texas by the Texas Legislature in 1977.

Tolbert's Original Texas Chili

2-4 ancho pepper pods or 4-8 japone pepper pods (substitute 1 heaping tablespoon chili powder per pod, if desired)

3 pounds lean chuck, cut into bite-sized pieces

2 ounces sweet beef kidney suet, devided (for greaseless chili, substitute vegetable oil)

⅓ cup garlic, finely chopped

Chopped onion, (optional)

2 tablespoons cumin

1 tablespoon oregano

½ cup paprika

1 sprig fresh cilantro, crushed (optional)

Water, as desired

Trim stems from peppers and purée with a little water. Reserve. Braise the beef with half the rendered suet in a large skillet; sprinkle with some garlic and onion, if desired. When meat is grey, pour off liquid into the chili pot along with the puréed pepper mixture. Add remaining suet to the skillet and continue to braise the meat until brown and almost dry; then add to the chili pot and simmer for 30 minutes.

Add cumin, oregano, paprika, garlic and onion to taste, and simmer for another 30 minutes or until meat is very tender. Let chili rest overnight, if possible, and skim off excess fat in the morning. Heat and serve.

Frank X. Tolbert

Dear Friends,

We at the Richardson Womans Club are proud to present you with this exciting selection of choice Texas recipes... a fantasy of good things to eat... guaranteed to please those who enjoy good food.

Family and friends will delight at trying these wonderful recipes. Among them are tempting new sweets, recognized favorites, and treasured family recipes many of which have been handed down from generation to generation.

We hope "The Texas Experience" will help you discover the many delicious foods of our state.

Cordially,
The Texas Experience
Cookbook Committee

Texas Flag Pledge —

A pledge to the Texas flag was adopted by the
Forty-Third Legislature and from 1933 until 1965
that pledge was used. It contained a phrase,
"Flag of 1836", which was historically incorrect, as
Texas did not have a flag in 1836. On April 3, 1965,
Gov. John Connally signed an act of the Fifty-ninth
Legislature officially designating the pledge to
the Texas flag as follows:

"Honor the Texas Flag.
I pledge allegiance to thee,
Texas, one and indivisible."

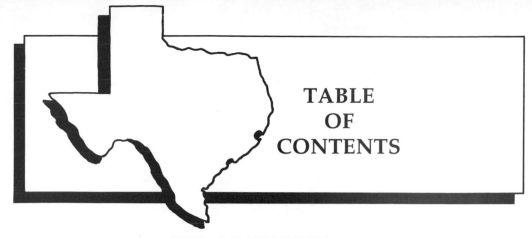

TABLE
OF
CONTENTS

Avocado Margarita Appetizer

Ripe avocados
Watercress or leaf lettuce
Lime juice

Tequila
Lime wedges

Halve and peel avocado and place on bed of salad greens. Salt generously. Squeeze lime juice over avocados. Just before serving, fill with tequila and garnish with lime wedges.

Goodies from Goodman by Jimmy and Bob

Stuffed Jalapeño Bites

1   (11 ounce) can pickled jalapeño peppers, drained
1   (3 ounce) package cream cheese

1   (6½ ounce) can water-packed tuna
½-¾ teaspoon Worcestershire

Drain and wash jalapeños, quarter lengthwise, and soak in ice water for 1 to 3 hours. This takes the bite out of the pepper. Blend cream cheese with tuna and Worcestershire. Fill pepper quarter with cheese mixture. Refrigerate until serving time.

Goodies from Goodman by Jimmy and Bob

Jalapeño Squares

2   (4 ounces each) cans jalapeño peppers
1   pound of bacon fried crisp and broken into small pieces
3   cups grated cheddar cheese

2   (4 ounces each) cans sliced mushrooms, stems and pieces
10   eggs, well beaten
Sliced black olives to taste
Water chestnuts to taste, or jicama, sliced, to taste.

Line bottom of 9 x 13 inch casserole with seeded jalapeños if you desire it to be HOT. Simply dot bottom of dish with peppers if you wish it mildly hot. Sprinkle bacon pieces, cheese and sliced mushrooms in layers; then sprinkle the black olives and jicama or water chestnuts over it. Add beaten eggs and cook at 300⁰ for 30 minutes. If the middle is soft, cook longer, until it will not shake. Let it stand 10 to 15 minutes before slicing. Serve hot. Serves 10-12.

Mary Bonfoey

☆   ☆   ☆

Mexican Chocolate

2 tablespoons cinnamon flavored hard candies, red hots
1½ cups milk

1½ cups whipping cream
½ cup semi-sweet chocolate pieces
1 tablespoon instant coffee

Blend cinnamon candies on medium speed until they are finely powdered. Heat milk and whipping cream. Add to blender container along with semi-sweet chocolate pieces and coffee. Blend on high until frothy or about 20 seconds. Add candy cane to each mug, if desired. Serves 4-6.

Irma O'Malley

Grandmother's Eggnog

12 eggs, separated
1½ cups sugar
¾ cup Kentucky Bourbon
1 quart milk

1 pint heavy cream, whipped
Grated nutmeg

Beat egg whites until soft peaks form. Beat yolks with sugar until creamy, add Bourbon to yolk mixture to cook the yolks. Add milk. Fold in egg whites and whipped cream into yolk mixture. Dust with grated nutmeg. Serves 12.

This was my grandmother's traditional Christmas day recipe, she kept the Bourbon hidden in the cedar chest for the rest of the year. This is really good because it's not too strong. Grandmother's theory was 1 tablespoon Bourbon to 1 egg.

Linda Juba

M.E.'s Texas Tea

3 quarts water
1 family size tea bag
15-20 lemon drops candy

1 cup fresh mint leaves, crushed

Bring water to a boil, add tea bag, lemon drops and mint leaves. Turn off heat and let cool; then remove tea bag and mint leaves. This is delicious. It has a light refreshing taste. *The Cookbook Committee*

☆ ☆ ☆

Gazpacho Dip

Make Ahead

3	tablespoons oil	1	(4 ounce) can chopped green chilies and liquid
1½	tablespoons cider vinegar		
1	teaspoon salt	2-3	tomatoes, finely chopped
1	teaspoon garlic salt	4-5	green onions, finely chopped
¼	teaspoon pepper		
1	(4 ounce) can chopped black olives and liquid	3-4	firm avocados, diced

Blend oil and vinegar. Add salt, garlic salt and pepper. Stir. Mix with olives, green chilies, tomatoes, onions and avocados. Chill for several hours for flavors to mix. Serve cold with tortilla chips.

Pat Williams and Carole Price

Variation: Omit 1 teaspoon salt and avocados.

Carla's Shrimp Dip

South of the Border Flavor

1	(10 ounce) can Rotel tomatoes with chilies	2	tablespoons lemon juice
1	(8 ounce) package cream cheese	½	teaspoon salt
		½	teaspoon pepper
1	tablespoon mayonnaise		Tabasco
2	(7½ ounces each) cans shrimp		

Drain tomatoes and reserve liquid. Set both aside. Soften cream cheese with mayonnaise in double boiler or in microwave. Drain and thoroughly wash shrimp. Add to cream cheese with lemon juice, salt, pepper and tomatoes. Add Tabasco to taste. If mixture needs to be thinned, use liquid from tomatoes.

Linda Juba

☆ ☆ ☆

Mild Guacamole

1	ripe avocado	½	teaspoon salt or seasoned salt
½	teaspoon lime juice		Pepper to taste
1	tomato, finely chopped		Dash of Worcestershire, optional
¼	cup chopped onion, optional		
1	tablespoon chopped green chilies, optional		

Mash avocado with fork until smooth. Add juice and mix. Add tomato, onion, chopped green chilies, salt, pepper and Worcestershire, if desired.

The Cookbook Committee

Hotter Guacamole

1	clove garlic, minced	1-3	tablespoons picante sauce
2	ripe avocados		Salt to taste
1	tablespoon lemon juice		Pepper to taste
1	tomato, chopped		Dash of Worcestershire, optional
½	cup grated onion		

You may drop garlic in food processor while processor is running. When minced, add all other ingredients and pulse once or twice. May also be made in blender or mashed with a potato masher.

The Cookbook Committee

Layered Guacamole Dip

6-8	ripe avocados	2	pints sour cream
1	lemon	1	cup picante sauce
1	pound grated Monterey Jack cheese	4-5	green onions, chopped

Mash avocados with juice of lemon. In a 9 x 13 glass dish layer mashed avocados, grated Jack cheese, sour cream, picante sauce and chopped green onions. Let set in refrigerator 2 to 3 hours. Serve with tostados. Beautiful and delicious!

Willena Harry

Variation: Additional bottom layer may be cream cheese or refried beans.

☆   ☆   ☆

Quick Mexican Dip

1   (8 ounce) package cream   Doritos
     cheese
1   (8 ounce) can Tostitos
     picante sauce

About 1 hour before serving, set out cream cheese to soften. Score cheese. Pour picante sauce over cheese and serve with chips. Easy, but so popular. Also good with wheat crackers.

I use Tostitos brand because it is not quite as hot as other brands and even people that can not tolerate "Mexican" food, love this.
                                                    Valerie McMahan

Marinated Black-Eyed Peas

1   (16 ounce) can or 1 (10   1   clove garlic
     ounce) package frozen   Sliced onion rings or chopped
     black-eyed peas   onion
Vinegar and oil dressing

Drain canned peas or cook and drain frozen peas. Add your favorite dressing, garlic and sliced onion rings. Chill. Remove garlic before serving.

Black-Eyed peas are traditionally served throughout the South on New Year's Day because legend says that eating Black-Eyed Peas brings good luck for the following year. This is a Texas way of serving them when they are out-of-season.
                                                The Cookbook Committee

Rotel Sausage Dip

Easy and Delicious!

1½   pounds ground beef   1   onion, chopped
1   pound hot sausage   2   pounds Velveeta
2   (10 ounces each) cans
     Rotel tomatoes with chilies

Brown ground beef and sausage. Add onion. Drain. Add tomatoes and cheese. Cut cheese into small chunks. Use medium heat to melt cheese. Serve with Fritos, Doritos, etc.   *Anna Wade Pierson*

☆   ☆   ☆

Sausage Con Queso

2   pounds hot sausage
2   pounds Velveeta, cubed
1   cup evaporated milk
1   (7 ounce) package Good
     Seasons Garlic salad
     dressing mix

1   (7 ounce) package Good
     Seasons Bleu Cheese salad
     dressing mix

Brown sausage well and drain thoroughly. Melt cheese with milk in top of double boiler; stir in salad dressing mixes and meat. To reheat, add additional evaporated milk. Serve warm with tostados. Fills a standard chafing dish.   *Pat Knott*

Green Chilies Queso

Make Ahead

1   cup chopped yellow onion
2   tablespoons margarine
3-4 (4 ounces each) cans chop-
     ped green chilies
1   (28 ounce) can tomatoes,
     drained and chopped

2   pounds Kraft Deluxe
     American cheese, grated
     (do not substitute)

In a Dutch oven, sauté onion in margarine until onions become transparent. Add green chilies and liquid. Sauté 2 or 3 minutes longer, but don't allow to brown. Add tomatoes. Add grated cheese and heat over low heat until melted. Cool slowly, stirring often to prevent film from forming. This improves with freezing. Thaw in refrigerator overnight. Serve warm with tortilla-style chips. Especially good to make ahead and freeze in small amounts or large containers for parties.

Ivanette Dennis

Variation: Increase margarine to 1 stick. Substitute 1 (10 ounce) can Rotel tomatoes with chilies for tomatoes for "hot" dip.

☆   ☆   ☆

Chilies Plus Chili Dip

Make Ahead

1	cup sour cream
1	(8 ounce) package cream cheese, softened
1	(4 ounce) can chopped green chilies and liquid
1½	teaspoons chili powder
¼	teaspoon garlic salt

Blend sour cream, cream cheese, chili powder and garlic salt. Fold in green chilies and liquid. Refrigerate. This must stand several hours for the flavors to blend well. Serves 12-16.   *Ivanette Dennis*

Lynn's Hot Cheese Dip

Hot, anyway you look at it!

1	(6 ounce) roll Kraft jalapeño cheese
1	(6 ounce) roll Kraft garlic cheese
1	(10¾ ounce) can cream of mushroom soup
1	bouillon cube, with just enough water to dissolve
1	(4 ounce) can chopped green chilies

Mix all ingredients in top of double boiler and heat until all are blended together and hot. Serve in chafing dish with Doritos or Tostitos. Serves 8-10.   *Lynn MacWithey*

Mother's Chile Relleños

2	(7 ounces each) cans whole mild green chilies
1	pound sharp Cheddar cheese, grated
16	ounces Monterey Jack cheese, grated
3	eggs
1	(16 ounce) container sour cream
	Salt to taste
	Pepper to taste

Remove seeds from chilies. In buttered 9 x 12 size casserole, layer chilies and cheeses to make two layers. Beat eggs, adding sour cream, salt and pepper. Pour over chilies. Bake 40 to 45 minutes at 350°. Serves 6.
          Pat Williams

☆   ☆   ☆

Chile Relleños Casserole

1 pound ground beef	1½ cups milk
½ cup chopped onion	2 tablespoons flour
½ teaspoon salt	⅔ teaspoon salt
½ teaspoon pepper	Pepper to taste
2 (4 ounces each) cans green chilies, divided	Hot sauce to taste
2½ cups shredded sharp Cheddar cheese, divided	3 eggs, beaten

Cook beef, onion, salt and pepper in a skillet until the meat begins to brown. Drain. Spread 1 can of the green chilies over the bottom of a 9 x 13 baking dish. Sprinkle with ½ the cheese and top with all of the meat mixture. Add the remaining cheese and second can of chilies. Combine milk, flour, salt, pepper, hot sauce and eggs. Pour over casserole and bake at 350° for 50 minutes or until knife inserted comes out clean. Cool 5 minutes. Cut in squares. May be frozen. Reheat while still frozen at 400° until heated through. Serves 4-6.   *Tura Bethune*

Squash Verole
Mexican Flavor

4-6 yellow squash, sliced or chopped	½ cup chopped green chilies
1 onion, chopped	½ teaspoon salt
4 tablespoons oil	½ teaspoon pepper
¼ cup milk	1 cup grated Parmesan or Cheddar cheese

Sauté squash and onion in oil, until tender. Add milk, chilies, salt and pepper. Cover and cook 15 minutes. Remove from heat and add cheese. Serve hot. Serves 6.   *Dot Prince*

Variation: Add 1 cup corn and substitute ⅓ cup grated Monterey Jack cheese for Parmesan or Cheddar cheese.   *Pat Williams*

☆   ☆   ☆

Chilies-Egg Puff

10	eggs	1	pound Monterey Jack cheese, shredded
½	cup flour		
1	teaspoon baking powder	1	stick butter or margarine, melted
½	teaspoon salt		
1	(16 ounce carton) cottage cheese	1-2	(4 ounces each) cans chopped green chilies

Preheat oven to 350⁰. Beat eggs until light and lemon colored. Add flour, baking powder, salt, cottage cheese, Jack cheese and butter. Blend until smooth. Stir in chilies. Pour mixture into a well buttered 9 x 13 inch baking pan. (A partially baked pie crust could be used if you prefer.) Bake for about 35 minutes or until top is browned and center appears firm. Serve immediately. Makes 12 servings. (One can of chilies makes a milder dish.) Picante sauce can be served to individual taste.

Roberta Madden

Mexican Quiche

1	cup heavy cream	4-5	strips cooked bacon, crumbled
4	eggs, beaten		
1	teaspoon dry mustard	¼	pound grated Cheddar cheese
1	(9 inch) baked pie shell		
6	thin slices of ham	¼	pound grated Baby Swiss cheese
½	onion, chopped		
3	jalapeños, chopped		Parsley, chopped
1	tomato, chopped		Nutmeg

Heat cream and add gradually to eggs. Add mustard. In the pie shell layer ½ the ham, onion, jalapeños, tomato and bacon. Add ½ the cheeses. Repeat. Pour egg mixture into the pie shell, jiggling the pan to settle the liquid. Sprinkle with parsley and nutmeg on top. Bake at 450⁰ for 30 to 40 minutes.

Jean Zinser

☆   ☆   ☆

Huevos Ranchero

1	bell pepper, cut in strips	8	soft tortillas
1	onion, chopped	½	stick butter (or more as needed)
1	tablespoon oil		
⅓	cup medium to hot red salsa	8	eggs
1	(12 ounce) can tomato juice		

Sauté bell pepper and onion in oil. Add salsa and tomato juice. Simmer. Soften tortillas in butter; stack on foil. Wrap and put in 200° oven to keep warm. Break 8 eggs in pan used to soften tortillas. Cook with lid on until whites are congealed. Place 2 tortillas on each plate, top with 2 eggs and circle the yolk with hot salsa (not on the yolk as the hot salsa will continue to cook and harden the yolk). Serve immediately.

Hat Madsen

Everybody's Texas Eggs

Must Be Made Ahead

2	dozen eggs	½ cup Cream Sherry
½	cup milk	1 (8 ounce) can sliced mushrooms
½	teaspoon salt	
¼	teaspoon pepper	8 ounces grated Cheddar cheese
½	cup butter	
2	cans (10¾ ounces each) cream of mushroom soup	

Beat eggs, add milk, salt and pepper. Scramble in butter. Mix mushroom soup, Sherry and sliced mushrooms. Layer eggs, soup mixture and cheese in 9 x 13 casserole. Let stand 8 hours or overnight in refrigerator. Return to room temperature 30 minutes before baking at 300° for 50 minutes. Freezes well. Serves 8-12.

Jean Zinser

☆　　☆　　☆

Green Chilies Casserole

Delicious Cheese and Chilies

Butter
2-3 (4 ounces each) cans green
chilies, drained
½ pound grated Monterey
Jack cheese
½ pound grated Cheddar
cheese
3 eggs, beaten

1 cup milk or half and half
or 1 (5.33 ounce) can
evaporated milk plus
water to equal 1 cup
¼ cup flour
1 (10 ounce) can Rotel
tomatoes with chilies

Butter a 2 quart casserole. Spread chilies and cheese alternately for three layers, saving small amount of cheese for topping. Beat eggs, milk and flour. Pour over casserole. Add tomatoes and top with cheese. Bake at 350⁰ for 1 hour. Serves 4-6. *Louise Propps*

Green Chilies Stew

2 pounds lean pork, cubed
Oil
1 cup chopped onion
1 clove garlic, minced
1 (10 ounce) can Rotel
tomatoes with chilies
1 (4 ounce) can chopped
green chilies

2 cups water
2 teaspoons instant chicken
bouillon
2 potatoes, peeled and
chopped

Brown cubed pork slowly in a small amount of oil; add onion and garlic and simmer for 5 minutes. Drain. Add tomatoes, green chilies, water, bouillon and potatoes. Simmer, covered at least 1 hour or until meat is fork tender. Serves 8.

Variation: Most recipes use beef round instead of pork.

☆   ☆   ☆

Micro-Mex Meat Loaves

Meat Loaves:

1	pound ground beef
2	green onions, chopped
1	egg
½	cup oatmeal
1	(4 ounce) can chopped green chilies, divided
1	(8 ounce) can tomato sauce, divided

½	teaspoon ground cominos
3	tablespoons Worcestershire
½	teaspoon ground chili pepper
⅛	teaspoon garlic powder
¼	teaspoon baking powder
¾	teaspoon seasoned salt
½	cup grated Cheddar cheese

Sauce:

Remaining tomato sauce
Remaining green chilies

½	teaspoon cominos
1	teaspoon ground chili pepper

⅛	teaspoon garlic powder
¼	teaspoon sugar

Dash of seasoned salt

MEAT LOAVES: Mix ground beef, onions, egg and oatmeal together. Add 2 tablespoons of green chilies, 3 tablespoons of tomato sauce, ground cominos, Worcestershire, chili pepper, garlic powder, baking powder and seasoned salt. Mix well. Shape into 6 small loaves. Heat browning grill 8 minutes at FULL POWER. Place meat on hot grill and cook on FULL POWER for 3 minutes. Turn loaves over and cook 5 more minutes on FULL POWER. Remove from oven and let stand on browning grill while mixing sauce.

SAUCE: Mix all ingredients in 2 cup measure and cover with paper towel. Cook on FULL POWER 2 minutes. Stir and cook 1 minute more. Pour over meat loaves on serving dish and cook 30 seconds on FULL POWER. Sprinkle grated cheese on top of loaves and serve. Garnish with cherry peppers and parsley.

The State Seal — The state seal was adopted in 1845 and readopted in 1876. Its design is a modified version of the seal adopted by the Republic of Texas in 1836. A single five pointed star is supported on the right by an olive branch, a symbol of peace, and on the left by a branch of live oak, a symbol of strength.

☆   ☆   ☆

Taco Filling

2-4 cloves garlic, minced or ½ teaspoon garlic powder
3 pounds lean ground beef
1½-2 ounces Gebhardt chili powder

2 teaspoons cumin
½ cup grated raw potato
2 teaspoons salt
6 cups water

Combine all ingredients and simmer for two hours. When the mixture is done, pour into a collander and drain well. Meat will not be greasy for tacos. Spoon meat into prepared taco shells. Top with shredded lettuce, chopped tomatoes, grated cheese and taco sauce if desired.

Layered Taco Salad

1 pound ground meat
2 tablespoons chopped onions
½ teaspoon salt
½ teaspoon garlic powder
¼ cup taco sauce
1 (23 ounce) can Ranch Style beans or Kidney beans
1 (12 ounce) bottle Catalina Salad dressing

1 head iceberg lettuce
2 tomatoes, diced
2 avocados, diced or 1 recipe guacamole (see index)
1 cup sour cream
½ cup Cheddar cheese
½ cup Monterey Jack cheese
½ red onion, sliced (optional)

Brown meat with chopped onion, salt, and garlic powder. Drain; combine with taco sauce, beans and salad dressing. Marinate 3 to 4 hours; drain and place in bottom of salad bowl. Tear ¾ head of lettuce into bite size pieces and layer on top of meat-bean mixture. Cover with sour cream. Continue to layer with tomatoes, avocados or guacamole and a combination of cheeses. Garnish with red onion. Chill until serving time. This makes a great lunch or light supper. Serve with tortilla chips. If desired pass additional taco sauce. This is very attractive served in a deep clear salad bowl. Serves 4 generously.

☆　☆　☆

Beef Enchilada Casserole

MEAT FILLING:

1	pound ground beef	1	tablespoon water
1	clove garlic	1	tablespoon chili powder
2	teaspoons salt	1	(1 pound) can chili beans
1	tablespoon vinegar		

TOMATO SAUCE:

1	clove garlic	1	cup boiling water
¼	cup chopped onion	½	teaspoon salt
3	tablespoons salad oil		Dash of pepper
2	tablespoons flour		Dash of cumin
2	(15 ounces each) cans enchilada sauce	2	tablespoons chopped green chilies
1	tablespoon vinegar	12	tortillas
1	beef bouillon cube	1	cup grated cheese

FILLING: In skillet sauté beef, garlic, salt, vinegar, water and chili powder until brown. Remove garlic clove and stir in beans. Set aside.

SAUCE: Brown garlic and onions in oil and remove from heat. To the skillet add flour, enchilada sauce, vinegar and bouillon cube dissolved in 1 cup boiling water. Bring to boil. While stirring, add salt, pepper, cumin and green chilies. Simmer uncovered about 5 minutes. Fill 9 x 13 baking dish with layers of tortillas, meat filling and tomato sauce. Repeat, finishing with tomato sauce on top. Sprinkle with grated cheese and bake at 350⁰ for 25 minutes. Serves 8-12.   *Pat Woodward*

Stack Enchiladas

1	(12 count) package soft corn tortillas	1	heaping tablespoon flour
1	(16-19 ounce) can chili without beans		1½ cups oil
	Water		Chopped ripe olives
			Onions
			Grated cheese

Brown heaping tablespoon flour in a frying pan (preferably iron skillet). Add one can chili to the flour. For each can of chili used, add a can of water. Simmer for 15 to 20 minutes. In another skillet heat 1½ cups oil. Dip tortilla in hot oil for no more than 30 to 45 seconds and then dip in chili. Combine chopped ripe olives, onions, and grated cheese. Sprinkle on tortilla. Repeat until you have 6 on a stack. Top with remaining chili when you have made all the enchiladas. Do ahead and reheat in 350⁰ oven for 15 to 20 minutes. Makes 2 stacks serving 4.   *Linda Juba*

☆　　☆　　☆

Green Enchiladas Mavis

ENCHILADAS:

1 dozen corn tortillas
Hot oil
2 onions, chopped
1 pound Monterey Jack
cheese, grated

1 (3½ pound) chicken,
cooked, boned, chopped

GREEN SAUCE:

1 (10 ounce) package frozen
chopped spinach
2 (10¾ ounces each) cans
cream of chicken soup
2 (4 ounces each) cans
chopped green chilies

¼ teaspoon salt
1 pint sour cream
1½ cups Monterey Jack
cheese, grated

ENCHILADAS: Soften each tortilla in hot oil for one minute and fill with generous mixture of onion, cheese and chicken. Roll and place in 8x10 greased shallow pan. Lightly cover with green sauce. Bake 350⁰ for 30 minutes. Serve with extra sauce which has been heated.

GREEN SAUCE: Slightly cook spinach until ice crystals break. Drain well. Mix spinach, soup, chilies, and salt in blender or food processor. Blend lightly. Add sour cream and blend lightly again. After the enchiladas have been covered with sauce cover with cheese. *Linda Juba*

Baked Enchiladas

2 pounds ground beef
1 onion, chopped
1 dozen tortillas cut in
quarters
1 (10¾ ounce) can cream of
mushroom soup
1 (10¾ ounce) can cream of
chicken soup

2 (4 ounces each) cans taco
sauce
1 (4 ounce) can chopped
green chilies
1 cup milk
2 cups grated cheese

Brown meat and onions. Cover bottom of 3 quart casserole with tortillas. Spread meat and onion mixture over tortillas. Mix soups, taco sauce, green chilies and milk. Pour over meat and top with cheese. Bake at 325° for 1 hour. A spoonful of sour cream may be used as a garnish on each serving. Serves 6-8. *Dot Prince*

☆　　☆　　☆

Chicken Enchiladas

2	large chicken breasts	1	teaspoon sugar
1	cup chopped onion	1	teaspoon ground cumin
1	clove garlic, minced	½	teaspoon salt
2	tablespoons margarine	½	teaspoon oregano
1	(16 ounce) can or 2 cups fresh cut-up tomatoes	½	teaspoon basil
		12	tortillas
¼	cup chopped green chilies or more to taste	2½	cups grated Monterey Jack cheese (about 10 ounces)
1	(8 ounce) can tomato sauce	¾	cups sour cream

Simmer chicken breast in water to cover 15 to 20 minutes. Remove skin and bones and cut in bite-size pieces. In saucepan saute onion and garlic in margarine 'til tender to make sauce. Add tomatoes, chilies, tomato sauce, sugar, cumin, salt, oregano and basil. Boil, reduce heat and simmer covered 20 minutes. Dip each tortilla in sauce to soften. Place chicken and 2 tablespoons grated cheese on each tortilla. Roll up and place seam side down in 9 x 13 dish. Blend sour cream into remaining sauce mixture; pour over tortillas. Sprinkle with remaining cheese. Cover and bake at 350⁰ for about 40 minutes. Serves 6.   *Anna Wade Pierson*

Whit's Chili

1½	onions, chopped	½	teaspoon crushed red pepper
¼	cup oil		
5	pounds ground round	½	teaspoon ground cumin
6	tablespoons chili powder	½	teaspoon Tabasco
1	(14½ ounce) can tomatoes	2	tablespoons salt
1	(6 ounce) can tomato paste	2	tablespoons paprika

Sauté onions in oil. Brown meat. Mix chili powder, tomatoes, tomato paste, crushed red pepper, cumin, Tabasco, salt and paprika with meat and onion mixture. Simmer for 2 to 4 hours. Add water if too thick. Serves 10-12.

First prize winner at Richardson Woman's Club Chili Cook Off.
Elsie Whitmarsh

☆   ☆   ☆

Chili Con Carne

3½ pounds chili-grind beef
1 cup Pace picante sauce, or
more to taste
1-2 cups water
2 tablespoons flour

½ teaspoon garlic salt
½ teaspoon oregano
2 teaspoons cumin
½ teaspoon salt

Brown beef and drain all but 2 tablespoons fat. Blend with flour. Add picante sauce, water, garlic salt, oregano, cumin and salt. Simmer about 1 hour, adding more water if necessary.

Tri Delta Chalupa Dinner
A Fun Party

MEAT:
20 pounds lean ground beef
20 onions, chopped
8-10 cloves garlic, minced
4 (2 ounces each) bottles
Mexene Chili Powder
2 (1.9 ounces each) jars
ground cumin

½ (.49 ounce) jar oregano
½ cup salt
12 (8 ounces each) cans
tomato sauce
8 (6 ounces each) cans
tomato paste
12 cups water

TOPPINGS:
Shredded lettuce
Chopped tomatoes
Guacamole (see index)
Chopped green onions and tops
Chopped ripe olives

Grated Cheddar or longhorn
cheese
Sour cream
Taco sauce

Brown meat, onions and garlic. Drain. Add chili powder, cumin, oregano, salt, tomato sauce, tomato paste and water. Simmer 2 hours. Serve on tostados, Fritos or Doritos, etc. Set out toppings. Let guests build their own. Serves 50 - 75.

We always have Chalupas at our first dinner meeting of the year and this is our favorite recipe.

Linda Juba

☆   ☆   ☆

Guadalajara Chalupas

MEAT:

2 pounds red beans soaked overnight and drained	1½ tablespoons cumin
	2-3 chicken bouillon cubes
4 pounds boneless pork, cut into cubes and remove fat	1 clove garlic, minced
	1 teaspoon salt
1½ tablespoons chili powder	1 teaspoon pepper

TOPPING:

Corn chips	Chopped avocado
Shredded Monterey Jack cheese	Chopped radishes
Shredded Cheddar cheese	Sliced jalapeños
Chopped onion	Sweet chilies
Shredded lettuce	Sour cream
Chopped tomato	Mexican hot sauce

MEAT: Combine beans, pork, chili powder, cumin, bouillon, garlic, salt and pepper in a large covered container, add water to cover. Cook 4 to 6 hours over low heat, stir frequently to keep from sticking. Mixture will become thick. Add a little water if needed. May be frozen at this point.

TOPPINGS: Arrange buffet table in this order, serving dishes of: regular sized corn chips, meat and bean mixture, shredded Monterey Jack, shredded Cheddar cheese, chopped onion, shredded lettuce, chopped tomato, chopped avocado, chopped radishes, sliced jalapeños, chilies, sour cream and Mexican hot sauce. Allow guests to assemble their own chalupas. Serves 18-20.   *Vivian Jackson*

Fajitas

Must Be Made Ahead

1 (12 ounce) can beer	Sour cream
1 (8 ounce) bottle Italian vinegar and oil dressing	Grated cheese
	Hot sauce
1 pound skirt or flank steak	

Pierce meat with sharp fork and put in a glass baking dish. Cover with mixture of beer and dressing. Marinate overnight. Pour off juices; reserve. Grill or bake steak 45 minutes at 350°. Baste with marinade. On a hot flour tortilla, place thinly sliced meat, sour cream, grated cheese and hot sauce. Roll and eat with fingers. Serves 3-4.   *Rich Myers*

☆   ☆   ☆

Flautas

The word "flauta", meaning flute in Spanish, describes the tubular shape of this Mexican·dish.

CHICKEN FILLING:

1	onion, finely chopped
1	small clove garlic, minced
6	tablespoons oil
1	(4 ounce) can chopped green chilies
1	teaspoon salt
½	teaspoon marjoram
1	(14½ ounce) can whole tomatoes

2	cups diced cooked chicken
½	pint sour cream
	Guacamole (see index)
1½	cups Monterey Jack cheese, grated
	Shredded lettuce
	Tortillas

BEEF FILLING:

1-1½	pounds ground meat
½	cup chopped onion
¼	teaspoon cumin
1	teaspoon salt
1	(10 ounce) can tomatoes and green chilies (optional)

	Shredded lettuce
	Chopped tomatoes
	Grated cheese
1	(4 ounce) can taco sauce
	Tortillas

CHICKEN FILLING: Sauté onion and garlic in oil until soft. Add chilies, salt, marjoram and drained tomatoes. Cut up tomatoes and cook mixture gently for 10 minutes. Add chicken and cook slowly until chicken is heated thoroughly (about 10 minutes). Before filling prepared shells, drain chicken mixture. Place 2 teaspoons chicken mixture on each tortilla.

BEEF FILLING: Brown meat and onion; drain. Add salt, cumin and tomato chilies. Simmer approximately 15 minutes. For each flauta, soften tortillas by dipping in hot oil or broth, lay tortillas flat. Spoon filling across the greatest length of the tortillas and roll. Bake at 350⁰ for 15 to 20 minutes, or fry in hot oil until crisp. Serve with guacamole and/or sour cream.   *Goodies from Goodman by Jimmy and Bob*

TEXAS was the only state recognized as an independent republic before being annexed by the United States.

☆   ☆   ☆

Mexican Influence

1 (3½-4 pounds) chicken, cooked, boned, chopped in bite-size pieces
2 cups uncooked rice (not instant)
2⅓ cups chicken broth or bouillon
6 tablespoons butter
2 onions, chopped, divided
½ cup flour
1 (13 ounce) can evaporated milk, divided
1 (8 ounce) can mushrooms and liquid
2 cups white Chablis wine
1 teaspoon garlic powder
1 teaspoon seasoning salt
½ teaspoon white pepper
½ teaspoon cumin powder
12 ounces Monterey Jack cheese, grated, divided
3-4 (4 ounces each) cans green chilies, chopped, and liquid
3 cups sour cream
1 bunch green onions, chopped
1 dozen tortillas, grilled to soften, cut into fourths
1 (2 ounce) can black olives
6 tomatoes, peeled and thinly sliced
Whole pimiento, optional

Wash rice until water is no longer cloudy. Drain thoroughly. Add broth to rice. Bring to a boil, lower temperature to simmer, cook for 10 minutes. Remove from heat, allow to set with lid on for 10 minutes more. Reserve. Rice should be cool before adding to casserole. Melt butter in large sauce pan, sauté 1½ onions until clear. Add flour, stir until well blended. Add 11 ounces milk, juice from mushrooms, wine, garlic powder, seasoning salt, white pepper and cumin powder. Sauce should be thin, if not add more milk. Add mushrooms to sauce, remove from heat and allow to cool somewhat. To sauce, add ½ cheese, chilies and sour cream. Grease two 9 x 13 baking dishes. Mix rice with green onions. Layer ingredients in this order: enough sauce to cover bottom of pan, tortillas, rice, sauce to cover rice, black olives, chicken pieces, tomatoes, remaining sauce, remaining cheese, remaining onion. Pimiento and green onion may be used as decoration. Bake at 375⁰ for 45 to 60 minutes. Serves 24.

State flower — The state flower of Texas is the bluebonnet, also called buffalo clover, wolf flower, "el conejo" (the rabbit). The bluebonnet was adopted as the state flower, on request of the Society of Colonial Dames in Texas, by the Twenty-seventh Legislature.

☆   ☆   ☆

Spanish Rice

1   cup uncooked rice
2   tablespoons oil
1   tablespoon diced onion
¾   of 1 (16 ounce) can of
     whole tomatoes

2½   cups water
Salt to taste
Pepper to taste

Brown rice in pot with oil. When brown add onions, tomatoes and water. Add salt and pepper. Cook over low heat until rice absorbs water and it is dry but not burned.

Arroz Con Jocoqui

2½   cups cooked rice (1 cup
     uncooked)
Salt to taste
Pepper to taste
Oregano to taste
1   pint sour cream

1   (4 ounce) can chopped
     green chilies, remove seeds
     and membrane, if whole
½-¾ pound grated Monterey
     Jack cheese
Chopped parsley

Season cooked rice with salt, pepper and oregano. Mix sour cream with green chilies. Layer rice, sour cream and grated cheese in casserole, ending with cheese. Bake for 30 minutes at 350⁰. Sprinkle with parsley last 10 minutes. Serves 6.   *Betty Johnson*

Variation: Add ½ cup grated Cheddar cheese. Omit oregano and parsley.
     Pat Cutler

Refried Beans

1   (1 pound) package pinto
     beans
1   cup Cheddar or Velveeta
     cheese

Bacon drippings

Cook pinto beans according to package directions. To refry, put bacon drippings into a frying pan, add beans with as little of liquid as possible. Mash beans with potato masher, add 1 cup cheese to them. As soon as cheese melts and mixes, the beans are done.

Refried beans can be reheated or refried as many times as necessary until all the leftovers are gone. That's why they're called refried beans.
     Cookbook Committee

☆   ☆   ☆

Fiesta Frijoles

2 pounds Mexican (pink) beans or pinto beans
1 pound salt pork, diced
2 cloves garlic, minced
4 slices bacon, cut fine
1 onion, diced
1 quart canned tomatoes
4-5 dried chili tepinos (careful, they're hot!)

3 tablespoons vinegar
1 tablespoon Worcestershire
3 tablespoons sugar
2 teaspoons chili powder
2 tablespoons finely chopped parsley
2 tablespoons grated Cheddar cheese
Salt to taste

Soak beans overnight. In the morning add pork and garlic; cook slowly in water in which beans were soaked for about 1 hour or until pork is tender. Add more water (boiling) if necessary to keep beans barely covered while cooking.

While beans are cooking, fry bacon; add onions and cook over low heat until tender. Add onions, tomatoes, chile tepinos, vinegar, Worcestershire, sugar, chili powder and parsley. Cook, stirring frequently, until mixture thickens. Just before removing from heat, stir in cheese. When beans and pork are tender, stir in thickened sauce and salt to taste. Continue cooking slowly about 1 hour. Serves 10-12.

Leftovers are even better warmed over the second or third day.

Green Chilies Corn Casserole

1 (16 ounce) can yellow cream style corn
1 cup biscuit mix
1 egg, beaten
2 tablespoons salad oil

½ cup milk
1 (4 ounce) can chopped green chilies, drained
6 ounces sharp Cheddar cheese, grated

Combine corn, biscuit mix, egg, oil and milk. Spread half of this mixture in a greased 8x8 inch square pan. Cover with chopped chili peppers and cheese. Spread remaining batter over the top. Bake at 400⁰ for 30 minutes. Serves 6-8. *Joyce Price and Yvonne Prevo*

☆　　☆　　☆

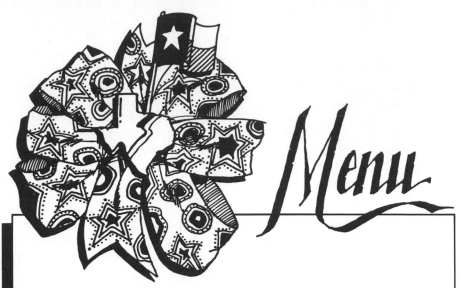

Menu

DINNER ON THE GROUNDS

Home Grown Sliced Tomatoes

Parsley Dressing

Crunchy Fried Chicken

Squash Verole   Okra & Tomatoes

Candied Sweet Potatoes

Anne's East Texas Biscuits

Coconut Lemon Cake

Strawberry Shortcake

Pecan Pie

M. E.'s Texas Tea

Dinner "On The Grounds" At Old City Park

A generation or so ago, in predominantly rural Texas, "dinner on the grounds" was the gastronomic culmination of revivals, cemetery workings, barn raisings, and family reunions. "On the grounds" meant outside on makeshift tables handsomely spread with linens and groaning under the weight of everybody's best home cooked food.

Here at the railroad depot, in Dallas' Old City Park, you can see the Dallas skyline and might wonder about the horse-and-buggy days of Dallas a century ago.

The Metroplex owes its incredible growth to the coming of the railroads in the 1870's. The Texas Pacific and the Houston and Texas Central were required by the Texas legislature to cross within a mile of Browder Springs, Dallas' first water supply, near the present downtown. This insured the growth of the old Indian trading center on the three forks of the Trinity River.

Richardson even owes its name to the railroads. When the Houston and Texas Central was extended north to Denton in 1873, a right of way and Richardson townsite were donated by John William "Billie" Wheeler. When he declined to have a town namesake, Richardson was named for the railroad contractor, E. H. Richardson.

Richardson remained a village until about the middle of the 20th century. The population in 1940 was 740, but today's vibrant city of 92,000 stretches north across Dallas County into Collin County.

Photography
Donna Rogers

Rotel Green Beans

3	(15 ounces each) cans green beans	3	tablespoons butter
¼	cup bacon drippings	3	tablespoons flour
1	onion, chopped	½	teaspoon salt
1	clove garlic, minced	1	cup milk
1	(10 ounce) can Rotel tomatoes and chilies	1	cup sharp cheese, grated
		½	cup cracker crumbs

Cook green beans over low heat in bacon drippings with onion and garlic for about 30 minutes. Drain, add Rotel tomatoes and chilies. Make a white sauce (see index) with butter, flour, salt and milk. Add cheese and stir until melted. Combine with green bean and tomato mixture. Pour into 2 quart casserole. Top with cracker crumbs. If serving immediately, bake in 350⁰ oven for 15 minutes. If prepared ahead and green beans have been refrigerated bake for 30 to 35 minutes until bubbly. Serves 6-8.

Linda Juba

Mexican Rice

1	clove garlic, chopped	3	cups rice
Pinch of fresh coriander		6	cups hot chicken broth
Pinch of oregano leaves		1	(3 pound) chicken, cooked
Achiote (see note)		Hot pepper such as jalapeño to taste	
Celery leaves			
2	sprigs parsley	½	of a (1 pound) can tomatoes, chopped
1	green onion top, chopped		
1	onion, chopped	Salt to taste	
Oil or bacon drippings		Pepper to taste	

Note: Achiote is a small red seed of the Annatto tree which is indigenous to tropical America and the Caribbean. It is found either as ground paste or seeds. The seeds are very hard and must be soaked in water or sautéd. Discard seeds. The best substitute is saffron.

DIRECTIONS: Sauté garlic, coriander, oregano, achiote, celery, parsley and onions in bacon drippings. Reserve, remove achiote seeds. Cover the skillet with melted bacon grease and fry rice until golden brown. Add more grease if necessary. Add hot chicken broth, chicken, onion mixture, hot pepper, tomatoes, salt and pepper. Bake at 300⁰ for 45 minutes; then at 250⁰ until light and fluffy.

☆   ☆   ☆

Mexican Zucchini Casserole

Corn chips as desired
1   (16 ounce) can zucchini
1   (16 ounce) can chili con
     carne
1   (16 ounce) can chili with
     beans

1   (4 ounce) can black olives
Cheddar cheese
Parmesan cheese

In a large bowl crumble corn chips. Add zucchini, reserving juice and both cans of chili. Stir, add olives and ¼ cup zucchini liquid. Place in a 2½ quart casserole. Top with desired amount of cheeses. Bake at 350⁰ 20 to 30 minutes or until bubbling. Serves 6-8.   *Tura Bethune*

TEXAS has more wild turkeys than any other state.

Pickled Venison

Never Tell What's In It!

1½-2 pounds venison roast,
     cooked (see index)
2   onions, sliced into rings
2   (4½ ounces each) jars
     mushrooms, drained
1   (3½ ounce) jar capers

Sugar to taste
Salt to taste
Pepper to taste
¼   cup red wine vinegar
¾   cup salad oil

Layer venison which has been cut into 1½ inch cubes, onion rings, mushrooms, and capers. Season with sugar, salt and pepper. Mix with vinegar and oil, (increase proportions as many times as necessary to cover layered items).

Refrigerate at least a day or two before serving. This is a good way to use the shoulder or less desireable cuts, however, the tenderloin or ham is preferable. Serve with party rye or wheat crackers.   *Linda Juba*

☆   ☆   ☆

Venison Casserole with Mushrooms

They'll Never Know It's Deer

1½-2 pounds tenderloin tips of Venison (may use round steak)	1 egg beaten
	Cracker Crumbs
	1 (10¾ ounce) can cream of mushroom soup
Milk	

Pound tips or steak until thin. Soak in milk for 30 minutes. Dip in egg; then roll in cracker crumbs. Fry in skillet with more oil than usual. (Crackers absorb it). When golden brown, remove from fat and place in 8x13 inch casserole. Pour mushroom soup over meat and bake 1 hour at 300⁰. Serves 4 hungry people.   *Shirley Caldwell*

Venison Stroganoff

A Montana Transplant

½	cup minced onion	¼	teaspoon pepper
4	tablespoons butter	¼	teaspoon paprika
½	cup chopped bell pepper	1	(4 ounce) can mushrooms
1	pound ground venison	1	(10¾ ounce) can cream of mushroom soup
1	clove garlic, minced		
2	tablespoons flour	1	cup sour cream
2	teaspoons salt		

Sauté onion in butter until golden. Stir in peppers, venison, garlic, flour, salt, pepper, paprika and mushrooms. Cook five minutes. Add soup, simmer 10 minutes. Stir in sour cream. Garnish with parsley. Serve over steamed rice. Serves 4-6.   *Eileen MacWithey*

Venison Roast

3-4	pound venison pot roast	Pepper to taste	
3	tablespoons bacon drippings	6	slices bacon
		¼	cup water
Salt to taste			

Remove all visible fat from roast. In a heavy Dutch oven brown on all sides in bacon drippings. Salt and pepper meat. Lay strips of bacon over the roast to baste it. Pour water in bottom of pan. Cover pan and place in 350⁰ oven for 2½ to 3 hours.   *Eileen MacWithey*

☆   ☆   ☆

Gene's Duck Gumbo

1	cup plus 2 tablespoons Mazola oil, divided	1½	teaspoons salt
2-3	ducks	½	teaspoon pepper
1	cup flour	¼	teaspoon cayenne pepper
1½	cups chopped onion	⅛	teaspoon crushed red pepper
2	cups red wine		Polish or venison sausage
2	teaspoons thyme		

Cover bottom of a large pot with Mazola oil. Salt and pepper ducks and brown in hot oil. Cover ducks with water and simmer 1 hour. Make roux while ducks simmer by browning 1 cup Mazola oil and 1 cup flour. Brown over low heat until copper color. Stir constantly and do not let burn. Add onions to roux. Cook 5 minutes. Add roux to ducks. Add thyme, salt, pepper, and crushed red pepper. Add to above and continue cooking until ducks are tender, about 2 hours. Skim fat as it cooks. Remove ducks and bone meat; reserve. Slice 1 ring polish sausage or venison sausage. Add to above and cook 10 minutes in broth. Add boned duck. Heat through and serve on white cooked rice. May cook day ahead and refrigerate to remove fat.   *Millie Fiedorek*

Wild Duck Casserole

Prepare One Day Ahead

3	ducks	2	eggs, beaten
1	onion	1	stick butter, melted
1	potato, halved	1½	cups chopped onion
1	bay leaf	½	cup chopped celery
1	(16 ounce) package Pepperidge Farm Herb Dressing Mix	1	cup mayonnaise
		1	(10¾ ounce) can cream of mushroom soup
1½	cups milk	1	cup grated Cheddar cheese

Cover ducks with water and simmer with potato, onion and bay leaf until tender, 2 or 3 hours. Save 1½ cups of broth. Bone duck and shred meat into bite-sized pieces. Combine duck and 1½ cups broth with dressing mix, milk, eggs, butter, chopped onion, chopped celery and mayonnaise. Fill 9x13 inch casserole with mixture, cover and refrigerate overnight. Uncover and spread soup over top. Bake at 400° for 1 hour. Add cheese and bake until melted. Serves 6-8.   *Dottie Pinch*

☆   ☆   ☆

Wild Duck Oriental

1	to 2 ducks	Salt to taste	
¼	cup melted butter	Pepper to taste	
1	(10 ounce) package frozen Oriental vegetables		

Skin the breast of one large or two medium wild ducks. Cut the meat off the breast bone into strips. Sauté in heavy pan in melted butter for about 5 minutes, stirring often. Add frozen vegetables, salt and pepper. Cover and steam for approximately 10 minutes or until vegetables are tender. Serve with cooked white rice and Chinese noodles. Additional sliced fresh mushrooms may be added with the Oriental vegetables if desired. Serves 3-4. *Vicky Nayes*

Duck and Wild Rice Casserole

Good with chicken, too!

2	medium ducks (3 cups cubed meat)	¼	cup flour
3	ribs celery	1	(4 ounce) can sliced mushrooms
1	onion, halved	1½	cups half and half
Salt and pepper to taste		1	tablespoon chopped parsley
1	(6 ounce) package seasoned wild and long grain rice	Slivered almonds	
1	stick margarine	1½	teaspoons salt
½	cup chopped onion	¼	teaspoon pepper

Boil ducks for 1 hour (or until tender) in water to cover, with celery, onion halves, salt and pepper. Remove and cube meat. Reserve broth. Cook the rice according to package directions. Reserve. Melt margarine, sauté chopped onion and stir in the flour. Drain mushrooms, reserving broth, add mushrooms to the onion mixture. Add enough duck broth to the mushroom broth to make 1½ cups of liquid; stir this into the onion mixture. Add duck and rice. Add half and half and parsley plus salt and pepper. Put into greased 2 quart casserole. Sprinkle almonds on top. Bake covered at 350⁰ for 15 to 20 minutes. Uncover and bake for 5 to 10 minutes more, or until very hot. (If casserole has been refrigerated it will take longer to heat). Serves 6. *Pate Stanphill*

☆　　☆　　☆

Mary Elizabeth Fite's Wild Ducks

6	wild ducks	2	onions
	Shortening or oil	2	strips of bacon for each
2	apples		duck
2	oranges	2	cups orange juice
2	ribs of celery	2	cups of red wine

Fry cleaned ducks in shortening or oil just long enough to slightly brown. (This can be done the day before you cook them.) Salt and pepper inside and out and stuff them with the apples, oranges, celery and onions that have been chopped in rather large pieces, leaving the peeling on the apples and oranges. Cover them with bacon and cook at 350⁰ in a roaster with the orange juice and wine mixed together. If very small ducks, such as Teal, they are tender in about 2 hours. Make gravy by thickening the drippings with cornstarch. Serve with Wild Rice Dressing. (See index).

Linda Juba

Mary's Baked Quail

4	tablespoons margarine	½	cup flour
1	tablespoon oil	8	quail
2	bunches green onions with tops, chopped	1	(10¾ ounce) can cream of chicken soup
	Salt	½	soup can Sherry
	Pepper		

Mix margarine and oil together. Sauté green onions with tops in margarine and oil mixture. Remove to dish. Mix salt, pepper and flour. Lightly flour quail with flour mixture. Brown quail in oil the onions were cooked in. Remove quail to casserole. Return onions to pan. Add soup and sherry. Mix together and heat to almost boiling. Pour mixture over quail. Cover casserole tightly and bake 2 hours at 225⁰. Serves 4.

Mary Newell Coil

State Bird — The mockingbird is the state bird of Texas, adopted by the legislature at the request of the Texas Federation of Women's Clubs.

☆   ☆   ☆

Broiled Quail

1 quail per person	Pepper to taste
Melted butter	Hot buttered toast
Salt to taste	Lemon slices

Clean birds and split down the back. Brush with melted butter. Sprinkle with salt and pepper. Place on greased broiler rack, split side down and broil about 10 minutes or until done. Serve on hot buttered toast with lemon slices.

Vicky Nayes

Quail with Wild Rice

10 quail	2 cloves garlic, minced
2½ sticks butter, divided	2½ cups cooked wild rice
1½ pounds chicken livers	2 cups chicken broth
2 onions, chopped	1½ cups Port wine
1 bell pepper, chopped	

Sauté quail in 1 stick butter until quail are browned. Place in baking dish. Cover, bake at 325⁰ for 30 minutes. Sauté livers, onion, pepper, and garlic in 1½ sticks butter. Do not let vegetables brown, but cook until clear in color. Add cooked rice, chicken broth and wine. Place mixture in 3 quart baking dish; cover and bake at 325⁰ for 20 minutes or until liquid is absorbed. Serve quail over wild rice.

Variation: Body cavity of quail may be sewed up and the quail lightly browned in butter and placed on top of the stuffing in baking dish. Mix chicken broth and wine and pour over quail and stuffing. Bake at 375⁰ for 30 minutes.

Willena Harry

☆　　☆　　☆

Game Birds a la Crème

2	pheasants or 6 quails or 8 doves or 2 Cornish game hens	2	(4 ounces each) cans sliced mushrooms and liquid
Salt to taste		1	onion, thinly sliced
Pepper to taste		½	cup finely chopped celery
Flour		½	cup pitted ripe olives, finely chopped
1	stick butter		
2	cups sour cream	2½	tablespoons chopped pimientos
2	tablespoons lemon juice		

Split larger birds in half; leave others whole. Sprinkle with salt, pepper and paprika. Dredge lightly with flour and brown in butter until golden. Put browned birds into a covered roaster skin side up. Add sour cream, lemon juice, mushrooms and liquid to butter in which birds were browned. Heat thoroughly and pour over birds. Cover and bake at 300° until tender, 1 to 2 hours. Sauce is good over rice. Rather a French taste in wild bird recipes. Delicious! Serves 4.   *Shirley Caldwell*

Wild Dove

12	doves, skinned breast only	¼	cup butter
Flour		¾	cup white wine
Salt to taste		Sliced fresh mushrooms	
Pepper to taste			

Coat birds lightly with flour. Salt and pepper and sauté in butter, turning often to brown evenly. Add white wine and mushrooms, stirring to mix well. Cover and simmer for about 30 minutes. If gravy is too thick add water to thin. Serve with cooked white or wild rice. Serves 2-3.   *Vicky Nayes*

Fried Jalapeño Dove Breasts

Dove breasts
For each breast:

1	jalapeño pepper	Fish fry mix
1	strip bacon	Hot fat or oil
Milk		

Bone dove breasts. Remove seeds from jalapeño peppers. Wrap breasts around pepper. Then wrap bacon strip around breasts and secure with toothpicks. Dip each breast in milk and dredge in fish fry mix. Fry in deep fat until brown.   *Pauline Stults*

☆   ☆   ☆

Fried Fish Fillets

Any small fish fillets
Beer
½ cup corn meal
½ cup flour

Salt to taste
Pepper to taste
Hot shortening or oil

Dip fillets in beer; then in a mixture of cornmeal and flour. Coat well. Season with salt and pepper and deep fry for 2 or 3 minutes or pan fry at high heat until golden brown. Turn pan fried fish once. This is very good for crappie and perch. *Vicky Nayes*

M.E.'s Wild Rice Dressing

1 pound wild rice
1 pound "hot" pork sausage
1 bell pepper, chopped
1 onion, chopped

1 bunch parsley, chopped
Butter
1 (14½ ounce) can chicken broth

Cook rice according to package directions. Fry sausage. Sauté peppers, onions and parsley in butter. Mix sausage, pepper, onion, parsley and chicken broth and simmer until vegetables are tender. Combine with cooked rice. Place in buttered 2½-3 quart casserole. Bake at 350⁰ until it bubbles, approximately 30 minutes. Serves 8. This is a very good accompaniment to duck and other game dishes. *Linda Juba*

Zippy Grits

1 cup quick grits
1 stick margarine
3 ounces garlic cheese

3 ounces jalapeño cheese
½ cup milk
2 eggs, well beaten

Cook grits according to package directions. While still hot, add butter and cheeses. Stir until they are melted. Add milk to eggs and blend well with grits mixture. Pour into 8x11 inch casserole. Bake at 350⁰ until mixture is set and top is golden brown, about 45 minutes. This is excellent with brisket or charcoal steak. Serves 4-6.

The Cookbook Committee

Variation: Omit garlic and jalapeño cheeses. Substitute 6 ounces Kraft Cracker Barrel extra sharp Cheddar cheese, grated. Add 1 (4 ounce) can chopped green chilies and liquid and 1-2 dashes of cayenne pepper. Sprinkle top of casserole with paprika and increase cooking time to 1 hour.

☆   ☆   ☆

Fried Apples

3-4 cooking apples
¾ cup sugar

¼ cup bacon drippings

Core and slice apples into rings about ¼ inch thick. Sauté in bacon drippings, cover with sugar and cook for about 15 to 20 minutes. Excellent for breakfast or a great accompaniment for pork dishes.

Baked Beans and Ground Beef

Great Picnic Dish

2 pounds lean ground beef
4 (21 ounces each) cans
   baked beans
1 (44 ounce) bottle ketchup
1 onion, chopped

2 tablespoons mustard
1 cup brown sugar
1 teaspoon garlic powder
2 tablespoons Worcestershire
2 slices bacon

Brown meat and drain. Mix baked beans, ketchup, onion, mustard, brown sugar, garlic powder and Worcestershire. Top with bacon. Place in greased 3 quart casserole. Cover and bake at 300⁰ for 2 to 2½ hours. Serves 8. *Linda Juba*

Variation: For typical Texas baked beans, omit ground beef.

Beef and Hominy Pie Casserole

Good cold weather quick supper.

1 pound ground beef
1 (1 pound) can hominy,
   drained
2 onions, chopped
½ teaspoon salt

½ teaspoon pepper
1 teaspoon chili powder
1 clove garlic, chopped fine
1 cup canned tomatoes
Grated Cheddar cheese

Brown ground beef. Brown hominy with onions and add to ground beef. Add salt, pepper, chili powder, garlic and tomatoes. Put in buttered 1½ quart casserole. Sprinkle with grated cheese. Bake 20 to 25 minutes at 350⁰. Serve with 24 hour coleslaw (see index) and red beans or pinto beans. Seves 6-8. *Novella Bailey*

☆   ☆   ☆

Texas Beef Skillet

1	pound ground chuck	3	tablespoons chopped bell
¾	cup chopped onion		pepper
1	(16 ounce) can tomatoes,	1½	teaspoon chili powder
	cut up	½	teaspoon salt
1	(15½ ounce) can red	½	teaspoon garlic salt
	kidney beans	¾	cup shredded American
½	cup quick cooking rice		cheese or Cheddar cheese
½	cup water		Corn chips, crushed

In skillet, cook ground chuck and onion until meat is brown and onions are tender. Drain off fat. Stir in undrained tomatoes, undrained beans, rice, water, bell pepper, chili powder, salt and garlic salt. Reduce heat; simmer covered for 20 minutes, stirring occasionally. Top with cheese, cover and heat about 3 minutes or until cheese melts. Sprinkle corn chips around edges. Serves 6.   *Ruth Canada*

Texas Steak K-bobs

MARINADE:

1-2	cloves garlic	1	bay leaf
1	cup dry red wine or		Dash of Tabasco
	Burgundy		Black peppercorns
¼	cup lemon juice		
1	tablespoon olive oil,		
	optional		

2	pounds sirloin or round,		Bell pepper chunks
	cut in 3 inch cubes		Fresh mushrooms
	Cherry tomatoes	1	beef bouillon cube
	Onion chunks	1	cup boiling water

Marinade: Cut garlic in half. Combine wine, lemon juice, oil, bay leaf, garlic, Tabasco and peppercorns. Add meat. Sirloin should marinate overnight. Round will be more tender if marinated two or three days. About 30 minutes before cooking, remove and discard garlic and peppercorns. Reserve marinade. Microwave or parboil onion chunks and bell pepper separately. Thread on skewers, alternating with meat and cherry tomatoes and mushrooms. Charbroil over hot coals *about* 3 minutes on each of 4 sides for medium rare. Dissolve beef bouillon in boiling water and combine with marinade. Heat to a boil. Skim and simmer a few minutes. Serve as gravy with white rice.

Hint: Do not attempt to turn skewer. To rotate, lift holding both ends so all four sides of meat and vegetables will cook evenly.

Ivanette Dennis

☆   ☆   ☆

Brisket

No one can count the ways!

Brisket is made a little differently by every one who cooks it. The basic method is to season the brisket the night before, bake slowly, about 275-300° for 45 minutes per pound. Cover the roasting pan tightly with foil. Amounts listed are approximate, to season 1 (6-7) pound brisket.

Sprinkle meat generously with garlic salt, onion salt, celery salt and liquid smoke. Cover with about ½ inch of Kraft Hickory Smoke Bar B Que sauce.   *Marjo Jeanes*

Mix 1 (5 ounce) bottle soy sauce, 1 (10 ounce) Campbell's consommé, 1 tablespoon liquid smoke, 1 tablespoon vinegar, 1 clove garlic and pour over brisket. Marinate overnight, turning once.   *Joyce Jenkins*

Season brisket with salt and pepper. Cover with 1 (12 ounce) bottle Heinz 57 sauce and 1 (5 ounce) bottle liquid smoke.   *Betsy Gibson*

Other optional ingredients are 2 teaspoons Worcestershire and black pepper.   *Linda Richardson*

Marinate brisket fat side down in about 2 inches of red wine seasoned with 1 tablespoon liquid smoke, whole celery seed and dehydrated onion flakes. When ready to bake, turn brisket so fat side is up, add a little more red wine, smoke and seasonings. Cover with approximately ½ bottle commercial BBQ sauce. Allow brisket to rest about 30 minutes after baking. Slice as thinly as possible against the grain of the meat.
                                                                     Yvonne Prevo

Cover brisket with sliced onions. Put in pan fat side up, pour 1 (12 ounce) can regular beer over brisket, cover tightly, and bake at 275° for 5 to 6 hours or until tender. Discard marinade and serve.
                                                                        Pat Horton

Hint: Most people prefer to refrigerate meat and juices separately. Lift off hardened grease and discard. Reheat meat with remaining sauce.

☆   ☆   ☆

Charcoal B-B-Que Round or Chuck Roast

3-7 pound round or chuck
roast, 1½ inch thick

Marinade: (For 3-4 pound
roast)

⅔	cup red wine vinegar	2	teaspoons prepared
½	cup Heinz chili sauce		mustard
4	tablespoons soy sauce	½	teaspoon black pepper
2	tablespoons Worcestershire		

Mix vinegar, chili sauce, soy sauce, Worcestershire, mustard and pepper in shallow glass baking dish. Add meat. Pierce often with sharp fork. Turn and repeat. Marinate 6 hours at room temperature, turning several times or overnight in refrigerator. Reserve marinade. Grill over charcoal until pink inside. Baste once or twice with marinade last 10 minutes of cooking time. Heat leftover marinade and serve as sauce. Good for cold sliced sandwiches. For thicker round steak marinate in refrigerator for two or three days. Serves 3-4 per pound of meat.

Ivanette Dennis

Mop

2	quarts bone stock	1½	tablespoons paprika
1½	tablespoons salt	1½	tablespoons M.S.G.
1	tablespoon garlic powder	1	tablespoon hot pepper
1½	tablespoons dry mustard		sauce
1	tablespoon chili powder	1	cup salad oil
½	tablespoon ground bay	1	pint Worcestershire
	leaf	1	cup vinegar

Mix all ingredients thoroughly. Keep in refrigerator and use on all grilled meats. Especially good on chicken. Makes about 2½ quarts.

Use a dish mop to apply to meat. Keep dish mop in mixture and it gets better and better as flavor is transferred from meat to mop mixture.

Elsie Whitmarsh

☆   ☆   ☆

Barbecue Sauce

2   sticks butter
1   cup ketchup
½   cup vinegar
Juice of 2 lemons
1   onion, grated
2   tablespoons prepared
      mustard

2   tablespoons prepared
      horseradish
2   tablespoons Worcestershire
1   tablespoon salt
Red pepper to taste

Melt butter. Combine ketchup, vinegar, lemon juice, onion, mustard, horseradish, Worcestershire, salt and pepper. Simmer for 45 minutes. Makes about 2 cups.

This is sufficient to baste 10 pounds of meat. Good on beef or pork.
Novella Bailey

Gourmet's Special for Ribs

½   cup chopped onions
2   tablespoons butter
½   teaspoon pepper
4   teaspoons sugar
1   teaspoon dry mustard
4   teaspoons Worcestershire

⅛   teaspoon Tabasco
1   teaspoon paprika
½   cup ketchup
¼   cup vinegar
¼   cup water

Cook onions slowly in butter until tender. Add pepper, sugar, dry mustard, Worcestershire, Tabasco, paprika, ketchup, vinegar and water and bring to a boil. Simmer gently for 5 minutes, stirring constantly. This amount is sufficient for 2 pounds of ribs.

Allow about ½ to ¾ pound of ribs for each serving. Spareribs should first be cut into serving sized pieces, then baked in a 325° oven for about 1 hour. Sauce is then poured over the meat and the ribs should bake for another half hour. Frequent basting is necessary.   *Pearl Leino*

☆   ☆   ☆

B.B.Q. Spareribs

1	side baby back pork ribs	1	tablespoon ketchup
2	scallions cut in 2 inch pieces	2	tablespoons soy sauce
		2	tablespoons water
2	cloves garlic, slightly crushed	1	tablespoon corn syrup
		½	teaspoon salt
1	tablespoon chili sauce	1	tablespoon honey

Preheat oven to 325⁰. Fill a baking pan with 2 inches of boiling water, add ribs and bake for 1 hour. Combine scallions, garlic, chili sauce, ketchup, soy sauce, water, corn syrup and salt. Remove steamed ribs to a shallow pan and cover with sauce. Bake 2 hours at 275⁰. Turn the ribs occasionally and baste with sauce while they are cooking. Brush both sides with honey. Increase heat to 375⁰ and brown for 10 minutes. Turn ribs and brown 10 minutes longer. Serves 4. *Tura Bethune*

TEXAS has more wildflowers than any other state.

Driskill Hotel Cheese Soup

For Texas Exes

4	cups milk	1	pound Old English or Kraft American cheese, cubed
4	cups chicken stock		
¼	cup butter		
½	cup finely diced onions	½-1	teaspoon salt
½	cup finely diced carrots		White pepper
½	cup finely diced celery		Dash of cayenne pepper
¼	cup flour	1	tablespoon dried parsley
1½	tablespoons cornstarch		Paprika
⅛	teaspoon baking soda		

Milk and stock should be at room temperature. Melt butter. Sauté onion, carrot and celery until tender. Stir in flour and cornstarch. Cook until bubbly. Add stock and milk gradually, blending into a smooth sauce. Add soda and cheese cubes. Stir until thickened. Season with salt, white pepper and cayenne pepper. Add parsley. Before serving, heat thoroughly over boiling water. Do not boil. Garnish with paprika. Serves 6-8.

Dolores Spence

☆　　☆　　☆

Chicken Fried Steak

2	pounds round steak, tenderized	1	teaspoon salt
		1	teaspoon pepper
½	cup flour	½	cup melted shortening

Cut meat into four pieces. Pound the meat until tender. Mix flour, salt and pepper together in a pie pan; dredge steak in mixture. Cook in hot melted shortening over medium-high heat until brown, turn and brown on the other side. The quicker the meat cooks the juicier it stays. Don't overcook steak. Make cream gravy (see index) with meat drippings to serve with the steak. Serves 4-6.

Variation: Some people prefer to beat 1 egg with 1 tablespoon water and dip meat in egg prior to dredging in flour.

Hint: Add ½ teaspoon baking powder to flour for fluffy crust on meat.

Cream Gravy

3	tablespoons drippings	½-1	teaspoon salt
3	tablespoons flour	½	teaspoon pepper
2	cups milk		

This gravy is to be made after frying chicken or chicken fried steak. Drain drippings from skillet leaving at least 3 tablespoons grease and the meat crumbs. Stir in flour to moisten and cook a few minutes until flour begins to brown. Gradually pour in milk, add salt and pepper and stir constantly until gravy thickens, about 5 minutes.

Uncle Billy's Asparagus Gravy

8-10 spears fresh asparagus	1	recipe Cream Gravy (see index)
Bacon drippings		

Wash, drain, and cut asparagus on bias. Simmer asparagus in small amount of water until fork tender and then sauté in bacon drippings. Proceed with directions for cream gravy. As far as I know this family favorite was created in Paris, Texas by my Great-Uncle Billy Crook 70 years ago. Serve for breakfast on biscuits. *Linda Juba*

☆　　☆　　☆

Fried Corn

10-12 ears corn
⅓ cup bacon drippings
1 teaspoon sugar

Salt to taste
Pepper to taste
Water

Cut the kernels off the cobs with a sharp knife being careful not to cut too close to cob. Melt bacon drippings in a skillet; add corn and sauté lightly for about 10 minutes. Scrape the milk from each cob into the skillet. Add sugar, salt and pepper. Cover with just enough water to cover corn and cook for about 25 minutes.

Greens

Mess of greens (turnip, mustard
    or collards)
2 quarts water

2 inch cube salt pork
1 teaspoon salt

Wash greens thoroughly. Strip leaves from stems. Put greens in a pot and add water, salt pork and salt. Cover tightly, bring to a boil, reduce heat and simmer until tender. The longer they cook — the better they taste.

The Proverbial Black-Eyed Pea

About 3 quarts of black-eyed
    peas
Water to cover
½ teaspoon salt, or more to
    taste

Salt pork, ham hock or bacon
    ends

Shell the peas, using some of the tender snaps. In a 3 quart pot, cover the peas with water and add salt. Add your choice of meat. (In an emergency when you're out of meat, peas may be seasoned with Lawry's seasoned salt.) Bring to a boil and simmer about 2 or 2½ hours. Taste and correct seasonings. This same method works for cream peas, crowder peas or purple-hulled peas. Serves 4-6.

Variation: Add a jalapeño or red pepper at the start of cooking time. Add ½ onion, chopped, the last 30 minutes of cooking. Serve with Fresh Relish (see index) and Cornbread (see index).

☆   ☆   ☆

Fried Okra

1-2 pints fresh okra (frozen may be used during emergencies)	Cornmeal or flour Salt Oil or bacon drippings

Wash okra and slice in ¼ inch pieces. Put cornmeal or flour or combination of both in a paper sack and shake until okra is well coated. Heat oil or bacon drippings to 375⁰. Add okra; fry until golden brown. Drain on paper towels and salt. Serve at once.

Variation: Whole okra pods. Use only small, tender pods. Cut off stem, but don't cut into the seed section. Par-boil 3 to 4 minutes. Drain. Dredge in yellow cornmeal. Deep-fat fry in bacon drippings at 400-425⁰ or just below smoking. Fry until golden brown.

Variation: Oven-fried okra: Cut into rounds, dredge in yellow cornmeal. Cover a non-stick skillet with a film of bacon drippings, stir coated okra in skillet. Put on jelly-roll pan in preheated 425⁰ oven. Bake until brown, about 10 minutes. Stir once. Watch carefully, it browns rapidly at the end of cooking time.

Okra and Tomatoes

2 pints fresh okra	Water
1 onion, chopped	Salt to taste
Bacon drippings	Pepper to taste
3-4 fresh tomatoes or 1 (16 ounce) can stewed tomatoes	

Wash and slice okra ½ inch thick. Sauté okra and onion in bacon drippings for about 25 minutes. This takes the slickness out of the okra that is so objectionable. Add tomatoes and enough water to cover. Season to taste. Continue to simmer for about 30 minutes.

Fresh Relish

2-3 tomatoes, diced	2 tablespoons water
1 bell pepper, diced	Salt to taste
½ onion, diced	Pepper to taste
½ cup vinegar	

Mix all of the ingredients and chill for about 30 minutes prior to serving. This is wonderful on black-eyed peas.

☆　　☆　　☆

Candied Sweet Potatoes or Carrots

6-8 sweet potatoes
1 stick margarine
1½ cups sugar
½ cup dark Karo syrup

½ cup orange juice
1 cup pecans, chopped
Marshmallows

Wash and peel potatoes, place in a pot with enough water to cover and let boil slowly for 35 to 40 minutes or until potatoes are just tender. Drain and cool. Cut into quarters or eighths. Place in a well greased 3 quart casserole. Dot with margarine and add sugar, Karo, orange juice and pecans. Bake for 1½ to 2 hours at 350° degrees. Place marshmallows over top and bake for 10 minutes. The secret to real candied sweet potatoes is to cook the syrup well into the potatoes, not to glaze the potatoes with a syrup.

Variation: For Candied Carrots use 2 pounds of carrots cut in 3 inch strips. Omit marshmallows and pecans. *Linda Juba*

Anne's East Texas Biscuits

4-5 cups flour
½ teaspoon baking soda
4 tablespoons baking powder
4 tablespoons sugar

6 tablespoons margarine, sliced
1½-2 cups buttermilk
4 tablespoons melted margarine

Sift flour into mixing bowl and make a hole or nest in the middle of the flour. Put the soda, baking powder, sugar, salt, margarine and milk in the hole and mix with fingers until there is enough flour in the milk to make a very soft dough. Roll out on a well floured board into a large rectangle. Brush one half dough with melted margarine, carefully fold unbuttered half over and cut out biscuits. Use remaining melted butter in pan which biscuits will be baked in. Flip biscuits over to coat each side of biscuits. Bake in hot oven 375° for 15 to 20 minutes.

Linda Juba

☆　　☆　　☆

Corn Pone

Fast and Easy

1	cup corn meal	2-3	green onions, chopped
¼	cup bacon drippings		Boiling water
½	teaspoon salt		

Mix cornmeal, bacon drippings, salt and green onions. Pour enough boiling water to stick mixture together without being too dry or mushy. Form into oval cakes and fry in bacon drippings in skillet, about 3 minutes on each side.

Jack's Hush Puppies

2	cups yellow corn meal	1	egg
1	cup white flour	1	cup milk
1½	teaspoons salt	½	cup water
1½	teaspoons baking powder	3	tablespoons bacon
1	onion, chopped		drippings

Mix corn meal, flour, salt, baking powder, onion, egg, milk, water and bacon drippings together and drop by teaspoonsful into hot deep fat. Cook until golden. Great for a fish fry. *Thecia Faulkner*

Iron Skillet Cornbread

¼	cup shortening	1⅓	cups boiling water
2	cups yellow corn meal	1	cup buttermilk
1	teaspoon salt	2	eggs, beaten
½	teaspoon baking soda	1	tablespoon baking powder
2	tablespoons sugar or 2 packages Sweet & Low		

Preheat oven to 450°. Put shortening in 9 inch iron skillet. Heat in oven because skillet must be very hot when batter is put into it. Mix corn meal, salt, soda and sugar in bowl. Add boiling water to coat the meal (improves texture). Add buttermilk, eggs and baking powder. Mix well. Remove hot skillet from oven, pour excess melted fat into batter, mix again quickly and pour batter into hot pan. Bake 20-25 minutes. Brown top quickly under broiler. (If using for turkey dressing omit sugar.) Serves 6-8. *Danna Almon*

☆ ☆ ☆

Cornbread Dressing

2	onions, chopped	1	teaspoon salt
1	stalk celery, chopped	1	teaspoon pepper
2	sticks margarine, melted	2-3	teaspoons sage
2	recipes Ranch Cornbread (see index)	2	eggs, beaten
2	cups crumbled biscuits	6	cups chicken or turkey broth

Sauté onions and celery in margarine. Combine with crumbled bread, seasonings and eggs. Add broth, stirring until all bread is moist and soft. Check seasonings and adjust according to taste. Stuff inside turkey or place in a greased 3 quart casserole and bake for 45 minutes at 375°.

Mexican Cornbread

A Southwestern Favorite

2	eggs	1	(4 ounce) can chopped green chilies
1	(16 ounce) can creamed corn	2	cups corn meal
2½	cups sweet milk or buttermilk	1	teaspoon baking soda
½	cup salad oil or bacon drippings	1	teaspoon salt
1	onion, chopped	1½	cups grated sharp Cheddar cheese

Mix eggs, corn, milk, oil, onion and green chilies. Mix together corn meal, soda and salt; combine with liquid mixture. Add cheese. Preheat oven to 375°, put well greased pans in oven to preheat and pour batter into warmed pan. Bake at 375° 45 to 60 minutes. Cut into squares and serve.

The Cookbook Committee

Variation: Substitute cornbread mix; omit baking soda and salt. You may also add a few chopped jalapeño peppers to give a zesty flavor.

Mary Rode

☆   ☆   ☆

Ranch Cornbread

1	cup buttermilk	1	teaspoon baking powder
1	egg	½	teaspoon baking soda
1	cup yellow cornmeal	1	teaspoon salt

Beat buttermilk and egg together slightly. Sift cornmeal, baking powder, soda and salt together and add to buttermilk and egg mixture. Pour into a *hot* 9 inch iron skillet, into which 2-3 tablespoons bacon drippings have been melted. Bake at 400° for 20 minutes.

Variation: Omit baking powder. Pour into greased 8x8 inch pan and bake at 450° for 18 to 20 minutes. Makes excellent base for cornbread dressing.

Ann Mize

Rocks

An Old Southern Cookie

1	cup soft butter	1	teaspoon salt
1½	cups sugar	1	pound coarsely chopped
3	eggs, separated		pecan meats
1	teaspoon vanilla	1	pound seeded raisins
3	cups flour	1	teaspoon baking soda
1	teaspoon ground cloves		dissolved in ⅛ cup boiling
1	teaspoon ground nutmeg		water
3	teaspoons ground cinnamon		

Cream butter and sugar. Add egg yolks and beat. Whip egg whites and fold in. Mix in vanilla. Remove ¼ cup flour and put aside. Sift flour with cloves, nutmeg, cinnamon and salt. Mix ¼ cup flour with nuts and raisins to separate them. Add flour mixture to sugar mixture. Stir well. Add soda in water and mix. Add floured nuts and raisins. Mix well. Drop by spoonsful about size of unshelled walnut on cookie sheet. Do not smooth down. Bake at 375° for 10 to 12 minutes. Keep in covered can. Makes 12-14 dozen cookies.

This cookie keeps well and ships well. My grandmother sent them overseas to my father in WWI. They were a Christmas tradition in my family.

Sally Kinne

☆　　☆　　☆

Boomer-Sooner Cake

Perfect for Football Season!

CAKE:

1½	cups sugar		2	ounces red food coloring
½	cup shortening			(for a burnt-orange cake
2	eggs			try 1½ ounces red and ½
2	cups sifted cake flour			ounce yellow food
¼	teaspoon salt			coloring)
1	tablespoon cocoa		1	teaspoon vanilla
¾	cup buttermilk		1	tablespoon vinegar
			1	teaspoon baking soda

PUDDING:

4	tablespoons flour		1	cup milk
½	teaspoon salt			

ICING:

1	cup sugar		½	cup shortening
1	stick butter		1	teaspoon vanilla

CAKE: Cream sugar and shortening, add eggs, beat. Add flour and salt gradually, beating after each addition. Add cocoa; beat in. Add buttermilk, food coloring, and vanilla. Add more buttermilk if buttermilk is very thick. Reduce buttermilk if buttermilk is thin. Beat well. Combine vinegar and soda. Fold in without beating. Bake at 350° for 30 to 35 minutes in three 8 inch round cake pans.

PUDDING: Blend ¼ cup milk with flour and salt, add remaining milk. Cook until thick. Chill thoroughly.

ICING: Cream sugar, shortening, and butter until fluffy; then add vanilla. Blend the chilled pudding and icing mixture by hand and chill again. Frost between layers, on top and on sides. You may sprinkle generously with Angel Flake or fresh coconut if you wish. Store in refrigerator. For larger cake, increase recipe to 1 and ½ times and increase baking time as necessary.

My traitor son and his wife substitute ½ ounce yellow food coloring for part of the red and call it Hook 'Em Horns cake.

Lynn Townsend

☆　　☆　　☆

Sombrero Cake

CAKE:

1 (18.5 ounce) package chocolate or dark chocolate cake mix
1 (3¾ ounce) package instant chocolate pudding mix

½ cup cooking oil
¾ cup milk
4 eggs
¼ cup Kahlúa
¼ cup vodka

GLAZE:

1½ tablespoons vodka
1½ tablespoons milk

1½ tablespoons Kahlúa
1 cup powdered sugar

CAKE: Mix all ingredients together for 4 minutes with electric mixer. Pour into well greased and floured Bundt or tube pan. Bake at 350⁰ for 45 to 50 minutes. Cool.

GLAZE: Mix ingredients and drizzle over warm cake.   *Linda Juba*

Fried Pies

PASTRY:

1 cup flour
¼ teaspoon salt
½ teaspoon baking powder
¼ cup shortening

3-4 tablespoons ice water
Fruit fillings
Oil

FRUIT FILLINGS:

1 (16 ounce) package dried apricots, apples or pears

½-1 cups sugar
2 tablespoons butter

PASTRY: Mix salt, flour and baking powder. Cut in shortening until mixture resembles cornmeal. Stir in water, mix until pastry forms a ball. Cover and chill 1 hour. Roll pastry to ¹⁄₁₆ inch thickness on a floured surface, cut into 4 inch rounds. Place 3 tablespoons filling on half of each pastry circle. Dip fingers in water and moisten edges of circles; fold in half, making sure edges are even. Dip a fork into flour and press edges together to seal. Heat 1 inch oil to 375⁰. Cook pies in hot oil until golden on both sides, turning once. Drain well on paper towels.

FILLING: Cook fruit according to package directions. Mash well until smooth. Blend in remaining ingredients.

☆   ☆   ☆

The Best Little Chocolate Pie in Texas

1¼	cups sugar	2	(1 ounce each) squares Baker's Chocolate
¼	teaspoon salt		
4	tablespoons cornstarch	2	tablespoons butter
2	cups milk, scalded	1	teaspoon vanilla
3	eggs, separated	1	(9 inch) baked pastry shell

Mix sugar, salt, and cornstarch. Then combine with scalded milk. Add chocolate. Cook slowly over low heat in a heavy pan or double boiler, stirring constantly, for 15 to 20 minutes. Beat egg yolks. Stir small amount of hot mixture into the yolks. Then return the yolk-chocolate mixture to the pan (this prevents the eggs from cooking). Cook for 5 more minutes. Add butter and vanilla and let cool to room temperature. (To prevent a crust from forming on the custard, cover with clear plastic wrap or wax paper.) Use reserved egg whites for meringue. (See index). Bake at 325° for 15 to 20 minutes.

The Cookbook Committee

Mrs. Harber's Famous Carmel Pie

1	cup sugar, divided	⅛	teaspoon salt
¼	cup water	1	teaspoon vanilla
1	tablespoon flour	1	tablespoon gelatin
1	tablespoon cornstarch	1	tablespoon cold water
1½	cups milk	1	(9 inch) baked pie crust
3	eggs, separated		

Brown ½ cup sugar in a skillet. When dark brown and melted, add water. When sugar is dissolved, remove from heat. Mix flour, cornstarch, milk, egg yolks, ½ cup sugar, salt and vanilla. Stir into this mixture the caramelized sugar. Cook until thick. Add gelatin dissolved in cold water. Cool and fill shell. Use egg whites to make meringue (see index).

Lemon Chess Pie

1	stick butter	1½	cups sugar
½	cup milk	3	tablespoons lemon juice
4	eggs	1	(9 inch) unbaked pie shell

Melt butter until caramel color. Add milk until almost scalded. Cool. Beat eggs, add sugar and lemon juice. Pour into pie shell, bake at 325° for 45 minutes.

Linda Juba

☆   ☆   ☆

Jeff Davis' Favorite Chess Pie

3	cups sugar	1	cup coconut
4	eggs, beaten	½	cup pecan halves
1	cup milk	2	unbaked deep dish (10
2	tablespoons flour		inch) pie shells or 3 (8
1	teaspoon vanilla		inch) unbaked pie shells
1	stick margarine, melted		

Beat sugar, eggs, milk, flour, vanilla and margarine until well mixed. Stir in coconut and pecans and pour into pie shells. Bake at 350° for one hour.

This version of the pie was given to me by the wife of my husband's World War I friend.   *Addie Spurlock*

Buttermilk Pie

Delicious and fattening!

2	cups sugar	3	tablespoons lemon juice
3	tablespoons flour	1	teaspoon vanilla
¼	teaspoon nutmeg	1	teaspoon grated lemon
½	cup melted butter		rind
3	eggs, lightly beaten	1	(9 inch) partially baked
1	cup buttermilk		pie crust

Mix sugar, flour and nutmeg. Add butter and beat until creamy. Stir in eggs, buttermilk, lemon juice, vanilla and lemon rind. Pour into pie crust. Cook at 350° about 1 hour. Test with toothpick. Serves 6-8.

Vivian Brotherton

Pecan Pie

1	stick butter	¼	teaspoon salt
3	eggs, beaten slightly	1	teaspoon vanilla
1	cup sugar	1	cup pecan halves
1	cup dark Karo syrup	1	(9 inch) unbaked pie shell

Melt butter in saucepan until golden brown or just before it starts to burn. Cool. (This is the secret to this pecan pie.) Beat eggs, add sugar, syrup, salt, vanilla and butter. Pour into pie shell, place pecans on top of filling. Bake at 400° for 10 minutes, reduce heat to 325° and continue baking for 35 minutes or until set.   *Linda Juba*

☆   ☆   ☆

Aunt Mae's Chess Pie

1	stick butter	1	cup sugar
¾	cup milk	1	teaspoon vanilla
3	eggs, room temperature	¼	teaspoon nutmeg
¼	teaspoon salt	1	(9 inch) unbaked pie shell

Melt butter until caramel color; add milk until milk is almost scalded. Cool. Beat eggs, add salt, sugar and vanilla. Pour into pie shell. Grate nutmeg on top of pie. Bake at 325⁰ for 45 minutes or until set.

The secret to this pie is to brown the butter and scald the milk. This chess pie is also different because there isn't any corn meal or flour in the recipe.   *Linda Juba*

Apple Dumplings

½	apple, peeled; sliced or chunked	¼	teaspoon cinnamon
		1	tablespoon margarine
2	tablespoons sugar	1	(6 inch) pastry circle

SIMPLE SAUCE:

½	cup sugar	1	teaspoon cinnamon
1	cup water	4	tablespoons margarine

This recipe is for 1 apple dumpling. Increase proportions for the number of dumplings you choose to make. Roll pastry, fill with apple, sprinkle sugar and cinnamon, top with margarine. Fold pastry around apple mixture, leaving vent in center. Place dumplings in baking pan and fill with ¼ inch water. Bake at 350⁰ for 45 minutes. Serve warm with sauce.

SAUCE: Bring sugar, water and cinnamon to a boil and simmer until thickened (about 5 to 7 minutes). Add margarine. Cool slightly. Spoon over dumpling at serving time. This can be made ahead and reheated just before serving.   *Linda Juba*

☆   ☆   ☆

Strawberry Shortcake

Fresh strawberries
Sugar to taste
2 (4 inches each) pastry
   rounds

1 recipe syrup, recipe
   follows

Syrup:
½ cup sugar
1 cup water

4 tablespoons margarine
¼ cup sliced berries

Wash and stem berries, slice. Sugar to taste, but leave slightly tart. Layer pastry with fresh berries and make a stack. Pour warm syrup over and serve.

SYRUP: Bring sugar and water to boil, simmer until thickened about 5 to 7 minutes. Add berries and cook for about 2 to 3 more minutes. Remove from heat, add margarine. Serve slightly warm over shortcake.

This is my all time favorite dessert that my grandmother used to prepare.
Linda Juba

Fruit Cobblers

1-2 quarts prepared fruit
   (peaches, dewberries or
   blackberries)
Sugar to taste
1 tablespoon lemon juice

1 stick margarine
1 cup water
1 recipe pastry for double
   crust pie

Prepare fruit, sugar to taste and add lemon juice. Grease a 9x12 pan, place fruit in pan; dot with margarine, and add water. Roll pastry into a rectangle and cut into strips and cover top of fruit. Sprinkle additional sugar over pastry and bake in 350⁰ oven until brown (about 45 to 50 minutes).

☆　　☆　　☆

Jalapeño Jelly

½-¾ cup chopped jalapeño peppers

½-¾ cup chopped bell peppers

5 cups sugar

1-1¼ cups vinegar (wine or white)

½ cup water

1 bottle Certo

Place peppers in a large pot. Add sugar, vinegar and water. Bring to a boil for 5 minutes. Remove from heat and let cool for 20 minutes. Add Certo; mix well and replace pot on heat. Allow jelly to come to a full boil; remove from heat. Stir well and pour into jelly glasses. Seal with paraffin when jelly has cooled. Makes 5-6 pint jars.

This jelly makes an excellent and unusual appetizer. Spread crackers with cream cheese and top with small amount of Jalapeño Jelly, or spread jelly over slightly softened cream cheese and serve with crackers on the side.

Imp Lightner

Variation:

¼ cup ground jalapeños, (8 or 10) seeds included

¾ cup ground bell peppers (seeded)

1½ cups white vinegar

6½ cups sugar

1 bottle Certo

Please wear rubber gloves when handling jalapeños. Mix jalapeños, bell peppers, vinegar and sugar in large saucepan or kettle. Boil 8 to 10 minutes. Remove from heat; add Certo and stir well. Cool slightly and put in sterilzied jelly jars. Seal with paraffin. If you use red ripe bell peppers and red jalapeños, your jelly will be a beautiful red color. If you use green bell pepper and green jalapeños, you may wish to add a little green food coloring. Makes 6-8 pints or several smaller containers.

Novella Bailey

State Holidays—Texas has two state holidays and several special observance days. The two holidays are Texas Independence Day, March 2, and San Jacinto Day, April 21.

☆   ☆   ☆

Buttermilk Pralines

1	cup buttermilk	1	tablespoon butter
2	cups sugar	1	teaspoon vanilla
1	teaspoon baking soda	2	cups pecans

Use heavy skillet. Cook buttermilk, sugar, and soda to a soft ball stage (234°). Add butter, vanilla and pecans. Beat until firm. Drop by spoonsful on waxed paper.   *Mildred Phillips*

Sour Cream Fudge

This candy does not do well on humid days.

2	cups sugar	2	tablespoons butter
1	cup sour cream	1	teaspoon vanilla
13	large marshmallows	1	cup chopped nuts

Combine sugar and sour cream. Cook over low heat. When mixture comes to a boil add marshmallows. Continue cooking over low heat until candy forms firm ball when dropped in cold water, (245°). Add butter and vanilla. Let candy cool. Beat until candy loses gloss; add nuts. Pour into a buttered 9x9 square pan.   *Linda Juba*

Divinity

3	cups sugar	4	egg whites (stiffly beaten)
1½	cups water	1	teaspoon vanilla
1	cup white corn syrup	1	cup chopped pecans

Cook sugar, water, and syrup to the soft ball stage (238°); then pour ½ of the syrup mixture slowly over the beaten egg whites. Add vanilla. Return remainder of syrup mixture to heat and cook to hard ball stage (250°) or until syrup crackles when dropped into cold water. Continue beating candy while the remaining syrup cooks, and then pour over candy and beat until mixture forms soft peaks and begins to lose its gloss. Add nuts. Drop from teaspoon, pushing off with a second spoon onto wax paper. If Divinity becomes too hard, beat in a few drops of hot water.

☆   ☆   ☆

Peanut Brittle

1	cup white corn syrup	2	tablespoons butter
2	cups sugar	2	teaspoons vanilla
½	cup water	2	teaspoons soda
1	pound raw peanuts	½	teaspoon salt

Combine syrup, sugar and water in heavy saucepan. Bring slowly to 230⁰ or until syrup spins a thread. Add peanuts and continue to cook to 300⁰. Stir to prevent burning. Remove from heat. Add butter, vanilla, soda and salt and stir until blended. Pour into well buttered cookie sheet. When cool, break into pieces. *Elizabeth Gross*

Strawberry Preserves

2	heaping cups fresh strawberries	3	tablespoons lemon juice
		3	cups sugar

Wash and stem berries. Bring berries and lemon juice to a rolling boil and cook for three minutes. Add sugar and bring back to boil and cook six minutes. Pour into hot sterilized jars, let stand 24 hours before sealing. Makes 2 pints.

Fig Preserves

6	cups peeled and chopped figs	1	thinly sliced lemon
		3	cups sugar

Combine the figs, lemon and sugar in a large pot. Cook on medium heat until thick, stirring just enough to prevent sticking, for about 1 hour. Spoon into hot sterilized jars; seal. Makes 6-7 half pints.

Kitty Brown

Wine Jelly

2	cups wine (Sherry, Port or your choice)	3	cups sugar
		1	envelope Certo

Put wine and sugar in top of double boiler over boiling water. Stir until all sugar melts and mixture is hot. Add Certo after removing from heat. Put into sterile jelly glasses and seal with paraffin. If you use white wine, you can color it red or green. Beautiful. *Novella Bailey*

☆   ☆   ☆

TEX-MEX
A TASTE OF THE BORDER

Avocado Margarita

Tostados   Texas Hot

Layered Guacamole Dip

Stack Enchiladas

Tacos

Green Enchiladas Mavis

Huevos Ranchero

Sombrero Cake

Buttermilk Pralines

Sangria

The DeGolyer Estate

Entertaining in Texas frequently favors colorful table settings and the flavors of spicy Tex-Mex foods. The Spanish-Mexican heritage is so ingrained in Texas culture it's hard to tell where the Mexican influence ends and Texas begins. That's why we call our food, Tex-Mex.

A comida of fiery Mexican dishes toned down a shade or two for visitors' palates blends with the style of the DeGolyer Estate. The Spanish colonial hacienda, built in 1939-1940 by Nell and Everette Lee DeGolyer, was named Rancho Encinal, or Ranch of the Oaks.

DeGolyer began his career as a geologist in the Mexican oil fields before World War I and gained international recognition as the founder of applied petroleum geophysics. He will probably be remembered as much for what he left above the earth as he will for what he discovered beneath its surface.

The DeGolyer estate and the neighboring Alex Camp property are now the home of the Dallas Arboretum and Botanical Society. The 66 acres of gardens, replanted seasonally, are open to the public year around. The Dallas Arboretum, perched on the southeast border of White Rock Lake, is a showplace, highly favored as a site for weddings, parties, receptions and seminars.

Recipes from **THE TEXAS EXPERIENCE**
prepared by

The Martinez Café
Dallas   Plano

Photography
Mike Flahive

Mama Jones' Peach Pickles

7	pounds cling peaches	½	teaspoon whole cloves
1	quart vinegar	1	large stick cinnamon
8	cups sugar		broken into bits.
1	teaspoon allspice		

Dip peaches into boiling water for 30 seconds to loosen skins. Cool in cold water; drain. Place in 4 quart bowl containing 1½ tablespoons salt and 2 quarts water to prevent darkening. Drain just before using.

Bring vinegar and spices to a boil; then add peaches. Cook until peaches are heated through, but not soft. Fill 4 quart jars. Boil syrup.15 to 20 minutes; then pour over peaches and seal. Process in boiling water bath 20 minutes.

Mama Jones' Chow Chow

1	peck green tomatoes	1	pound brown sugar
1	head cabbage (about 2 pounds)	2	tablespoons pickling spices
1	bell pepper	2	tablespoons tumeric or enough for desired color
4-6	onions (1 pint)		Vinegar (about 1 gallon)
1	cup uniodized salt		

Grind tomatoes, cabbage, bell pepper and onions. Put in an earthenware jar. Sprinkle with salt. Let stand several hours or overnight. Drain. Put in large enamel or stainless steel kettle and sprinkle with sugar. Put pickling spices and tumeric in a cheesecloth bag. Cover with vinegar. Simmer until the chow chow reaches desired color. Ladle into 18 hot pint jars. Process in boiling water bath for 15 minutes. Seal jars.

Hint: When working with pickles it is best to always use either plastic, enamel or stainless steel utensils. Never cook pickles in aluminum.

Hint: Always use pickling or uniodized salt in pickles or when canning food.

☆   ☆   ☆

Richardson Woman's Club Pickles

We started selling these at bake sales in 1958!

1	gallon whole dill or sour pickles	1	teaspoon allspice
5	pounds sugar	3	tablespoons celery seed
3	tablespoons mustard seed	3	tablespoons whole cloves
8	sticks cinnamon	8	cloves garlic
		4	Jalapeño pods, optional

Drain and discard juice from pickles. Cut into ¾ inch thick slices and place in a two gallon crock. (Don't use aluminum!) Pour sugar and spices over pickle slices. After 24 hours stir with wooden or stainless steel spoon. Then stir 2 or 3 times daily. They are ready to eat after the third day. May be left in crock (covered) or packed into four one-quart jars and sealed.

There will be lots of juice left when pickles are gone. Don't throw it away! It's wonderful for basting a baked ham. Also gives a delightful flavor to tuna or chicken salad. (Put some pickles in the salad, too!)

Novella Bailey

RWC Sweet Crispy Pickles

7	pounds fresh cucumbers	1	tablespoon mixed pickling spice
2	quarts white vinegar		
4	pounds sugar	1	tablespoon whole cloves
1	tablespoon celery seed	1	tablespoon pickling salt (do not substitute)

Peel cucumbers and slice ¾ inch thick. Seed cucumbers with a doughnut cutter. Soak cucumbers overnight in lime water (2 cups builders lime to 2 gallons of water). Rinse very well. Cover with ice water for 3 hours. Drain. Cover with vinegar, sugar spice mix and allow to stand overnight. Bring to a boil and cook 35 minutes. Jar and seal. Makes 6-7 pints.

Variation: Color red or green with food coloring. They look like apple slices and are wonderful.

Juice from both pickle recipes may also be used for flavoring drained, plain sweet "store-boughten" pickles or canned beets. Novella Bailey

☆　　☆　　☆

Pickled Okra

1	quart cider vinegar	Garlic bud
2	quarts water	Celery sticks
1	cup salt	Bell pepper strips
1-1½	tablespoons dill seed	Okra, 3 to 4 inches long

Boil vinegar, water, salt and dill seed. Strain. Place garlic bud in bottom of jar. Pack sterilized jar in this order; 2 celery sticks, 2 bell pepper strips, and okra. As you fill jar with okra reverse okra in jar with one stem up and one down; jars are easier to fill. Reheat vinegar mixture to boiling point and pour over vegetables and seal jars. A water bath is not necessary. Keep 6 weeks before opening. This works beautifully for green tomatoes (patio or cherry). The marinade will keep indefinitely in a sterilized container; this is neat if you grow okra and you want to pickle a small amount at a time. Pickled okra is great on the cocktail table as an appetizer.

Hot Pickled Okra

3	pounds young tender okra, no pod over 4 inches long	½	cup uniodized salt
		6	jalapeño peppers
4	cups water	6	cloves garlic
2	cups acid strength (5%) cider vinegar	6	heads dill (the flower)

Leave okra whole, without stemming, but pierce with a fork. Bring water, vinegar and salt to a boil. Pack okra lengthwise into 6 sterilized hot pint jars. To each jar add 1 jalapeño, 1 clove garlic and 1 head dill. Pour boiling vinegar into each jar within ¼ inch of jar top. Process in water bath 5 minutes. Seal jars. Let stand 3 to 4 weeks before serving.

Novella Bailey

Variation: For an Okie-tini add one pod to your favorite martini instead of an olive.

Glenn Dennis

☆   ☆   ☆

Mexican Hot Sauce

3 bell peppers	Jalapeños to taste
6 carrots	5 (16 ounces each) cans
2 onions	stewed tomatoes

Cut bell pepper, carrots, onions and jalapeños in large chunks. Put in a saucepan and cover with cold water. Heat until the water comes to a boil. (Canned jalapeños don't need to be parboiled.) Process vegetables in a blender (this is too liquid for the food processor) until well blended. Add 3 cans stewed tomatoes to blender. Chop other tomatoes by hand for texture. Fill sterilized pint jars and seal. Use a water bath for 20 minutes. *Carole Price*

Texas Hot

Tour of Homes Favorite

6-8 tomatoes or 1 (28 ounce) can of tomatoes	1 teaspoon celery seed
5-6 red bell peppers	1 teaspoon mustard seed
5-6 green bell peppers	1 cup vinegar
8-10 jalapeños, including seeds	1 tablespoon pickling salt
1 onion, chopped fine	1 tablespoon fresh dill, chopped

Grind all peppers in blender. Add tomatoes and blend again. Add jalapeños, onion, celery seed, mustard seed, vinegar, pickling salt and dill and cook 30 minutes. Seal in sterilized jars. May be processed in hot water bath, if desired. Makes 2 pints. *Novella Bailey*

Homemade Picante

13½ pounds ripe tomatoes	¼ cup salt
5 pounds onions	¼ cup black pepper
2½ pounds jalapeño peppers	3½ cups vinegar

For "HOT" sauce leave seeds in the jalapeños. For milder sauce, remove the seeds before beginning the recipe.

Grind tomatoes, onions and jalapeños. Pour over salt, pepper and vinegar. Mix well. Cook in stainless steel or enamel kettle until desired thickness. Pour in scalded jars and seal with NEW lids and NEW jar rings. Do not substitute for new lids and rings. Yield 14-15 pints. *Shirley Rind*

☆   ☆   ☆

Our Specialties

Our favorite recipes include the foods we serve to our families and to our friends. Many of the recipes we have adapted from each other, tasting and cooking together in our Clubhouse kitchen. Our members have lived in every state and many foreign countries, so these recipes are seasoned from everywhere.

☆   ☆   ☆

Chicken Liver Pâté

Make Ahead

1	pound chicken livers	½	teaspoon salt
4	tablespoons grated onion	½	teaspoon nutmeg
1	stick soft margarine	2	teaspoons dry mustard
Dash of cayenne pepper		¼	teaspoon ground cloves

Drop the chicken livers into just enough boiling water to cover them. Simmer, covered, for 15 minutes. Drain well. Put the livers through the finest blade of a food chopper. Add onion, margarine, cayenne, salt, nutmeg, dry mustard, cloves and blend well. Pack in a crock or small glass jar. Store the pâté in the refrigerator for at least 12 hours. The pâté will keep for about 1 week. Makes about 2 cups.   *Lynda Corbin*

Tuna Pâté

Must Be Made Ahead

1	(8 ounce) package cream cheese, softened	1	teaspoon instant minced onions
2	tablespoons chili sauce	½	teaspoon Tabasco
2	tablespoons snipped parsley	2	(7¾ ounces each) cans tuna, drained and flaked

Mix cream cheese with chili sauce, parsley, onions and Tabasco. Gradually add tuna. Blend well. Pack in mold or bowl to shape. Chill three hours. Unmold and serve with crackers.   *Dolores Spence*

Almond Pâté

1	(8 ounce) package ripe Brie, rind discarded, room temperature	½	cup slivered almonds, toasted
1½	sticks butter, softened	2	tablespoons dry Sherry
		¼	teaspoon thyme

Whip the Brie, butter, almonds, Sherry and thyme together. Spoon into cheese crock, cover and chill for 2 hours. Let stand at room temperature for 1 hour before serving. Makes 2½ cups.   *Hat Madsen*

☆　　☆　　☆

Salted Pecans

1   quart shelled pecans   Salt to taste

Soak shelled pecans in ice water for 10 minutes. Drain on paper towels.
Spread out on cookie sheet and sprinkle very generously with salt. It's
nearly impossible to use too much salt. Roast in 300° oven for about 45
minutes, stirring about every ten minutes. Cook until crisp. To test
pecans, let one cool a minute and check for crispness.

*Do not use any butter or margarine. They'll be the best you ever ate
and think of the calories you'll save!*   *Meredith Marston*

Prunes and Stuff

Must Be Made in Advance

1   (1 pound) box seeded   1   tablespoon mayonnaise or
     prunes   1 tablespoon milk
Burgundy or Port wine   ½   cup chopped Black
1   (8 ounce) package cream   Walnuts
     cheese

Cover prunes with wine and let stand 3 days. Drain. Soften cream cheese,
add mayonnaise and nuts. Make into small balls and fill the prunes.

Variation: May also use a strong Cheddar cheese mixed with pecans.
                                                          Novella Bailey

Sweet Bacon Roll-Ups

1   pound bacon   1   (8 ounce) package pitted
1   cup pineapple juice   dates
¼   cup honey   1   tablespoon soy sauce

Slice each piece of bacon in half. Wrap around a date and secure with
a toothpick. Blend pineapple juice, soy sauce and honey and use as a
marinade. Marinate the roll-ups about 1 hour, turning occasionally.
Remove from marinade and broil until bacon is cooked.

Variation: An almond may be placed in the date before wrapping in
bacon.   *Hat Madsen*

☆   ☆   ☆

Woodcook's Bacon
Water Chestnut Hors d'Oeuvre

1	(8 ounce) can water chestnuts, drained	2	tablespoons soy sauce
¼	cup dark rum (80 proof)	4	bacon slices
			Sugar

Marinate water chestnuts in rum and soy sauce 1 hour. Turn occasionally. Roll each in sugar. Coat well. Cut 4 bacon slices in ½. Then cut lengthwise in ½ again to make 16 strips. Wrap bacon strips around water chestnuts. Fasten with wooden picks. Bake at 400⁰ for 15-18 minutes. Drain well. Serves 10.

Cocktail Dates

1	(16 ounce) package pitted dates	Bacon slices, cut in thirds
1	(8 ounce) package cream cheese	

Fill dates with cream cheese. Wrap bacon slice around date and secure with toothpick. Broil 3 to 4 minutes on a broiling pan. *Elizabeth Gross*

Drunk Pineapple

1	(20 ounce) can pineapple chunks	1	cup vodka

Drain pineapple. Cover with vodka and put into freezer. Serve slightly icy with toothpicks. Great sweet for a cocktail buffet.

Cheese Biscuits

½	pound Old English cheese, grated	½	teaspoon red pepper
2	sticks butter	1	teaspoon salt
1	cup finely chopped pecans	2½	cups flour

Blend cheese and butter thoroughly. Add pecans, red pepper, salt and flour. Mix well. Make 4 logs, 8 inches long. Wrap in waxed paper and place in refrigerator until ready to bake. Slice ⅛ inch thick and place on lightly greased cookie sheet. Bake at 350⁰ for 20 minutes.

Carol Garrigues

☆   ☆   ☆

Cheese Wafers

2	sticks margarine	⅛	teaspoon cayenne pepper
2	cups sharp Cheddar cheese, grated		Dash of salt
2	cups flour, sifted	2	cups Rice Krispies

Preheat oven to 350⁰. Blend margarine and Cheddar cheese. Add flour, cayenne pepper and salt. Fold in Rice Krispies and roll into balls the size of a marble. Place on greased cookie sheet and mash with floured fork. Bake 10 minutes or until lightly brown. Makes 120. Serves 30-40. Freezes well.

Gail McAda

Magnificent Mushrooms

1	pound mushrooms halved or, if large, sliced	1	tablespoon basil
½	cup dry vermouth	1	teaspoon salt
½	cup olive oil	½	teaspoon pepper
½	cup wine vinegar	½	teaspoon sugar
1	garlic clove, crushed	½	teaspoon dry mustard
2	tablespoons chopped onion		

Put mushrooms in a jar. Combine remaining ingredients and mix well. Pour over mushrooms. Serves 8-10 for cocktails. Sealed and refrigerated these will keep for several weeks.

Goodies from Goodman By Jimmy and Bob

Ginger's Fried Mushrooms

1	pound fresh mushrooms	½	cup milk
	Flour	¼	teaspoon salt
1	egg, beaten	2	cups cornflakes, crushed

Clean and stem mushrooms. Dredge lightly in flour. Dip in batter of egg, milk and salt. Roll in crushed cornflakes. Fry one minute on both sides. Take out and lightly salt. Serve while hot. *Linda Juba*

☆　☆　☆

Mushroom Puffs

Very Good Hors d'Oeuvre

1½	pounds fresh mushrooms	2	tablespoons chopped parsley
2	tablespoons oil	½	teaspoon onion powder
½	cup milk	¼	teaspoon salt
1	tablespoon flour		Dash of pepper
2	eggs, separated		
2	tablespoons chopped pimiento		

Clean mushrooms. Carefully remove stems from mushroom caps and lightly brush with oil. Place on baking sheet and set aside. In a small saucepan combine milk with flour and mix well. Cook and stir until medium thick. Cool slightly. Beat egg yolks in small bowl and stir in milk mixture. Add pimiento, parsley, onion powder, salt and pepper and mix. Beat egg whites until stiff and fold into sauce mixture. Fill mushroom caps with souffle mixture. Bake at 375° for 15 to 20 minutes. Makes 25-30. *Martha Crowley*

Parmesan Mushrooms

12	mushrooms	⅛	teaspoon oregano
2	tablespoons butter	½	teaspoon salt
¼	cup chopped onion	1	tablespoon chopped parsley
2	cloves garlic, chopped	1	tablespoon sour cream, if needed
⅓	cup seasoned bread crumbs		
3	tablespoons grated Parmesan cheese		

Wash mushrooms, break off stems and remove a little meat to make a deeper cavity for the stuffing. Chop stems and scraped meat. Sauté onions, garlic and chopped mushrooms in butter. Combine bread crumbs, Parmesan cheese, oregano, salt and parsley with the sautéed mixture. Pile into mushroom caps. (If mixture seems too dry to hold together well, mix with 1 tablespoon sour cream before stuffing.) Place on oiled baking pan and bake for 15 minutes in 400° oven. Serves 6.

Delicious served with meats at dinner, too! *Ruth Dirks*

☆　　☆　　☆

Julie Benell's Stuffed Mushrooms

24	mushrooms (1¾-2 inches in diameter)	⅓	cup chopped ripe olives
⅔	cup Sauterne	⅓	cup grated Parmesan cheese
¼	teaspoon dill weed	2	tablespoons chopped parsley
¼	cup chopped onion		Salt to taste
2	tablespoons butter or margarine		Pepper to taste
1	cup finely chopped cooked chicken		

Clean mushrooms and remove stems. Chop stems and set aside. Place caps in frying pan; add Sauterne and sprinkle with dill. Cover and simmer 5 minutes. Drain the mushrooms well, saving the wine. Sauté onions and chopped stems in butter. Add wine from mushroom caps, and simmer until liquid is evaporated. Remove from heat, and mix with chicken, olives, cheese and parsley. Season to taste with salt and pepper. Place mushroom caps, stem side up, in a buttered baking dish, and sprinkle with salt. Heap chicken mixture into caps, packing tightly. You may freeze at this point. Allow to thaw. Bake at 350⁰ about 15 minutes until thoroughly heated.   *Lynn Townsend*

Cheesy Mushroom Puffs

1	(3 ounce) package cream cheese, softened	2	drops pepper sauce
2	(8 ounce cans) mushrooms, drained and chopped	1	(9 ounce) can refrigerated quick crescent dinner rolls
2	tablespoons chopped pimiento	⅓	cup finely chopped nuts, and/or grated cheese if preferred
1	teaspoon instant minced onion or 1 tablespoon chopped onion		

Preheat oven to 375⁰. In small bowl blend cream cheese, chopped mushrooms, pimiento, onion and pepper sauce. Separate crescent dough into four rectangles; press perforations to seal. Spread each with about 1-2 tablespoons mushroom mixture. Starting at longer side roll up. Seal. Cut each into six pieces. Roll in nuts, or sprinkle grated cheese on top. Bake on ungreased cookie sheet 15 to 20 minutes or until golden brown. If cheese topping is used, do not put on until the last five minutes of baking. Serve warm.   *Corrine Shaw*

☆   ☆   ☆

Cucumber Sandwich Spread
(or Dip)

1	(8 ounce) package cream cheese	1	teaspoon minced dry onion
¼	teaspoon salt	2	tablespoons mayonnaise
¼	teaspoon pepper	1	small cucumber
¼	teaspoon lemon juice	3	drops green food coloring

Soften cream cheese. Add salt, pepper, lemon juice, onion, mayonnaise and coloring. Beat until smooth. Peel cucumber and dice very fine. Drain well. (Important!) Fold cucumber into seasoned cheese.

An excellent spread for party tea sandwiches. Also a good dip.
Virginia Matzen

If cucumbers are sliced very thin and put on top of sandwich; then use enough milk with cheese to make it spreadable. If this method is used, omit adding cucumbers to cheese spread. Sprinkle a little dill weed or parsley on top of cucumber slices. About 1 and ¾ loaves of thin sliced bread with crusts removed will make 100 party sandwiches. This is 25 sandwiches cut in fourths. A thin coating of soft margarine on the bread before the cheese is spread will help prevent the sandwich from getting soggy. *Patsy Blankinship*

Geron's Swiss Cheese Spread

Original Family Recipe

1	pound Swiss cheese, grated	3-4	green onions, finely chopped, including tops
1	(3 ounce) jar real bacon bits	1	cup homemade mayonnaise (see index)

Mix cheese, bacon bits, onions and mayonnaise. This recipe must be made with homemade not "store-bought" mayonnaise and must have the real bacon bits. One pound of bacon, fried, drained and crumbled may be used instead of the jar of bacon bits. Serve on party rye.

Pretty served in a red cabbage hollowed out for a cocktail buffet.
Linda Juba

☆   ☆   ☆

Everlasting Cheese Spread

A Tour of Homes Recipe

1	pound Cheddar cheese, grated	1	teaspoon dry mustard
4	ounces Philadelphia cream cheese, softened	8	teaspoons brandy
8	teaspoons salad oil	1	teaspoon caraway seeds, optional

Blend cheese, cream cheese, oil, mustard and brandy. Stir in caraway seeds if desired. Mix well. Store in covered jar in refrigerator. Do not freeze. Serve at room temperature with crackers.

Variation: Use Port wine instead of brandy.   *Jonelle Jordan*

Chutney Cheese Ball

2	(8 ounces each) packages cream cheese	2	teaspoons curry powder
½	cup chutney		Chopped nuts
			Chopped parsley

Combine cream cheese, chutney and curry and mix well until blended. Roll in chopped nuts or parsley. Makes 1 large ball or 2 small ones. May be frozen.

Variation: Add 1 cup grated Cheddar cheese to cream cheese. Garnish with chives.   *Hat Madsen*

Martha's Cheese Ball

1	pound Cheddar cheese	1	teaspoon chopped onion
1	pound cream cheese	¼	teaspoon garlic powder
¼	pound Blue cheese		Sherry or Port wine
1	teaspoon prepared mustard	1	cup chopped nuts

Soften Cheddar cheese by running through food processor. Mix Cheddar cheese, cream cheese, Blue cheese, mustard, onion and garlic powder. Add enough wine to soften. Wrap in wax paper and chill well. Shape in log or ball. Roll in nuts and refrigerate. Taste improves after 24 hours. Serves 16.   *Martha Brott*

☆   ☆   ☆

Cheese Ball

2   (8 ounces each) packages   1   (2½ ounce) jar Armour
    cream cheese   dried beef, chopped
1   teaspoon horseradish   Chopped pecans or chopped
    mustard   parsley

Whip cheese. Add mustard and beef and shape into ball. Roll in chopped
pecans or parsley. Serve with crackers.   *Patricia Brott*

Olive and Chive Cheese Ball

12 ounces cream cheese,   2   tablespoons chopped
    softened   chives
6   ounces Bleu cheese,   1   (2 ounce) can chopped
    crumbled   ripe olives, drained
2   tablespoons softened   ¾   cup chopped pecans,
    margarine   divided
Dash of Worcestershire

By hand, blend cream cheese, Bleu cheese, margarine, Worcestershire
and chives. Add olives and ¼ cup of pecans and blend well. Place in
bowl for several hours or shape by hand. Roll ball in ½ cup chopped
pecans. Serve with crackers. Serves 8-12.   *Dolores Spence*

Cheese Surprise Ball

1   pound Old English Cheese   ½   teaspoon Worcestershire
1   stick margarine   ¼   teaspoon cayenne pepper
1   (3 ounce) package cream   ½   teaspoon paprika
    cheese with chives   Heinz 57 Steak Sauce

Let cheeses and margarine soften at room temperature. Cream together
with Worcestershire, cayenne and paprika. Put in refrigerator until firm
enough to be worked into 2 balls.

Scrape out middle of each ball with teaspoon, reserving cheese. Fill each
hole with Heinz 57 Steak Sauce. Use reserved cheese to cover holes.
Reshape balls. Roll in finely chopped pecans. Wrap in waxed paper and
refrigerate. One hour before serving remove from refrigerator. Serve with
crackers. This will freeze well.   *Kitty Brown*

☆　　☆　　☆

Curried Shrimp Balls

11	ounces cream cheese, softened	1	cup toasted slivered almonds
2	tablespoons mayonnaise	½	teaspoon salt
1	cup chopped frozen or canned tiny shrimp	1-2	tablespoons curry powder
			Coconut

Blend cream cheese and mayonnaise, salt and curry. Fold in shrimp and almonds. Form into one inch balls. Roll in coconut. Chill.

Hat Madsen

Tuna Puffs

PUFF:

½	cup water	½	cup flour
¼	cup butter	2	eggs
Dash of salt			

FILLING:

2	(6½-7 ounces each) cans tuna	2	tablespoons chopped sweet pickle
1	cup finely chopped celery	½	cup mayonnaise or salad dressing
2	tablespoons chopped onion		Salt to taste

PUFFS: Combine water, butter and salt in a saucepan and bring to a boil. Add flour all at one time and stir vigorously until mixture forms a ball and leaves the sides of the pan. Remove from heat. Add eggs one at a time. Beat until satiny. Drop by level teaspoons on a cookie sheet. Bake at 450° for 10 minutes; then lower temperature to 350° and continue baking 10 more minutes.

FILLING: Drain and flake tuna. Combine with celery, onion, pickle, mayonnaise and salt; mix thoroughly. Cut tops from puff shells. Fill each puff shell with approximately 2 teaspoons of salad. Makes approximately 55 hors d'oeuvres.

Variation: Fill with egg, ham, chicken or shrimp salad.

Florence Whiting

☆　　☆　　☆

M. E.'s Crunchy Asparagus

1   bunch fresh asparagus
1   (.6 ounce) package Good
     Seasons Onion Dressing or
     Italian Dressing Mix

Drop asparagus in shallow pan and boil for 3 minutes only. Drain. Immediately place in flat glass 3 quart container and cover with ice cubes. Refrigerate for 30 minutes. Remove after chilling; drain and pat very dry. This is important. Return to dry dish and sprinkle with dressing mix. Chill again.

Wonderful, low calorie appetizer.   *Linda Juba*

Baked Italian Appetizer

6	eggs	¼	pound salami
4-6	ounces Mozzarella cheese	1	pound hot sausage
½	stick pepperoni	1	cup grated Romano cheese

Beat eggs. Cut Mozzarella, pepperoni and salami into small pieces. Fry the sausage and pour off all the fat. Combine eggs, pepperoni, sausage, Mozzarella cheese, Romano cheese and salami. Bake in a greased 8 inch square pan for 25 to 30 minutes at 350°. Cut into 1 inch squares when cooled.   *Hat Madsen*

Seafood Antipasto

1	(14 ounce) bottle ketchup	1	onion, sliced into rings
¼	cup Worcestershire	1	cup pitted ripe olives
1	teaspoon garlic powder	1	cup stuffed green olives
1	(4½ ounce) can shrimp, drained	1	(3 ounce) can button mushrooms, undrained
1	(4½ ounce) can tuna, undrained	1	cup cauliflower flowerettes
			Ritz Crackers

Combine ketchup, Worcestershire, garlic powder, shrimp, tuna, onion, ripe olives, green olives, and mushrooms in a saucepan. Top with cauliflower flowerettes and cook over low heat 1 hour. Cool and refrigerate. Serve with Ritz Crackers only. This may be prepared 2 to 3 days in advance as it becomes tastier with age.   *Tura Bethune*

☆   ☆   ☆

Oysters Joy

3   cloves garlic, minced
¾   cup chopped green onions
2   tablespoons chopped parsley
4   tablespoons margarine
4   tablespoons flour

2½   dozen raw oysters
2   dashes of cayenne pepper
1½   tablespoons lemon juice
1   (10¾ ounce) can cream of mushroom soup

Sauté garlic, onions, and parsley in margarine. Add flour slowly. Let simmer 5 to 8 minutes. Cover oysters with water and boil for approximately 8 minutes. Reserve stock and chop oysters finely. Slowly mix soup with sautéed vegetables, add pepper, lemon juice and ½ cup stock from oysters. Mixture should be gravy consistency, so you may need to add more stock. Serve from chafing dish as a hot dip or over small pastry shells for a hot hors d'oeuvre.

Tura Bethune

Crabmeat Mousse

Chill Overnight

1   package unflavored gelatin
¼   cup cold water
1   cup cream of mushroom soup
1   (8 ounce) package cream cheese

1   cup mayonnaise
1   (6-7 ounce) can crabmeat
¾   cup finely chopped celery
1   tablespoon grated onion
1½   teaspoons Worcestershire

Dissolve gelatin in cold water. Heat soup until bubbly, add dissolved gelatin, soup, cream cheese, mayonnaise, crab, celery, onion and Worcestershire. Mix well. Pour into greased mold and chill overnight.

Louise Propps

Hint: Grease mold with mayonnaise for easy release.

☆   ☆   ☆

Salmon Mousse

A favorite at the New Member Tea.

1	(15½ ounce) can Red Sockeye Salmon	½	teaspoon dried dillweed
2	envelopes unflavored gelatin	¼	teaspoon pepper
2	cups mayonnaise	1	(6 ounce) can tuna
½	cup chili sauce	4	hard-cooked eggs, finely chopped
2	tablespoons lemon juice	½	cup chopped, stuffed green olives or salad olives
1	tablespoon Worcestershire	¼	cup finely chopped onion

Drain the salmon, but reserve the liquid, adding water to make ½ cup. Bone, flake and reserve the salmon. In a Pyrex cup combine the reserved liquid and the gelatin. Place the cup in a pan of hot water and stir until the gelatin is dissolved. Transfer the gelatin to a large mixing bowl and gradually blend in the mayonnaise. Stir in the chili sauce, lemon juice, Worcestershire, dillweed and pepper. Fold in the salmon, tuna, eggs, olives and onion. Turn into a 6 cup mold and chill until firm. Serve with crackers. Serves 12-15.

Lynda Corbin

Tuna Nuggets

Chill Before Serving

2	(7 ounces each) cans tuna	Worcestershire to taste
2	(3 ounces each) packages cream cheese, softened	¼ teaspoon Tabasco
1	tablespoon lemon juice	1 cup chopped parsley

Drain and flake tuna. Whip cheese, lemon juice, Worcestershire and Tabasco until smooth. Add tuna and mix thoroughly. Use teaspoons to form about 40 balls and roll each ball in parsley. Chill 2 or 3 hours. Serves 12-16 people.

Variation: Use salmon or chipped beef instead of tuna.

Ivanette Dennis

☆   ☆   ☆

Caroline's Caviar Pie

Outstanding!

2	envelopes Knox gelatin	1	cup onions, finely chopped
¼	cup cold water	1	(4 ounce) jar caviar,
2	chicken bouillon cubes		divided
½	cup boiling water	1	tablespoon capers
1	dozen hard-cooked eggs, chopped	½	cup sour cream
¾	cup mayonnaise	1	teaspoon salt

Soften gelatin in cold water. Combine with bouillon dissolved in hot water. Add to chopped eggs, mayonnaise, onions, 3 ounces caviar, capers, sour cream and salt. Mix carefully. Put into glass pie plate. Garnish around edge with 1 ounce of caviar (red or black). Refrigerate. Serve with crackers. Serves 12-15. *Willena Harry*

Sweet and Sour Hot Sausages

2	(8 ounces each) packages smokey link sausages	⅓	cup vinegar
1	(13½ ounce) can pineapple chunks	1	bell pepper, chopped
4	teaspoons corn starch	½	cup Maraschino cherries drained
½	teaspoon salt		Bite-sized cubes of ham, if desired
½	cup maple syrup	1	(8 ounce) can whole water chestnuts, cut in half.
¼	cup brown sugar		
⅓	cup water		

Cut sausages in bite-sized pieces, brown and drain. Drain pineapple, reserve syrup; then blend corn starch, salt, maple syrup, sugar, water, vinegar and pineapple syrup. Heat to boiling, stirring constantly. Add sausage, pineapple, bell pepper, cherries, ham and water chestnuts. Cook 5 minutes. Keep warm while serving. To freeze, double the liquid ingredients. Serves 12-16. *The Cookbook Committee*

☆   ☆   ☆

Ham Roll Ups

Make Ahead

1 (8 ounce) package cream cheese, softened
½ package dried onion soup, or less to taste
2 tablespoons chopped ripe olives

1 (4 ounce) package thin sliced ham (rectangular slices)

Mix cream cheese, onion soup mix and olives. Spread over ham slices. Roll and chill at least 12 hours. Use sharp knife and cut in ¼ inch slices. Rolled horizontally makes 5 dozen pieces. Rolled lengthwise makes 8 dozen pieces. May be frozen.   *Charlotte Clark*

Hot Chicken Bites

⅔ cup minced cooked chicken
1 cup plus 1½ tablespoons dried bread crumbs, divided

1 tablespoon curry powder
1 tablespoon minced onion
2 tablespoons minced parsley
2½-3 tablespoons mayonnaise
1 egg

Mix chicken, 1½ tablespoons bread crumbs, curry, onion and parsley and mayonaise to form into small balls. Roll in beaten egg; then in bread crumbs. Bake at 450° for 10 to 15 minutes until golden brown. May be made ahead and refrigerated before baking. Serve with dip made of equal parts of prepared mustard and plum jam or marmalade.

Vivian Jackson

☆   ☆   ☆

Meatballs for Cocktails

Oriental Style

MEATBALLS:

1½	pounds ground beef
¾	cup rolled oats
1	(5 ounce) can water chestnuts, drained and chopped
½	cup milk
1	egg, slightly beaten
1	tablespoon soy sauce
1	teaspoon M.S.G.
½	teaspoon onion salt
½	teaspoon garlic salt
¼	teaspoon salt
	Dash of hot pepper sauce

SAUCE:

1	(8 ounce) can crushed pineapple
1	cup firmly packed brown sugar
2	tablespoons cornstarch
1	cup beef bouillon
½	cup vinegar or lemon juice
1	teaspoon soy sauce
⅓	cup chopped bell pepper

MEATBALLS: Thoroughly combine all ingredients. Shape to form balls using 1 tablespoon for small and 1 rounded teaspoon for miniature. Brown in small amount of oil, drain off fat. (Or put on cookie sheet and brown in oven.)

SAUCE: Drain pineapple, reserving juice. Mix brown sugar and cornstarch in saucepan. Gradually stir in juice, bouillon, vinegar and soy sauce. Cook, stir until thick and clear. Stir in bell pepper and pineapple. Add sauce to meatballs. Simmer about 10 minutes. Serve hot with picks. Serves 20.   *Marge Alesch*

Hint: Meatballs will cook better if they are the same size. Use either size of melon scoop or a small ice cream scoop.

Hint: Instead of browning meatballs in a skillet, place them on a broiler pan and bake at 375° for 10 minutes. Fat will drain off as the meatballs brown. Turn once, using tongs, about ½ way through the cooking time.

☆   ☆   ☆

Sweet & Sour Meatballs

MEATBALLS:

¾ pound ground beef
¼ pound ground pork
¾ cup oatmeal
¼ teaspoon Worcestershire

½ cup milk
½ teaspoon onion salt
½ teaspoon garlic salt
Dash of Tabasco

SAUCE:

1 cup sugar
¾ cup vinegar
¾ cup water
1 teaspoon paprika

½ teaspoon salt
1 tablespoon cornstarch
mixed with 1 tablespoon
water

MEATBALLS: Mix all ingredients. Shape into small balls. Brown lightly and cook about 5 minutes.

SAUCE: Mix all ingredients. Simmer until thickened. Pour over meatballs. Serve with toothpicks. *Betsy Gibson*

Texas Cocktail Meatballs

MEATBALLS:

1 pound ground beef
1 egg, beaten
½ cup fine dry bread crumbs

Salt to taste
Pepper to taste

SAUCE:

1 clove garlic, quartered
2-3 tablespoons oil
1 . cup Dr. Pepper
¼ teaspoon dry mustard

2 tablespoons ketchup
⅛ teaspoon black pepper
1 tablespoon vinegar
1 tablespoon soy sauce

MEATBALLS: Mix all ingredients. Shape into bite-sized balls and set aside.

SAUCE: Over low heat sauté garlic in oil until pieces are tender. Discard garlic. Brown meatballs on all sides. Remove. Save 1 tablespoon fat and add Dr. Pepper, mustard, ketchup, pepper, vinegar and soy sauce. Bring to boil. Add meatballs, cook over low heat until sauce is thick. Makes about 40 balls. *Chris Norman*

☆ ☆ ☆

Quick & Easy Swedish Meatballs

MEATBALLS:

2-2½ pounds ground beef
1 grated onion
2 eggs

Salt to taste
Pepper to taste
Garlic salt to taste

SAUCE:

1 (12 ounce) bottle Heinz
Chili Sauce
1 bottle water

3 heaping tablespoons grape
jelly

MEATBALLS: Mix all ingredients and form into small meatballs.

SAUCE: Combine all ingredients. Simmer meatballs in sauce for 20 minutes. Serve on toothpicks in chafing dish. Serves about 10 people. These may be made ahead and frozen.

Variation: This sauce will also work for wieners cut into 1 inch pieces or cocktail franks.   *Phyllis Roberts*

New Mexico Cocktail Meatballs

MEATBALLS:

2 pounds lean ground beef
2 cups Pepperidge Farm
Herb Seasoned Stuffing
2 eggs
¼ cup evaporated milk

1 clove garlic, crushed
¼ cup chopped canned
mushrooms
2 teaspoons salt

SAUCE:

¼ cup butter or margarine
½ cup chopped onions
2 tablespoons flour
1 (16 ounce) can tomatoes
1 cup hot water

3-4 (4 ounces each) cans green
chilies
2 cloves garlic, chopped
1 teaspoon salt

MEATBALLS: Mix all ingredients together and form small balls. Place on broiler pan and bake at 375⁰ for 10 minutes. Remove meatballs to casserole and keep warm.

SAUCE: Sauté onions in margarine until onions are clear. Add flour and brown a bit; then add tomatoes, mashing well. Add hot water, green chilies, garlic and salt. Simmer 10 to 15 minutes. Pour sauce over meatballs and gently mix. Serve in chafing dish. Makes 80-85 small meatballs or about 65 larger ones. Freezes well.

The Cookbook Committee

☆   ☆   ☆

Cheese Dip in Round Rye

Progressive Dinner Favorite

3   (6 ounces each) packages garlic cheese
2   (1 ounce) packages Blue cheese. (If there are 3 or 4 in package, only use 2.)
2   tablespoons soft margarine
1   onion, finely chopped
1   teaspoon Worcestershire
½   teaspoon Tabasco
½   cup beer
1   loaf round rye bread
    Paprika

Melt garlic cheese, Blue cheese and margarine. Add onion, Worcestershire, Tabasco and beer. Heat until thoroughly blended. Hollow out round rye loaf of bread and fill cavity with warm cheese mix. Sprinkle paprika over top. Use the broken chunks from center of bread, and crackers to dip into cheese.   *Helen Grieve*

Shrimp Pizza Hors d'Oeuvre

Pretty and Yummy

1   (8 ounce) package cream cheese, softened
1   (12 ounce) bottle Heinz chili sauce
2   cups shredded Mozzarella cheese
4   green onions, finely sliced
½   bell pepper, minced
1   (6½ ounce) can small shrimp, rinsed and drained
1   (4¼ ounce) can sliced ripe olives
    Parsley, minced, optional

Drain shrimp and rinse in cold water. Spread cream cheese on a round flat platter to resemble pizza dough. Spread about ¾ bottle of chili sauce to within ½ inch of edge. Use more if necessary. Sprinkle with Mozarella cheese, onions and peppers. Top with shrimp and black olives. Sprinkle with parsley if desired. Chill until serving time. Serve with corn chips. Serves 12.   *Pat Williams*

☆   ☆   ☆

The Moveable Feasts' Spinach Dip

1	(10 ounce) package frozen chopped spinach, defrosted and squeezed	½	teaspoon celery salt
1	cup sour cream	½	cup mayonnaise
½	cup minced parsley	½	cup minced onion
1	teaspoon salt	¼	teaspoon pepper
		⅛	teaspoon nutmeg
		1	head red cabbage

Combine spinach, sour cream, parsley, salt, celery salt, mayonnaise, onion, pepper and nutmeg. Chill. Serve in a hollowed out head of red cabbage surrounded with crackers or corn chips.   *Hat Madsen*

Helen's Clam Dip

Make Several Hours Ahead

1	cup sour cream	1-2	dashes of cayenne pepper
1	(7½ ounce) can clams, well drained		
2-3	teaspoons Old Bay seasoning or McCormick Chesapeake Bay Style Seafood seasoning		

Combine all the ingredients and chill for several hours to allow the seasonings to blend. Serve with potato chips.

This is hot. I recommend you start with the smaller amounts of seasonings. It's supposed to burn your lips slightly as if you were eating steamed crabs in Maryland.   *Ivanette Dennis*

Oriental Dip

½	cup chopped water chestnuts	1	cup mayonnaise
½	cup chopped onion	2	tablespoons parsley
1	cup sour cream	1	tablespoon soy sauce

Mix all ingredients. Chill and serve with vegetables. *Connie Altemus*

☆　　☆　　☆

Food Processor Vegetable Dip

Follow recipe for Food Processor mayonnaise (see index).
Leave mayonnaise in bowl and add:

½ ounce Blue cheese   1   green onion
1 (3 ounce) package cream
  cheese
1 tablespoon Wilson's B.V.
  concentrate or 1
  tablespoon instant beef
  bouillon

Process with a quick on-off pulse until blended. If using instant bouillon
allow to stand several hours before serving. Serve as a dip with assorted
fresh vegetable slices, such as cucumbers, carrots, zucchini squash, bell
pepper, cauliflower or cherry tomatoes.   *Liz Willson*

Artichoke Dip

1 (6 ounce) jar artichoke hearts,   1   cup mayonnaise
  drained and finely chopped   1   cup freshly grated
1 tablespoon finely chopped   Parmesan cheese
  onion   Dash of pepper

Combine all ingredients and mix well. Pour into a buttered 1 quart baking dish. Bake at 350⁰ for 20 to 25 minutes. Serve with crackers. May be
heated in a microwave until hot.   *Clara Lemming*

Variation: ½ cup grated Cheddar cheese may be added.

Variation: 1 (4¼ ounce) can ripe olives may be added.

Barbara's Crab Fondue

1 (8 ounce) package cream   ½   teaspoon Worcestershire
  cheese   ¼   teaspoon cayenne
1 (5 ounce) jar Old English   ¼   teaspoon garlic salt
  cheese   1   (6-7 ounce) can crab
¼ cup cream

Melt cream cheese and Old English cheese in the top of a double boiler;
then add cream, Worcestershire, cayenne, garlic salt and mix well. Fold
in crab. Heat slowly. Serve with melba toast or chunks of French bread.

☆   ☆   ☆

Hot Crab Dip

8 ounces sharp Cracker Barrel Cheddar cheese	½ stick butter
8 ounces American cheese	1 (6-7 ounce can) white claw crabmeat, drained and picked
½ cup Sauterne	

Melt cheeses and butter together. Add Sauterne and half of shredded crabmeat. Serve in chafing dish, topping with remaining shredded crabmeat. Serve with Triscuits. *Dottie Pinch*

Curried Crab Dip

CRAB MIXTURE:

4 tablespoons margarine	2 ribs of celery, chopped
1 bell pepper, chopped	1 (6-7 ounce) can crab meat, drained and flaked
1 onion, chopped	

WHITE SAUCE:

2 tablespoons butter or margarine	Paprika
2 tablespoons flour	1 cup milk or a combination of cream and milk
½ teaspoon salt	Curry powder to taste
Dash of pepper	

Sauté bell pepper, onion and celery in margarine until tender. Add crab. Cook 10 minutes longer. Make white sauce (see index). Pour over crab mixture and season to taste with curry powder. Serve in chafing dish with melba toast. *Tura Bethune*

Party Favorite Crab Dip

Easy To Do!

1 onion, chopped	1 (12 ounce) package cream cheese, softened
1 stick butter or margarine	1 (6-7 ounce) can crab meat, drained
1 (10¾ ounce) can cream of mushroom soup	

Sauté chopped onion in butter. Add mushroom soup and cream cheese. Blend until you have a nice, creamy mixture. Fold in crab. Serve in a chafing dish with Doritos. *Mary Pittman*

☆   ☆   ☆

Crab Dip Supreme

Party Favorite

1	(6-7 ounce) can crab, drained	1	tablespoon Sherry
1	cup mayonnaise	1	teaspoon lemon juice
½	cup sour cream		Salt to taste
1	teaspoon chopped parsley		Pepper to taste

Pick crab to remove shell fragments. Combine all ingredients. Chill at least 2 hours before serving. Makes 2 cups. *Pate Stanphill*

Alsatian Cheesepot

3	ounces Camembert cheese	2	cups cream
1	ounce Liederkranz cheese	½	cup chopped ripe olives
2	sticks butter	1	tablespoon pimiento
2	tablespoons flour	½	cup chives
1	cup milk	½	teaspoon salt
½	pound cottage cheese		Dash of cayenne
¼	pound Roquefort cheese		

Remove rind from Camembert and Liederkranz. Heat butter, blend in flour and add milk stirring until smooth and thick. Make a smooth mixture of cottage cheese, Roquefort and cream. Add olives, pimiento, chives, salt and cayenne. Combine with Camembert mixture. Blend well. Serve cold as a dip for raw cauliflower floweretes. Makes 4-5 cups.

Tura Bethune

Cheese Chunks

1	(3 ounce) package Philadelphia cream cheese	2	egg whites
½	cup sharp Cheddar cheese		Sourdough French bread
1	stick butter (do not substitute)		

Melt cream cheese, Cheddar cheese and butter in top of double boiler. Fold in beaten egg whites. Dip squares of sourdough French bread in mixture. Bake 10 to 15 minutes in 450⁰ oven. Serve hot. *Dottie Pinch*

☆   ☆   ☆

Bleu Olive Dip or Spread

New Member Tea Sandwiches

1 (8 ounce) package cream cheese
3 ounces Bleu cheese, crumbled

1 (4½ ounce) can chopped ripe olives, drained
Milk, as desired

Let cheeses soften. Whip in a mixer with chopped ripe olives. Use amount of milk as needed to make proper consistency for a dip or a spread. Serve as a spread for openface or finger sandwiches or as a dip for chips.

Eileen MacWithey

Variation:
1 (4½ ounce) can chopped black olives and liquid
2 (8 ounces each) packages cream cheese

1 teaspoon Beau Monde seasoning
1 tablespoon lemon juice

Follow directions as above. Whip well. Makes 26 sandwiches, about 2½ loaves of thin sliced bread.

Ivanette Dennis

Ginger's Cheese Puffs

1 loaf thin sliced sandwich bread
1 cup mayonnaise
4 green onions, finely chopped, including tops
½ teaspoon mustard

½ teaspoon Worcestershire
½ scant teaspoon sugar
2 tablespoons Parmesan cheese
3-4 drops of Tabasco

Trim crusts from bread and cut into squares, toast one side only under broiler. Mix mayonnaise, onions, mustard, Worcestershire, sugar, cheese and Tabasco. Put one heaping teaspoon of mixture on untoasted side of toast square, sprinkle extra Parmesan cheese on top and bake at 350° until bubbly. Serve immediately. The toast squares and mixture can be made ahead and assembled just prior to serving.

Hint: The scant teaspoon of sugar is the secret of this recipe.

Linda Juba

☆ ☆ ☆

Hot Shrimp Hors d'Oeuvres

1½ cups mayonnaise
¾ cup sharp Cheddar cheese,
    grated
1   tablespoon lemon juice
2   tablespoons minced onion
Worcestershire to taste

Salt to taste
Accent to taste
1   loaf white bread, cut in
    squares (crusts removed)
20-25 boiled shrimp, sliced
    in half

Mix together mayonnaise, cheese, lemon juice, minced onion, Worcestershire, salt and Accent. Mayonnaise and cheese mixture may be reserved for some time in the refrigerator. Toast both sides of bread under broiler, top with pieces of shrimp. Spoon mayonnaise and cheese mixture on top. Broil at 500° for 3 to 4 minutes, until bubbly. Watch carefully. Serve hot. Makes 40-50. *Dottie Pinch*

Mushroom Triangles

1   (4 ounce) jar sliced
    mushrooms, drained
2   tablespoons butter
1   (8 ounce) package cream
    cheese

1   egg yolk
¼ teaspoon salt
¼ teaspoon garlic powder
⅛ teaspoon celery seed
8   slices bread

Sauté mushrooms and butter in saucepan. Mix softened cream cheese and egg yolk. Add salt, garlic powder, and celery seed. Combine the mushrooms and butter with this mixture. Cut the crusts off the bread. Toast one side of the bread under the broiler until light brown. Spread the mixture on the untoasted side. Before serving, place under the broiler until bubbly and light brown. Cut into triangles and serve warm. May be made the night before or ahead of time and frozen. Makes 32 appetizers. *Carol Garrigues*

☆   ☆   ☆

Crab Canapes

Must Be Made Ahead

1	stick margarine	½	teaspoon seasoned salt
1	(5 ounce) jar Old English cheese spread	1	(6-7 ounce) can crabmeat, drained
½	teaspoon mayonnaise	9	English muffins, split
½	teaspoon garlic salt		

Mix margarine, cheese, mayonnaise, garlic salt, seasoned salt and crabmeat together. Spread on muffins and freeze in single layer. Cut into 6 pieces; wrap and store in freezer. Just before serving, broil until light brown. *Pat Woodward*

Toasted Rounds with Cherry Tomatoes

40-50 cherry tomatoes		2	tablespoons grated onion
Seasoned salt		2	teaspoons hot mustard
2	cups mayonnaise		Toasted melba rounds
½	cup grated Parmesan cheese		

Wash, chill and cover cherry tomatoes with seasoned salt. Mix mayonnaise, Parmesan cheese, onion and mustard and spread thickly on toasted melba rounds. Broil 6 inches from heat for 2 minutes. Serve toasted rounds on a tray surrounding the chilled tomatoes in a bowl. Use toothpicks for serving tomatoes or, after broiling, put ½ of tomato, cut side down, on each round. *Phyllis Roberts*

☆　　☆　　☆

Hot Cranberry Spice Punch

1	quart cranberry juice cocktail	1	teaspoon cloves
2	cups pineapple juice	1	teaspoon allspice
1	cup apricot nectar	2	sticks (2 inches long) cinnamon

Put cranberry cocktail, pineapple juice and apricot nectar in 10 cup percolator and cloves, allspice and cinnamon in the basket. Let perk according to your coffeepot. Makes 10 cups.   *Joyce Price*

Old Virginia Wassail

2	quarts sweet apple cider		Sugar to taste
2	cups orange juice	1	stick of cinnamon
1	cup lemon juice	1	teaspoon whole cloves
4	cups pineapple juice		

Combine apple cider, orange juice, lemon juice, pineapple juice and sugar in stainless steel percolator. Place cinnamon and cloves in percolator basket; perk 18 to 20 minutes. Serves 30 when using 4 ounce cups.

Dolores M. Spence

Mock Champagne

Chill Before Serving

½	cup sugar	2	cups ginger ale
½	cup water	3	tablespoons Grenadine syrup
½	cup grapefruit juice		
¼	cup orange juice		

Boil sugar and water together until sugar is dissolved. Mix with grapefruit juice and orange juice and chill until ready to use. Just before serving, mix with ginger ale and Grenadine. Recipe makes 1 quart of punch, so you will need to multiply according to your needs. Most punch cups hold 4 ounces of liquid.   *Judy West*

☆　　☆　　☆

Richardson Woman's Club Coffee Punch

1	(2 ounce) jar instant coffee	1	pint heavy cream, whipped
2	quarts hot water		
2	cups sugar	½	gallon French Vanilla ice cream
2	quarts half and half		
1	quart ginger ale		

Dissolve instant coffee in hot water. Cool. Add sugar and half and half and mix well. At serving time, add ginger ale, heavy cream and ice cream. Stir to mix. Makes 60 four ounce servings.

The New Member Tea, held the first Thursday afternoon in September, is a special event of the Richardson Woman's Club. Several of the recipes are traditional and this punch has been a favorite for 25 years. We are sorry we were unable to discover who served it first.

Strawberry Sunday School Punch

1	(16 ounce) can frozen orange juice	1	(16 ounce) package frozen strawberries
1	(16 ounce) can frozen lemonade	1	(32 ounce) bottle ginger ale
6	(16 ounces each) cans water	1	quart water

Mix all ingredients in punch bowl and top with fruit slices and ice rings. Serves approximately 25. *Dot Prince*

Honolulu Tea

2	quarts strong cold tea	1	cup Maraschino cherries and their syrup
	Juice of 6 lemons		
2	cups crushed pineapple and its syrup	2	cups sugar
		1	cup water

Brew tea. Add lemon juice, pineapple, pineapple syrup, cherries and cherry syrup. Boil the sugar and water for 5 minutes. Stir into tea mixture. Chill and serve over cracked ice. Yields 2½ quarts.

Eileen MacWithey

☆   ☆   ☆

Sangria Base

4	seedless oranges, divided	3	pounds sugar
5	lemons, divided	2½	quarts water
2	limes		

Cut 2 oranges, 3 lemons, and 2 limes in thin wedges. Bring to a boil and simmer slowly in saucepan with sugar and water to form a simple syrup. Taste often to see that mixture doesn't get a bitter taste. Mash and squeeze remaining fruit, add to hot syrup and let stand. Chill base. This will store indefinitely in refrigerator in tightly sealed jar.

Sangria Rojo

5	ounces Sangria Base	1	orange, sliced
1	(750 ml.) bottle dry red wine	2	lemons, sliced
½	(32 ounce) bottle club soda	1	fresh peach, sliced

Combine base, wine and club soda in pitcher. Add fruit. Eight 4 ounce servings.

Variation: For Sangria Blanco use dry white wine. Strawberries and grapes are nice additions to this mixture.

White Sangria

2	cups grapefruit juice (fresh is best; may use frozen)	1	magnum white wine
1	cup fresh orange juice		Sliced oranges
1	cup sugar		Sliced lemons

Pour grapefruit juice, orange juice, sugar and white wine over sliced oranges and lemons. Chill and serve in pitcher. Serves 8-12.

Barbara England

Variation: You may also fill glass ⅔ full with Sangria and fill remainder with club soda.

☆   ☆   ☆

Breakfast Milkshake

1 egg
1 (6 ounce) can frozen
   orange juice
2 cups milk

1 pint vanilla ice cream
2 teaspoons non-dairy
   powdered creamer
   (optional)

Mix egg and orange juice in blender. Add milk, ice cream and non-dairy powdered creamer. Blend until smooth and almost fluffy. Serves 4.

Barbara England

Blender Eggnog

2 eggs
1½ cups milk
Cinnamon to taste
Nutmeg to taste

1-1½ cups vanilla ice cream
2 tablespoons sugar
Vanilla to taste

Mix all ingredients in blender and blend to desired consistency. Serves 4.

Jean Zinser

Pink Chablis Punch

5 cups pink Chablis
¾ cup sugar
1 (6 ounce) can pink
   lemonade

1 cup water
2 tablespoons lemon juice

Combine all ingredients. Freeze in a flat shallow container. Thaw slightly, stir and serve when slushy. Serves 16.   *The Cookbook Committee*

Party Punch

1 (750 ml.) bottle Taylor
   Sauterne
1 teaspoon Angostura bitters

2 (750 ml. each) bottles dry
   Champagne

Use a block of ice in a punch bowl. Mix Sauterne and Angostura bitters. Pour over ice. Add Champagne.

Hint: It is pretty to use ice ring with cherries or fruit in it.

Eileen MacWithey

☆   ☆   ☆

Pink Elephant Punch

2	quarts cranberry juice	1	quart ginger ale
2	cups pineapple juice	1	(750 ml.) bottle vodka

Chill all ingredients. Combine prior to serving, add ice ring. Yield: 48 servings.

Frozen bunches of white grapes make beautiful ice.

The Cookbook Committee

Artillery Punch

2	(1.75 liters each) bottles rum	1	pint lime juice
2	quarts grapefruit juice	2	quarts soda water
1	quart pineapple juice	3	cups sugar
2	quarts Claret wine		Lemon to taste

Mix all ingredients and chill. Makes approximately 3 gallons.

Watch out! This has character!   *Jean Zinser*

Spicy Cranberry Punch

2	cups water	1½	cups frozen lemon juice
1	cup sugar	2	cups orange juice
4	cinnamon sticks	2	cups pineapple juice
12	whole cloves	1	quart ginger ale, chilled
4	cups cranberry juice	1	liter vodka, chilled

Combine water, sugar, cinnamon and cloves. Boil until sugar dissolves. Add cranberry juice and cook over low heat for 5 minutes. Chill over night. Remove spices and add fruit juices. Just before serving add ginger ale and vodka. Pour over ice ring. Serves 35. If non-alcoholic punch is desired substitute a second bottle of ginger ale.

The Cookbook Committee

☆   ☆   ☆

Bourbon Milk Punch

Potent!

2	cups vanilla ice cream	¼	cup white rum
1	cup sweet milk	1	jigger dry brandy
½	cup Bourbon		Nutmeg

In a blender, mix and blend the ice cream, sweet milk, Bourbon, rum and brandy for 5 or 6 seconds and pour into a punch bowl. Serve in mugs with a dash of nutmeg on top. Will make about five 4 ounce punch cups. This may be doubled or tripled when making. Just be sure that it is served very cold.   *Dottie Pinch*

Holiday Eggnog

May Be Made Ahead

FOR 50 SERVINGS:

1	dozen eggs	1½	cups Drambuie
2	cups sugar	½	teaspoon salt
3	cups Apricot brandy	2	tablespoons vanilla
3	cups rum	3	pints whipping cream
2	cups Grand Marnier	1	gallon milk
3	cups mild blend Bourbon		

FOR 16 SERVINGS:

4	eggs	½	cup Drambuie
¾	cup sugar		Dash of salt
1	cup Apricot brandy	1	tablespoon vanilla
1	cup rum	1	pint whipping cream
¾	cup Grand Marnier	1	quart plus 1½ cups milk
1	cup Bourbon		

Separate eggs, beat yolks, add sugar, brandy, rum, Grand Marnier, Bourbon, Drambuie, salt and vanilla. Chill. Beat egg whites until stiff. Beat whipping cream until peaks form, fold in egg whites and add to milk. Stir; then stir both milk and liquor mixtures together. Chill at least 1 hour before serving. Will keep 2 weeks in refrigerator.*Lynn Trentham*

☆   ☆   ☆

Alice's Bloody Mary Recipe

1 (46 ounce) can vegetable juice (V-8)	⅓ cup Worcestershire sauce
1 (32 ounce) bottle Snappy Tom	3 cups vodka

Mix all ingredients. Will keep in refrigerator several weeks.

Variation: Add 1 tablespoon lemon juice, 2 to 3 tablespoons prepared horseradish, and 3 to 4 drops Tabasco to above mixture. *Jean Zinser*

Fruit Daiquiris

Great for a Crowd

1 (16 ounce) can frozen orange juice	8 lemonade cans water
1 (6 ounce) can frozen lime juice	1 (10 ounce) bottle Maraschino cherries with juice
2 (7.5 ounces each) cans frozen lemon juice	1 cup powdered sugar
1 (16 ounce) can pink lemonade	1 (liter) bottle light Bacardi rum

Thaw orange juice, lime juice, lemon juice, and lemonade. Combine with water, cherries, sugar and rum. Put in container or containers and freeze 24 hours before serving. Stir several times during freezing process. Serves 36-40. *Linda Juba*

Glenn's Peach Daiquiris

3 ounces light rum	3 tablespoons syrup from peaches
Juice of 1 lime	
½ cup sliced frozen or canned peaches	1 cup finely cracked ice

Blend all ingredients in blender or food processor about 5 seconds. Serve immediately. These are delicious without rum as a summer cooler, brunch drink or for children. *Ivanette Dennis*

☆   ☆   ☆

Whiskey Sour Punch

1	(12 ounce) can frozen lemonade	24	ounces Bourbon
1	(6 ounce) can frozen orange juice	1	quart white soda

Thaw lemonade and orange juice. Blend with Bourbon. Add white soda just before serving. Makes 20 servings for 4 ounce punch cups.

Virginia Matzen

Hot Buttered Rum

1	pint vanilla ice cream	½	teaspoon cinnamon
1	pound brown sugar	½	teaspoon allspice
2	sticks margarine	Rum	
½	teaspoon nutmeg		

Cream ice cream, brown sugar, margarine, nutmeg, cinnamon and allspice together. Put 2 teaspoons batter in 1 cup; add 1 jigger of rum and add hot water to fill. Batter may be stored in refrigerator.

Jere Wagenhals

Cappuccino

A Tour of Homes Recipe

1	(8 quart) box instant non-fat dry milk	1	pound powdered sugar
1	(8 ounce) jar instant coffee	1	pound Nestles Chocolate Quik
1	(16 ounce) jar Coffee Mate		

Mix instant non-fat dry milk, instant coffee, Coffee Mate, powdered sugar and Nestles Chocolate Quik together and store. This mixture will keep for several months. To serve add 4 tablespoons to a mug of hot water. Liqueur or brandy may be added. Top with whipped cream. Makes 12 quarts.

Lynn Trentham

☆   ☆   ☆

Soupe A L'Oignon (Onion Soup Gratinée)

1½	pounds or 5 cups thinly sliced yellow onions	½	cup vermouth
			Pepper to taste
3	tablespoons butter or margarine	3	tablespoons Cognac
		8	slices French bread
1	tablespoon oil		Butter
1	teaspoon salt		Grated raw onions
¼	teaspoon sugar	1½	cup grated Swiss cheese
3	tablespoons flour		Parmesan cheese
2	quarts beef bouillon		

Cook onions slowly with butter and oil in covered heavy pot for 15 minutes. Uncover, raise heat to moderate and stir in salt and sugar. Cook 30 to 40 minutes stirring frequently until onions have turned golden brown. Stir in flour and blend well. Remove from heat and add bouillon and wine. Simmer partially covered 40 minutes. (You may freeze or set aside here). Reheat to simmer, add Cognac. Pour into ovenproof soup pots. Sprinkle in a few grated fresh onions. Cover with croutons. See below. Top with lots of Swiss cheese. Sprinkle on Parmesan, dot with butter. Bake 20 minutes at 350⁰. Broil until brown, about 1 minute. Serves 6.

Croutons: Place bread in one layer on pan, bake 325⁰ for 15 minutes. Spread with butter and bake 15 more minutes until brown. Cut to size.

Lois Williams

Cream of Broccoli Soup

1	(10 ounce) package frozen chopped broccoli	½	cup water
		2	cups half and half
2	tablespoons minced onion		Salt to taste
2	beef bouillon cubes		Pepper to taste

Cook broccoli according to package directions and drain well. Add bouillon cubes dissolved in boiling water. Place in blender or food processor and purée. Remove and add half and half. Heat and serve. Garnish with crisp bacon crumbles. Serves 6-8. *Flora Anderson*

☆　　☆　　☆

Spinach Soup

2	(10 ounces each) packages frozen chopped spinach	1	teaspoon salt
¼	cup oil	¼	teaspoon pepper
½	cup minced onion		Dash of nutmeg
⅓	cup flour	4	cups chicken broth
		6	cups milk

Cook spinach according to package directions. Drain well and purée in food processor or blender. Heat oil in large saucepan. Add onions and sauté until transparent. Remove from heat. Blend in flour, salt, pepper, nutmeg and broth. Gradually add milk, stirring constantly. Add spinach. Cook over medium heat for about 15 minutes, stirring often. Do not boil. Serve hot. Serves 8. *Valerie McMahan*

Cream of Potato Soup

4	cups diced potatoes	2	tablespoons flour
1	onion, thickly sliced	1	teaspoon salt
2	cups milk		Dash of pepper
4	tablespoons butter		
2	tablespoons chopped parsley		

Cook potatoes and onion in 4 cups water until tender. Scald milk in top of double boiler. Melt butter in small skillet; add parsley. Cook until wilted; stir in flour and seasonings. Add butter mixture to warm milk. Cook, stirring constantly, until slightly thickened. Purée potatoes, onion and liquid; then combine with white sauce. Stir until well blended. May be garnished with additional chopped parsley. Keeps well in refrigerator, but do not freeze. Serves 6-8. *Irene Howland*

☆　　☆　　☆

Zucchini Soup

Unusual and Delicious

3	pounds zucchini	Salt to taste
6	cups chicken broth	Pepper to taste
1	onion, chopped	Nutmeg to taste
2	tablespoons margarine	Minced jalapeño, optional
2	(8 ounces each) packages cream cheese	Minced carrots, optional

Cook zucchini in chicken broth for about 15 or 20 minutes. Sauté onion in margarine. Put half of zucchini and broth in blender and blend to make smooth. Repeat with remaining zucchini and broth. Add cream cheese, salt, pepper, nutmeg and jalapeño and carrots as desired. Blend again if necessary. Serve hot in winter or cold in summer. Serves 12.

Geri Smith

Grandmother's Garden Soup

4	potatoes, cubed	3 fresh tomatoes, cut up
4	ribs celery, sliced	2 (13 ounces each) cans evaporated milk
4-5	carrots, sliced	
1	onion, diced	4 tablespoons butter
6	cups water	Salt to taste
2	teaspoons salt	Pepper to taste
6	cups shredded cabbage	

Cook potatoes, celery, carrots and onion in salted water for 20 to 25 minutes, or until almost tender. Add cabbage and tomatoes and cook 10 minutes more. Add canned milk and butter. Heat to serving temperature. Salt and pepper to taste. Serves 6-8.

Eileen MacWithey

☆   ☆   ☆

Tura's Super Special Lentil Soup

1	pound of lentils, soaked overnight	½	pound mushrooms, sliced
1	beef soup bone	2	potatoes, diced
1	ham bone	2	carrots, sliced
1	onion, chopped	1	teaspoon thyme
A handful of chopped parsley		¾	teaspoon oregano
3	ribs of celery, sliced with finely chopped tops	Schillings seasoned pepper to taste	
¾	pound ground beef, browned and drained	McCormick's Season-all salt to taste	
½	pound Eckrich Smoked Sausage, sliced	1	tablespoon salt
		1	pound cleaned fresh shrimp

Simmer lentils with bones, skimming foam, for 45 minutes to an hour. Add onions, parsley, celery tops and ground beef. Add celery slices, sausage, mushrooms, potatoes, carrots, thyme, oregano and pepper. When vegetables are done, add seasoning and salt; simmer, and adjust to taste. Add shrimp and boil 2 minutes longer. Serves 8.

Hint: Don't add salt until last minute for any dried beans because salt will make the beans tough.

The Cookbook Committee

Clear Mushroom Soup

Unusual

½	onion, chopped	1	soup can water
½	teaspoon curry powder	1	teaspoon Worcestershire
2	tablespoons butter	1	tablespoon fresh lemon juice
½	pound fresh mushrooms, sliced	¼	teaspoon basil
1	clove garlic, minced	2	green onions, chopped
1	(10½ ounce) can beef bouillon		

Sauté onion and curry powder in butter 3 minutes. Add mushrooms and garlic. Sauté 5 minutes more. Add bouillon, water, Worcestershire, lemon juice and basil. Simmer one minute. Garnish with green onions and tops. Serves 4-6.

Claire Hine

☆   ☆   ☆

Curry Soup

3	tablespoons butter	1	quart chicken stock
1	onion, diced	1	raw apple, peeled and
1	clove garlic, crushed		chopped
2	tablespoons flour		Salt to taste
1	tablespoon curry powder		Pepper to taste
2	cups half and half cream		Thyme to taste

Melt butter in a large soup kettle. Add onion and garlic and cook over low heat until onion is soft. Add flour and curry powder and cook about 3 minutes. Add cream and chicken stock, cooking and stirring with a wire whisk until smooth, about 15 minutes. Add the apple and season to taste with salt, pepper and thyme. Simmer 10 minutes longer. Serve in demitasse cups before dinner. Serves 12.   *Jean Wallace*

Gazpacho

1	quart Snap-E-Tom,	¼	cup vinegar
	divided	¼	cup oil
2	tomatoes	1	tablespoon sugar
1	cucumber, halved	1	teaspoon dried onion

Put 1¼ cups Snap-E-Tom, one tomato, one half cucumber, vinegar, oil, and sugar in blender and process until ingredients are smooth. Chop one tomato, remainder of cucumber and add to puréed mixture with onion and remaining Snap-E-Tom. Serves 10-12.

This recipe is terrific before lunch or for an afternoon snack.
Willena Harry

White Gazpacho

Good As It Looks!

3	medium cucumbers, peeled	2	teaspoons salt
	and cut in chunks	1	clove garlic, crushed
3	cups chicken broth, cooled		Green onions, thinly sliced
3	cups sour cream		Parsley, chopped
3	tablespoons white wine		Tomato pulp
	vinegar		

Whirl cucumber chunks in blender a very short time, with a little broth. Combine with remaining broth, sour cream, vinegar and salt in bowl. Add garlic. Stir just enough to mix. Chill. Serve in chilled cups or bowls. Sprinkle thinly sliced green onions, parsley and tomato pulp on top. Serves 8-12.   *Charleye Conrey*

☆   ☆   ☆

Gazpacho and Croutons

SOUP:

1	cucumber	1	egg
½	onion		Juice of ½ lemon
2	tomatoes	5	tablespoons cooking oil
1	clove garlic	2	teaspoons salt
½	cup sour cream	½	teaspoon black pepper

CROUTONS:

1	slice bread diced in ¼ inch cubes		Olive oil
			Garlic powder

SOUP: Chop cucumber, onion and tomatoes coarsely and place with garlic, sour cream, egg, lemon juice, oil, salt and pepper in blender. Mix at high speed until desired smoothness is reached. Taste and correct seasonings, if necessary. Serve very cold with hot fresh croutons.

CROUTONS: Heat olive oil and garlic powder in heavy skillet, using enough oil to cover bottom of skillet. Toss bread cubes until coated with oil. Brown in 400⁰ oven. Serve while hot. Serves 4.   *Ruth Dirks*

Mother's Shrimp Gumbo

1	cup Crisco or bacon drippings	½	cup chopped bell pepper
1½	cups flour	½-¾	pound sliced okra
1½	cups chopped onion	3	ripe tomatoes, peeled
2	teaspoons chopped garlic	3	bay leaves
4-5	quarts *cold* water	3	pounds shrimp, shelled and deveined
1	cup chopped celery		

Melt Crisco or drippings and add flour stirring constantly and cooking slowly over low heat until very dark brown (this is the roux). Add onions and wilt. Add garlic. Add water. Stir until mixed over high heat. When hot add celery and bell pepper. Fry okra in bacon drippings until slime is gone. Add tomatoes to okra. Add to gumbo. Add bay leaves. "Cook until tastes good." Add shrimp. Continue cooking 3 to 5 minutes. To serve place ½ cup of cooked rice in soup bowl. Fill with gumbo. Serves 10.   *Pat Bailey*

Seasoning gumbos is a matter of individual preference. Begin cooking with ½ teaspoon salt, ¼ teaspoon black pepper and 1 or 2 dashes of cayenne pepper. Simmer 10 minutes; taste, and add more seasonings. Repeat several times. (After all "tasting" is the best part of cooking!)

☆   ☆   ☆

Seafood Gumbo

2	pounds fresh shrimp	1	(28 ounce) can tomatoes
½	teaspoon crab boil	1	bell pepper, chopped
2	tablespoons bacon drippings	1	clove garlic, mashed
2	tablespoons flour	1	teapsoon salt
1	onion, chopped	½	teaspoon freshly ground pepper
1	cup cooked, chopped ham	¼	teaspoon dried thyme
2	pounds fresh okra, chopped	¼	teaspoon ground oregano
3	ribs celery, chopped	2	bay leaves
2	tablespoons chopped parsley	1	pound crab, fresh or frozen

Cover washed shrimp with water and crab boil. Cook until shrimp are tender, about 10 minutes. Drain and save the water. Peel shrimp and reserve. In an iron pot or Dutch oven make a roux (melt bacon drippings and blend with flour. Cook very slowly over low heat until brown). Immediately add the chopped onion and sauté until transparent; add ham and okra. Cook about 10 minutes over medium heat, stirring constantly. Add the shrimp, water, celery, parsley, tomatoes, bell pepper, garlic, salt and pepper. Simmer mixture for 1 hour. Add thyme, oregano and bay leaves. Cook for 15 minutes. Add crab and peeled shrimp and cook 5 minutes longer or until heated thoroughly. Remove bay leaves. Serve with rice. Serves 8-10.   *Tura Bethune*

Easy Chicken Gumbo

1	(2-3 pound) fryer, cut up	1	(16 ounce) can tomatoes
Oil		1-2	tablespoons filé gumbo powder
1	onion, chopped		
1	bell pepper, sliced	1	quart water
2	cloves garlic	1-2	cups cut okra

Brown fryer pieces in oil. Remove chicken to plate. Sauté onion, pepper and garlic. Drain excess fat. Combine chicken, vegetables, tomatoes, filé and water. Add okra. Cook until chicken is tender — 1 to 2 hours. Serve over rice. Serves 4.   *Mildred Phillips*

☆   ☆   ☆

Steamboat's Cream of Crab Soup

Exceptional

1	pound fresh backfin crabmeat	1	quart plus 1 cup half and half
¼	cup butter	½	cup dry Sherry
¼	cup flour	½-1	teaspoon salt
1	cup chicken broth	¼	teaspoon white pepper

Remove and discard cartilage from crabmeat; then set crabmeat aside. Melt butter in a Dutch oven over low heat; add flour, stirring until smooth. Cook 1 minute, stirring constantly. Gradually add broth; cook over medium heat, stirring constantly, until thickened and bubbly. Add crabmeat, half and half, Sherry, salt and pepper. Cook over low heat 10 to 15 minutes (do not boil), stirring frequently. Makes 2 quarts.

The Cookbook Committee

Smoky Corn Chowder

Make Ahead of Time

½	cup chopped onion	2	(16 ounces each) cans cream style corn
4	tablespoons butter or margarine	1	(8 ounce) package frozen lima beans, cooked and drained
¼	cup flour		
1	teaspoon salt		
⅛	teaspoon pepper		
4	cups milk		
2	(12 ounces each) packages smoked sausage links, sliced		

In saucepan sauté onion in melted butter until tender, but not brown. Blend in flour, salt, and pepper. Add milk all at once and cook and stir until thickened and bubbly. Stir in sausage links, corn and lima beans. Simmer 10 minutes. Make a day ahead of time; the smoked sausage taste is much better.

Lynne Karp

☆ ☆ ☆

Quick Clam Chowder

1 (5-6 ounce) package scalloped potatoes with seasoned sauce mix	2½ cups water
	2 cups milk
	1 tablespoon butter
1 (7-8 ounce) can minced or chopped clams (do not drain)	Ground pepper to taste
	Chopped parsley

Mix scalloped potatoes and clams with 2½ cups water in large pan. Bring to boil, stirring occasionally. Simmer 15 to 20 minutes until potatoes are tender. Add milk, butter, pepper and parsley. Serves 4.

Marian Rose

Steak Soup

Golden Ox Restaurant, Kansas City

1½ pounds round steak, fat removed	½ teaspoon peppercorns
2 sticks margarine	1 (10 ounce) package frozen mixed vegetables
2 cups flour	1 (16 ounce) can tomatoes
4 cups water	1 (3¾ ounce) jar beef bouillon
1 rib celery, chopped	
1-2 pounds carrots, chopped	12 more cups water
2-3 onions, chopped	

Brown round steak and cut into bite-sized pieces. In 16 quart pot, make a roux of margarine, flour and water. Add celery, carrots, onions, peppercorns, mixed vegetables, tomatoes, beef bouillon, water and round steak. Cook 4½ to 6 hours, stirring occasionally. Serves 12-16.

Barbara Israel

☆　　☆　　☆

Soccer Soup

1 pound ground beef
1 (8 ounce) can tomato sauce
1 can stewed tomatoes (size depending on how much soup you want)

3 cans water (stewed tomato can)
1 package Lipton onion soup mix
1 tablespoon sugar
1 (16 ounce) can Veg-All

Brown meat in large roaster pan. When browned, pour off most of the fat. Add tomato sauce, stewed tomatoes, water, onion soup mix, sugar, Veg-All and liquid. Heat over low heat. Serves 8-10. Serve with Hot Dog Bun Bread Sticks (see index). *Carole Price*

Stew Soup

3 pounds lean stew meat cut into ½ inch pieces
4 tablespoons bacon drippings
2 large soup bones
3 (10½ ounces each) cans beef consommé
8 cups water
2 (15½ ounces each) cans peeled tomatoes, chopped
1 package dry onion soup mix
1 package French's or Lawry's meat stew seasoning
4-6 cloves garlic, chopped or pressed

V-8 juice, optional
2 cups chopped onion
2 cups diced celery, including leaves
1 turnip or parsnip, diced (optional)
2 tablespoons salt
1 teaspoon coarse ground pepper
2 (10 ounces each) packages frozen mixed vegetables
1 (10 ounce) package frozen chopped okra
8 ounces shell macaroni

Brown stew meat in 4 tablespoons of bacon drippings in a large kettle or roaster. Drain well. Cover meat and bones with consommé, water and chopped tomatoes. Add the onion soup mix, stew seasoning, garlic, V-8 juice, onions, celery, turnip, salt and pepper. Cook over low heat until meat is fork tender, about 2 hours. Remove bones. Set aside if desired. About 30 minutes before serving, add frozen vegetables, okra and macaroni. Do not over cook after vegetables are added as they lose their color and identity. If necessary to add more liquid (and it usually is after adding macaroni), add either water, V-8 juice, or consommé. This is intended to make a thick soup. Freezes well. Serves 16.
Eloise McIntosh

☆ ☆ ☆

Pimiento Cheese Soup

2 (10¾ ounces each) cans cream of chicken soup diluted with 2 cans water

1 (4 ounce) jar pimientos

4 tablespoons grated sharp Cheddar cheese

4 tablespoons grated Parmesan or Romano cheese

6 fresh mushrooms thinly sliced

Stir chicken soup and water until there are no lumps. Add pimientos, Cheddar cheese, Parmesan or Romano cheese and mushrooms and heat, but do not boil. You may use this as a base for creating many other soups. Add, for instance, 1 potato, boiled and diced, or cauliflower flowerets, steamed or boiled. Other variations might be the addition of your favorite vegetables. Serves 4-6. *Novella Bailey*

Cheese Soup

1 stick margarine or butter

1 bunch green onions, chopped

2 ribs celery, chopped

2 cups chicken broth

1 cup grated carrots

1 (10¾ ounces) can or 2 cups cream of potato soup

Pinch of chopped parsley

Dash of Tabasco

Salt to taste

Pepper to taste

8 ounces sharp Cheddar cheese, grated

½ cup Sherry

½ cup sour cream

Melt margarine; sauté onions and celery. Add chicken broth and carrots. Simmer until vegetables are tender. Add potato soup, parsley, Tabasco, salt and pepper. Add cheese. Keep warm. Before serving stir in Sherry and sour cream. *Flora Anderson*

☆　☆　☆

A Word About Salads

Gone are the days of the standard iceberg lettuce and tomato combination salad. Let your imagination run riot! Combine your favorite vegetables with; seafood, chunks of chicken, leftover beef or lamb, snow peas, artichoke hearts or chilled transparent Japanese noodles. Try different cheeses, and use any of the dressings in the book from creamy to members of the vinaigrette family. Try substituting some of the different vinegars on the market; garlic, herb, pear, raspberry, blueberry or champagne vinegar. Garnish salads with alfalfa sprouts, bean sprouts or toasted sesame seeds. Don't forget that citrus combines well with marinades, and blends well with spinach and different varieties of lettuce.

Bon Appétit.

Grannie's Cucumbers

4	cucumbers	1	cup vinegar
1	cup sugar	1	tablespoon salt
1	cup water		

Slice cucumbers. Mix sugar, water, vinegar and salt, pour over cucumbers and marinate several hours or overnight until crisp and chilled.

Doris Trcka

Cauliflower-Pea Salad

Make Ahead

1	head cauliflower	1	cup mayonnaise
1	(8 ounce) can green peas, drained	3-4	tablespoons milk
		1½	teaspoons salt
1	onion, chopped	½	teaspoon pepper

Cut cauliflower into flowerets and toss with peas and onions. Blend mayonnaise, milk, salt and pepper. Pour over vegetables and refrigerate for several hours. Serves 8. *Patricia Brott*

☆　☆　☆

Orange Avocado Tossed Salad

Make Dressing in Advance

¼ cup salad oil
2 tablespoons red wine vinegar
½ cup fresh orange juice
½ teaspoon grated orange peel

¼ teaspoon salt
2 tablespoons sugar
1 tablespoon fresh lemon juice

SALAD:
1 head lettuce, broken into small pieces
1 (11 ounce) can mandarin oranges, drained
2 avocados, sliced lengthwise

1 cucumber, sliced
1 red onion, sliced and separated into rings

DRESSING: Mix salad oil, red wine vinegar, orange juice, grated orange peel, salt, sugar and lemon juice. Store in refrigerator.

SALAD: Arrange pieces of lettuce in large bowl. Place mandarin oranges in the center and top with avocado and cucumber slices. Arrange red onion rings around the oranges. Salad may be served with dressing poured over the top, or may be tossed to make a tastier dish. Serves 10-12.

Vivian Brotherton

Simply Super Salad

1-2 heads of lettuce, broken into bite-sized chunks
1 carrot, thinly sliced
2 ribs celery, diced
Other greens as desired
2 fresh tomatoes, diced

1 can (4½ ounce) small shrimp, rinsed and drained
1 cup grated Cheddar cheese
½ cup sunflower nuts
Croutons if desired

Prepare vegetables for salad. Add cheese. Just before serving add tomatoes, shrimp, sunflower nuts and croutons. Pass vinaigrette dressing if desired. Serves 6-8.

This salad needs very little dressing. It has its own natural flavor. A small amount of oil adds sheen.
Mary Cooprider

☆ ☆ ☆

Indian Spinach Salad

DRESSING:
⅔   cup salad oil
1   teaspoon Worcestershire
1   tablespoon chutney

1   teaspoon curry powder
1   teaspoon salt
Dash of Tabasco

SALAD:
1   (10 ounce) bag fresh
     spinach
1   tablespoon sesame seed
¾   cup unsalted roasted
     peanuts

1   apple, chopped
¼   cup chopped green onions
½   cup raisins

DRESSING: Combine salad oil, Worcestershire, chutney, curry powder, salt and Tabasco.

SALAD: Toss spinach with salad dressing until the spinach is well coated with dressing. Add sesame seed, peanuts, apple, onions and raisins. Toss *very* lightly.   *Barbara Eveleth*

Spinach Salad Oriental

Make Dressing a Day Ahead

DRESSING:
1   cup oil
¼   cup vinegar
⅓   cup ketchup
2   tablespoons Worcestershire

¾   cup sugar
½   teaspoon salt
1   onion, grated

SALAD:
1   (8 ounce) bag fresh
     spinach
16   ounces bean sprouts
     (better if fresh)
1   (8 ounce) can sliced water
     chestnuts, drained

8   strips crisp bacon,
     crumbled
3   hard-cooked eggs,
     chopped

DRESSING: Combine dressing day ahead. Combine oil, vinegar, ketchup, Worcestershire, sugar, salt and onion. Refrigerate. Use only as much as needed for salad.

SALAD: Toss spinach, sprouts, water chestnuts, bacon and eggs. Add as much dressing as desired. Serves 8.

Charlotte Clark and Gerry Spicer

☆   ☆   ☆

Caesar Salad

6	tablespoons salad oil	¼	cup wine vinegar
2	cloves garlic, peeled	1	(2 ounce) can anchovy
2	slices day-old bread, cubed		fillets
2	quarts crisp, mixed salad greens such as lettuce, chicory and water cress	¼	cup grated Parmesan cheese
		Salt to taste	
1	egg	Pepper to taste	

Combine salad oil and garlic and let stand several hours. Discard garlic. Put 2 tablespoons of garlic-oil in a skillet. Sauté bread cubes until crisp and brown. Place mixed greens in a deep salad bowl. Break egg over greens. Add remaining garlic-oil, vinegar, anchovies, grated cheese and browned bread cubes. Sprinkle with salt and pepper to taste. Toss until greens glisten with dressing and all trace of the egg has disappeared. Serves 6-8.

Tura Bethune

Mennonite Salad

1½	times the amount of lettuce usually used for specified number of servings	Salt to taste	
		Pepper to taste	
		1	slice bacon
Green onions, finely chopped, optional		1	teaspoon brown sugar
		1	teaspoon wine vinegar
		2	tablespoons sour cream

Wash, dry, and shred lettuce in bite-sized pieces. Add green onion; toss. Season to taste. Cook bacon until crisp; drain; reserve bacon drippings. To drippings, add sugar and vinegar. Salad and dressing may be held for an hour or more at this point. Just before serving add sour cream to sugar, vinegar, fat mixture and heat until steaming but not boiling. Pour over greens, toss and serve immediately. Garnish the salad or each serving with crumbled bacon. Serves 1.

Use fresh garden lettuce or red leaf lettuce for this salad. Many say this is the best darn wilted lettuce they have ever tasted.

Ruth Dirks

☆　　☆　　☆

Stuffed Lettuce Slices

1   (3 ounce) package cream
    cheese
2   tablespoons Roquefort
    cheese
2   tablespoons grated carrot

1   teaspoon minced onion
2   tablespoons minced bell
    pepper
2   tablespoons diced fresh
    tomatoes

Wash a firm head of lettuce; remove core. Stuff with above mixture, packing firmly into cavity. Wrap lettuce in damp cloth and chill for several hours. Slice the head cross wise so that each portion has a cheese center for serving. Serves 4.   *Mary Ann Myers*

Sour Cream Noodle Salad

1   (8 ounce) package fine egg
    noodles
1   (10 ounce) package frozen
    green peas
½-1 cup grated carrots
1   bell pepper, diced
1   cup sour cream
1   cup mayonnaise

1   teaspoon sugar
2   tablespoons lemon juice
1   tablespoon Worcestershire
1   teaspoon Beau Monde
    Seasoning
½   teaspoon onion powder
½   teaspoon garlic salt
Dash of Tabasco

Cook egg noodles according to package directions. Drain and cool. Cook peas for 5 minutes, drain and cool. Combine carrots and bell pepper with noodles and peas. Mix sour cream and mayonnaise with sugar, lemon juice, Worcestershire, Beau Monde, onion powder, garlic salt and Tabasco. Fold into noodles and vegetable mixture. Chill. Great for picnics.   *Linda Juba*

Tossed Avocado Do-Ahead Salad

Juice of 2 lemons
¾   cup oil
Accent
Beau Monde Seasoning

6   green onions
2   avocados
2   heads Romaine lettuce
Parmesan cheese

Squeeze lemon juice in the bottom of a salad bowl. Add oil, Accent and Beau Monde. Stir together. Chop onions, slice avocados and add to the lemon juice mixture. Fill the bowl with lettuce and sprinkle Parmesan cheese on top. Cover with Saran Wrap and refrigerate. Toss at serving time. Serves 12.   *Barbara England*

☆   ☆   ☆

New Potato Salad

20	new potatoes	1	(16 ounce) package frozen
1	tablespoon Dijon mustard		green peas
1	cup sour cream	1	cup chopped watercress
Lemon juice, as desired			leaves

Scrub and dice potatoes. Cover with cold water and boil 6 to 10 minutes. Meanwhile, mix Dijon mustard, sour cream and lemon juice. Reserve. Add the peas to the potatoes and cook 2 to 4 minutes longer. Drain. Add to dressing mixture and toss with desired greens. Serve hot. Serves 6-8. *Connie Altemus*

Variation: Chopped parsley or green onions and herbs may be substituted for watercress.

H. A. Bachman's German Potato Salad

SALAD:

12-14	new potatoes, as big as possible	3	tablespoons parsley, chopped fine
2	bunches green onions, finely diced		

DRESSING:

½	cup sugar	½	cup salad oil
1	tablespoon salt	1	cup white wine vinegar
½	teaspoon pepper	1	cup chicken broth
½	teaspoon dry mustard		

SALAD: Boil potatoes with jackets on and peel while warm. Slice thin and add enough dressing to warm potatoes to moisten (not too wet). Add onions and parsley. Mix and marinate well. This can be served warm, but is truly best chilled.

DRESSING: Combine all ingredients in saucepan. Heat to boiling point. Add to potatoes.

This recipe was given to me by Bachman's Catering in Lawrence, Massachusetts, when I visited there as a bride. He would not share it with me until my husband and I returned to Texas. Mr. Bachman is no longer living and his family business is closed, so I really feel free to share this now. *Linda Juba*

☆　　☆　　☆

Salmon Salad

1   (15½ ounce) can Red
    Sockeye Salmon
1   cup mashed potatoes,
    seasoned with butter and
    salt to taste
12   slices bread and butter
    pickles, chopped

1   onion, chopped
2   hard-cooked eggs,
    chopped
⅓   cup mayonnaise
Salt to taste

Drain salmon; remove skin and bones and flake. Add potatoes, pickles, onion and eggs. Mix gently with mayonnaise until desired consistency. Add salt to taste. Chill 1 to 2 hours. Also good as an appetizer with crackers or as a sandwich. Serves 6-8.

This salad has been served by my family for Christmas dinner for more than 100 years.

Hint: Instant mashed potatoes work well.   *Ivanette Dennis*

Red Bean Slaw

5   slices bacon
¾   cup chopped onion
1   cup mayonnaise
¼   cup vinegar
1   tablespoon sugar
2   tablespoons parsley flakes
1   teaspoon salt

1   teaspoon oregano
½   teaspoon pepper
3   cups shredded cabbage
2   (16 ounces each) cans
    kidney beans, drained
1   cup diced celery

Cook bacon; drain, reserving ¼ cup drippings. Set bacon aside. Sauté onions in bacon drippings until tender; remove from heat. Stir in mayonnaise, vinegar, sugar, parsley, salt, oregano, pepper and mix well. Crumble bacon and add cabbage, beans and celery and stir into mayonnaise mixture.   *Paula King*

☆   ☆   ☆

Flora's Slaw

4	cups cabbage, shredded	1	onion, chopped
1	cup diced bell pepper	2	carrots, grated

DRESSING:

1	cup mayonnaise	1	teaspoon dry mustard
2	teaspoons sugar	1	teaspoon curry

Combine mayonnaise, sugar, dry mustard and curry and blend until smooth. Add to Flora's Slaw and toss.   *Flora Anderson*

Creamy Cole Slaw

2	tablespoons sugar	4	cups shredded cabbage
3	tablespoons vinegar		Diced bell pepper
½	cup cream or canned evaporated milk		Diced pimiento
			Grated onion
¼	teaspoon salt		

Combine sugar, vinegar, cream and salt in small bowl. Pour over cabbage, bell pepper, pimiento and onion. Chill. Serves 8.

Mary Cummins

Poppy Seed Cole Slaw

1	head cabbage, shredded	½	cup mayonnaise
1	carrot, grated	1	tablespoon vinegar
5-6	green onions, chopped	2	tablespoons sugar
½	cup sour cream	1	tablespoon poppy seeds

Combine cabbage, carrot and onions in a large bowl. In a small bowl, blend sour cream, mayonnaise, vinegar, sugar and poppy seeds. Pour over vegetables and toss. Serves 6.   *Marge Grogg*

☆   ☆   ☆

24 Hour Cole Slaw

SLAW:

1	head cabbage	2	onions
1	bell pepper	1	carrot
1	cup sugar		

DRESSING:

2	tablespoons sugar	1	teaspoon dry mustard
1	cup vinegar	1	tablespoon salt
¾	cup salad oil	1	teaspoon celery seed

SLAW: Chop cabbage, pepper, onion and carrot as fine as desired. Put in large bowl and sprinkle with sugar.

DRESSING: In pan, bring to boil the sugar, vinegar, salad oil, mustard, salt and celery seed. Pour over cabbage. Do not stir until ready to serve. Refrigerate. Will keep a week. Serves 8. You may vary the amount of sugar or vinegar according to your taste. *The Cookbook Committee*

Scandinavian Cole Slaw

1	cabbage	1	cup vinegar
2	onions, thinly sliced	1	teaspoon sugar
¾	cup sugar	1	teaspoons salt
1	teaspoon celery seed	¾	cup salad oil
1	teaspoon prepared mustard		

Shred cabbage and alternate cabbage with onions in Pyrex bowl or 3 quart heat-proof casserole. Cover with sugar. Heat celery seed, mustard, vinegar, sugar and salt together. Bring to a boil while stirring. Add oil. Bring to a boil again. Pour over slaw. Cover and refrigerate for at least 3 hours. Mix after one hour. Will keep refrigerated for several weeks. Serves 12. *Rae Taylor*

☆　　☆　　☆

Rice and Pea Salad

Make Ahead

1	tablespoon vinegar	2	tablespoons chopped onion
2	tablespoons corn oil	1	cup chopped celery
1	teaspoon salt	1	(10 ounce) package frozen green peas, undercooked
½	teaspoon curry powder		
¾	cup mayonnaise		
1½	cups cooked rice		

Mix vinegar, oil, salt, curry powder and mayonnaise. Add to the warm rice. When cool add onion, celery and peas. Make 24 hours ahead of time so that flavors may blend. Serves 6-8.

Variation: Increase the curry to 2 tablespoons.

Variation: Add shrimp, ham or poultry chunks.

Frances Hough

Curried Artichoke Rice Salad

1	(6-7 ounce) package chicken flavored rice mix	2	(6 ounces each) jars marinated artichoke hearts
2-3	green onions, thinly sliced with tops	1	teaspoon curry powder
½	bell pepper, chopped	⅓	cup mayonnaise
8-10	pimiento stuffed green olives, sliced		

Cook rice according to package directions, but omit butter. Cool. Add onions, bell pepper and olives. Drain artichokes, reserving marinade. Add artichoke to rice mixture. Mix mayonnaise with desired amount marinade and curry powder. Blend all together and chill 6 hours or overnight. Serve on romaine lettuce with tomato wedge and green or black olives. Serves 4-6.

Mickey Laue

☆　　☆　　☆

Anne's Zucchini and Tomato Salad with Lemon Dressing

SALAD:

3	medium zucchini	2	tomatoes

DRESSING:

1	lemon	¼	teaspoon dry mustard
1	teaspoon salt	½	cup salad oil
½	teaspoon seasoned pepper	1	teaspoon sugar

SALAD: Cut zucchini crosswise in half, then cut each half lengthwise. Cut tomatoes in chunks. Place zucchini and tomatoes in 9 x 13 inch dish or plastic container with lid.

DRESSING: Grate lemon rind and squeeze lemon juice into small bowl. Add salt, pepper, mustard, oil and sugar to lemon juice and rind. Pour dressing over zucchini and tomatoes and chill. Stir occasionally. Make 6 to 8 hours before serving. Serves 4-6. *Jean Zinser*

Variation: Substitute 2 tablespoons white vinegar for lemon juice and add ½ teaspoon marjoram in dressing. One (8 ounce) can sliced mushrooms and ½ cup sliced scallions may be added to the zucchini and tomatoes. *Martha Crowley*

Variation: May use about ½ yellow squash and ½ zucchini. Add 1 bell pepper, diced; 2 onions, diced and 1 rib celery, diced. *Patricia Brott*

24 Hour Marinated Tomatoes

6	tomatoes	1	clove garlic, crushed
4	tablespoons salad oil	1	teaspoon salt
4	tablespoons red wine vinegar	½	teaspoon thyme

Peel tomatoes and cut into wedges or slices. Combine all other ingredients and pour over tomatoes. Cover and refrigerate. Stir several times or use a bowl that can be turned over. Prepare at least the night before. Serves 6-8. *Martha Clem*

☆   ☆   ☆

Stewart's Rice Salad

2 cups cooked rice	½ cup chopped green onion
1 (4 ounce) can sliced black olives	1 (12 ounce) package frozen baby shrimp, thawed
2 jars (6 ounces each) marinated artichoke hearts, chopped	½ (12 ounce) jar Marie's Creamy Italian Dressing

Toss all ingredients and chill.

Tura Bethune

Marinated Vegetables with Green Chilies

Must Be Made Ahead

1 cup sliced fresh carrots	1 tablespoon olive oil
1 cup fresh or frozen cut green beans	½ cup pimiento-stuffed green olives, sliced
1 cup fresh or frozen green peas	¼ cup chopped onion
½ teaspoon seasoned salt	¼ cup lemon juice
½ cup boiling water	1 (4 ounce) can chopped green chilies and liquid
1 cup tiny cauliflower flowerets	2 bay leaves, crushed
	1-2 whole cloves if desired

In a saucepan cook carrots, fresh beans, fresh peas and salt in boiling water about 10 minutes. Add cauliflower flowerets and cook 5 minutes more or until just tender. (If using frozen beans, cook fresh carrots in salted water 10 minutes and then add beans, peas and cauliflower flowerets for 5 minutes etc.) Add oil, olives, onions, lemon juice and chilies with liquid. Stir gently. Tie bay leaves and clove in a cheesecloth bag. Add to vegetables. Cover and refrigerate several hours or overnight, stirring occasionally. Drain; remove cheesecloth bag. Taste for seasonings. Garnish with onion rings and whole green olives if desired. Serves 8.

Variation: Cook 1 pint drained fresh oysters in 2 tablespoons oil until the edges curl, 3 to 4 minutes. May substitute 2 tablespoons finely chopped fresh green chili pepper for canned green chilies. Add oysters with spice bag and continue with recipe.

☆　　☆　　☆

Marinated Green Beans

Mediterranean Delight

1 onion, finely chopped	½ cup water
¼ cup olive oil	1 teaspoon sugar
2 tomatoes, peeled and cut up	1 teaspoon salt
1 pound fresh green beans, cut	

Fry onions in oil until transparent. Add tomatoes to cooked onions along with water, beans, salt and sugar. Cook until beans are tender. Chill and serve. Never serve hot. Serves 4.   *Tura Bethune*

Variation: 1 tablespoon tomato paste may be substituted for fresh tomatoes.

Matchstick Carrots

Must Be Made Ahead

2 pounds carrots	1 onion, chopped fine
¼ cup Italian Dressing	2-3 teaspoons fresh or dry dill
¼ cup Green Goddess Dressing	

Cut carrots into matchstick size, cook to crunchy stage about 2 or 3 minutes. Drain, combine with dressings and onion. Sprinkle lightly with dill. Marinate overnight.   *Tura Bethune*

Brussel Sprout Salad

Make Ahead

1 (10 ounce) package frozen brussel sprouts	1 clove garlic, pressed
¼ cup black olives, sliced	1 teaspoon salt
¼ cup minced onion	1 teaspoon sugar
⅔ cup salad oil or less	¼ teaspoon dry mustard
⅓ cup cider vinegar	⅛ teaspoon crushed red pepper

Cook sprouts until just tender. Drain and cool. Slice in half. Combine with olives, onion, oil, vinegar, garlic, salt, sugar, mustard and red pepper. Marinate several hours or overnight. Serve on lettuce. Serves 4.
Nancy Brown

☆   ☆   ☆

TEXAS STATE FARE

Food Memories That Live Forever

Snow Cones   Salt Water Taffy

Corny Dogs

Hamburger and French Fries

Corn on the Cob

Belgium Waffles

Cotton Candy   Ice Cream Bars

Lemonade

Coke

Dr. Pepper

Pepsi Cola

The State Fair of Texas

Simple Simon met a pieman
Going to the fair.
Says Simple Simon to the pieman,
"Let me taste your ware."

As the old nursery rhyme says, people have been going to the fair for centuries to show off their wares and to taste the wares of others.

Every year Texans hold their county fairs and in October come to Dallas for the really big one, The State Fair of Texas, the nation's largest.

Highlights of the fair include the midway, livestock shows, arts and crafts, exhibits, entertainment, cooking contests and special events. Tasting the wares is delicious! Texas food at its prize-winning best is found in the Creative Arts building where cooks vie for blue ribbons in every food category imaginable.

Entries from creative arts categories such as needlework, crafts and art are featured in the photograph with Big Tex, the 52 foot tall fair landmark. In the background is the giant ferris wheel, Texas Star, which towers over the other midway rides.

Although Dallas had its first county fair in 1859, the state fair dates back to the 1880's when two rival shows merged. The annual exposition became nationally known in 1936 during the enormous Texas Centennial celebration. Average attendance is over three million, but almost four million people visited the 1986 Texas Sesquicentennial, the largest crowd ever recorded at an American state fair.

Photography
Mike Flahive

Mayonnaise Chicken Watson

2	envelopes Knox gelatin	1	(16 ounce) can peas, drained
1	cup chicken broth		
2	cups mayonnaise	2	cups celery, diced
4-6	cups cooked, diced chicken	2	tablespoons chow-chow or sliced olives
4	hard-cooked eggs, diced	1	cup slivered almonds

Dissolve gelatin in cold water and add to hot broth and mayonnaise. Add chicken, eggs, peas, celery, chow-chow or olives and slivered almonds. Pour into individual molds or one large one. Chill. Serves 12.

Frances Hough

Chinese Shredded Chicken Salad

DRESSING:

2	tablespoons sugar	1	teaspoon salt
1	teaspoon M.S.G., optional	¼	teaspoon white pepper
3	tablespoons white wine vinegar		

SALAD:

¼	pound rice sticks	3	scallions
1	whole chicken breast, boiled	1	head lettuce, shredded
3	ribs of celery		Sesame seeds or toasted almonds, optional

DRESSING: Blend all ingredients. Reserve.

SALAD: Fry rice sticks in hot oil, but do not let them brown. Drain on paper towel. May be prepared in advance and stored in plastic bag. Shred chicken finely and chop celery and scallions into 2 inch lengths. Combine with chicken and shredded lettuce. Toss with dressing. Add desired amount of rice sticks and garnish with toasted sesame seeds or toasted almonds. Serves 6-8.

Variation: Substitute sliced jicama for rice sticks.

Novella Bailey

☆　☆　☆

Curried Chicken Salad

Must Be Made Ahead

2	cups uncooked rice	1	tablespoon salt
1	cup raw cauliflower	1½	teaspoons pepper
1	(8 ounce) bottle Kraft	½	cup milk
	Creamy French Dressing	6-7	cups cooked chicken, large
1	cup mayonnaise		chunks
1	tablespoon curry powder	1	cup thinly sliced red
1	cup thin strips bell pepper		onions
2	cups diced celery		

Cook rice until tender and chill. Toss chilled rice with cauliflower and french dressing. Refrigerate at least 2 hours. In another bowl, combine mayonnaise, curry powder, salt and pepper. Slowly stir in milk. Add chicken and mix well. Refrigerate at least 2 hours. When ready to serve combine both mixtures. Add bell pepper, celery and onion. (It's best to do this at least 1 hour before serving.) Serves 8-12.

The Cookbook Committee

Party Chicken or Turkey Salad

DRESSING:

3	cups Hellmann's Mayonnaise	2	tablespoons soy sauce
		1	tablespoon curry powder

SALAD:

8	cups cooked and chopped chicken or turkey		
2	pounds seedless green grapes	2	(8 ounces each) cans sliced water chestnuts
2	cups finely diced celery	2	cups whole roasted almonds

DRESSING: Combine mayonnaise, soy sauce and curry powder. Allow to stand several hours for flavors to blend.

SALAD: Combine meat, grapes, celery, water chestnuts and almonds. Pour dressing on just before serving. Serves 12-14.

This may be made from frozen turkey rolls. One roll yields 4 cups.

Jere Wagenhals

☆　　☆　　☆

Oriental Chicken Salad
Make Ahead

CHICKEN:
Cook 4 chicken breast halves.
   Skin, bone and cut into
   slivers.

MARINADE:

½   cup chicken broth
¼   cup soy sauce
⅓   cup wine vinegar
¼   cup sugar
1   teaspoon dry mustard

½   teaspoon salt
1   tablespoon fresh ginger
1   teaspoon sesame oil
1   pound fresh bean sprouts,
   parboiled and drained

MARINADE: Bring chicken broth, soy sauce, wine vinegar, sugar, dry mustard, salt, fresh ginger, sesame oil to a boil. Pour over chicken and marinate for 12 to 24 hours. Toss with bean sprouts and garnish with green onion and radish slivers. Serves 6-8.

Variation: Substitute 1 small head of cabbage for bean sprouts.

Elbie Guindon

Neiman-Marcus Zodiac Room Seafood Salad

2   cups rice, cooked and
   chilled
½   cup king crabmeat or
   lobster, chopped
½   cup ham, slivered
½   cup celery, finely chopped
2   hard-cooked eggs, finely
   chopped

1   tablespoon chopped chives
¼   cup parsley, chopped
1   tablespoon olive oil
1   tablespoon red wine
   vinegar
½   cup mayonnaise
Salt to taste
Pepper to taste

Combine and toss lightly rice, crabmeat, ham, celery, eggs, chives and parsley. Sprinkle with oil and vinegar. Add mayonnaise, salt and pepper. Mix all ingredients. Let stand in refrigerator a few hours before serving for better flavor. Serves 6.

Vicky Nayes

A specialty of the late Helen Corbitt, this has been a Neiman-Marcus favorite for many years.

☆   ☆   ☆

Wild Tuna Salad

1	(6 ounce) package Uncle Ben's Wild & Long Grain Rice	2	tablespoons finely chopped onion
1	cup mayonnaise	1	(12½ ounce) can white albacore tuna (do not substitute)
½	cup sour cream		
½	cup finely chopped celery	1	cup salted cashews

Cook rice according to package directions. Chill. Add mayonnaise, sour cream, celery, onion, tuna and cashews. Serve in lettuce cup. If desired garnish with alfalfa sprouts. Serves 4 generously. To make ahead, do not add nuts until just before serving. *Linda Juba*

Variation: Chicken or shrimp may be substituted for tuna.

Deluxe Frozen Fruit Salad

1	(3 ounce) package cream cheese, softened	¼	cup drained, chopped Mandarin orange slices
⅓	cup mayonnaise	1	(6 ounce) can pineapple chunks, drained
1	teaspoon lemon juice		
2	egg whites	2	tablespoons chopped Maraschino cherries
⅓	cup sugar		
1	cup whipping cream	1-2	tablespoons toasted almonds
1	(16 ounce) can apricots, drained and diced		

Blend cream cheese, mayonnaise and lemon juice. Beat egg whites until foamy. Beat in sugar, a tablespoon at a time until stiff peaks form. Beat cream until stiff. Fold cream into egg whites. Fold into cream cheese mixture. Fold in apricots, Mandarin oranges, pineapple, cherries and almonds. Pour into 8 inch square pan. Freeze. Or freeze in muffin pans in cupcake liners. Serves 8. *The Cookbook Committee*

☆   ☆   ☆

Frozen Cherry Salad

1 (14 ounce) can Eagle Brand milk
Juice of 2 lemons
1 (8 ounce) can crushed pineapple, drained

1 (21 ounce) can cherry pie filling
½ pint whipping cream
1 cup pecans, coarsely chopped

Combine Eagle Brand milk, lemon juice, crushed pineapple and cherry pie filling. Fold in whipped cream and add chopped pecans. Freeze in 9x13 inch pan. Serves 8.   *Brenda Chattaway*

Frozen Fruit Salad

½ cup Miracle Whip salad dressing
1 (8 ounce) package cream cheese, softened
2 cups vanilla ice cream, softened

1 (10 ounce) package frozen raspberries
1 (1 pound) can sliced peaches, drained
Lemon juice (optional)

Gradually add salad dressing to softened cream cheese until well blended. Add ice cream, fold in fruits and place in 9 inch square glass dish and freeze. Serves 10-12.   *Martha Aldridge*

Easy Frozen Fruit Salad

1 (8 ounce) package cream cheese
¼ teaspoon salt
½ cup mayonnaise
Juice of 1 lemon
1 (6 ounce) jar Maraschino cherries, chopped, reserve juice

1 (6 ounce) can crushed pineapple
2 bananas, diced
½ pint whipping cream, whipped
1 cup miniature marshmallows
½ cup pecans

Mix cream cheese with salt, mayonnaise, lemon juice and cherry juice. Add crushed pineapple and juice, bananas, nuts, cherries and marshmallows. Fold in whipped cream and put in dish to freeze. Cut in squares when serving. Serves 8-10.   *Anna Wade Pierson*

☆   ☆   ☆

Hot Curried Fruit Salad

Make a Day Ahead

FRUIT:

1 (16 ounce) can pear halves
1 (16 ounce) can apricot halves
1 (20 ounce) can peach halves

1 (20 ounce) can pineapple slices, cut in half
Cherries, sweet, dark or Maraschino, optional

SAUCE:

¾ cup brown sugar
1 stick margarine

3-4 tablespoons curry powder

FRUIT: Drain all fruits. Mix in a 2½ quart casserole.

SAUCE: Mix sugar, margarine and curry and heat until melted. Pour over fruit. Bake for 30 minutes at 350⁰. Cool and refrigerate. Reheat before serving the following day. This goes well as an accompaniment for meat and chicken dishes.   *Sally Kinne*

Red Hot Peaches

Make a Day Ahead

Canned peach halves
Red Hots

Lemon juice

Drain peaches, place in shallow dish. Fill each peach half with red hots and add 1 teaspoon lemon juice per peach. This needs to be made a day in advance of serving as the lemon juice dissolves the red hots. This is delightful and so easy to prepare. The peach really makes a nice accent for many dishes.

☆   ☆   ☆

Cranberry Salad Delight

Make Ahead

1 pound cranberries, ground
2 cups sugar
1 (15 ounce) can pineapple tidbits
2 cups Tokay grapes, halved and seeded
1 cup bite-sized marshmallows
½ cup nuts
½ pint whipped cream

Let cranberries and sugar stand overnight. Drain thoroughly. Add pineapple, grapes, marshmallows and nuts. Fold in whipped cream. Let stand at least 2 hours. Serves 10-12.   *The Cookbook Committee*

Fruit Salad

1 (21 ounce) can Comstock cherry pie filling
1 (8 ounce) can crushed pineapple
1 (12 ounce) container Cool Whip
1 (11 ounce) can mandarin oranges, drained
½ package marshmallows
1 (7 ounce) package coconut
1 cup chopped nuts

Mix all ingredients and chill a few hours before serving. Serves 8-10.
Ann Long

Variation: Apricot pie filling may be substituted.

Tangy Salad

1 (10¾ ounce) can tomato soup
1 (3 ounce) package lemon Jello
1 tablespoon sugar
1 teaspoon salt
1 cup Miracle Whip
1 (8 ounce) carton small curd cottage cheese
1 cup chopped onion
1 cup chopped bell pepper
1 cup chopped celery

Heat undiluted soup. Pour over dry Jello, sugar and salt. When dissolved, add Miracle Whip. Mix well. Add cottage cheese, onions, peppers and celery. Chill. Makes 8 individual molds. Sets quickly.
Ivanette Dennis

☆   ☆   ☆

Frosted Avocado Mold

MOLD:

1	(6 ounce) package lemon gelatin	1	avocado, chunked
2	cups boiling water	½	cup sliced celery
2	tablespoons lemon juice	2	hard-cooked eggs, diced
1	cup cold water	1	tablespoon sweet pickle relish
1	tablespoon minced onion		
2	(6-7 ounces each) cans of tuna, drained		

FROSTING:

1	avocado, mashed	½	teaspoon seasoned salt
¼	cup mayonnaise		

Dissolve gelatin in boiling water. Stir in lemon juice, water and onion. Chill until partially set. Add tuna, avocado, celery, eggs and relish. Spoon into 1½ quart mold. Chill until firm. Unmold salad on platter and spread frosting mixture over top and down the sides. Serve immediately. Serves 8. *Ruth Holzschuh*

Avocado Tomato Aspic

May Be Made Ahead

4	envelopes unflavored gelatin	3	tablespoons grated onion
¾	cup cold water	3	tablespoons vinegar
7	cups tomato juice	1	tablespoon salt
Light green, tender, celery leaves, as desired		1	tablespoon sugar
1	bay leaf	1	avocado
		Lemon juice	

Sprinkle gelatin over cold water. Let stand 5 minutes. Meanwhile heat tomato juice with celery leaves, bay leaf, onion, vinegar, salt and sugar. Simmer 10 minutes. Strain. Add softened gelatin to hot juice and stir until dissolved. Chill until thick and syrupy. Cut avocado into thin slices. Dip in lemon juice to prevent darkening. Arrange the slices in a pattern in the bottom of a 10 inch ring mold. Pour in a little of the tomato mixture and chill until firm. Pour in rest of tomato mixture and chill until firm. Cover with wax paper to keep overnight in the refrigerator. Serves 12. *Tura Bethune*

☆　　☆　　☆

Avocado Lime Salad

½ cup boiling water
1 (3 ounce) package lime Jello
1 (8 ounce) can crushed pineapple drained, reserve juice
½ teaspoon salt
1 ripe avocado, mashed
2 teaspoons lemon juice
½ cup mayonnaise
¾ cup heavy cream, whipped
½ cup nuts

Add boiling water to Jello. Drain pineapple and add juice to Jello mixture. Set aside until mixture begins to thicken; then add pineapple and salt. Mash avocado and mix with lemon. Fold in mayonnaise, whipped cream, nuts and avocado into Jello. Pour into greased mold. Serves 8.

The Cookbook Committee

Lemon Raspberry Salad

1 (3 ounce) package lemon Jello
1 cup hot water
1 (20 ounce) can crushed pineapple
½ pound marshmallows cut fine, about 32 large
1 (8 ounce) package cream cheese, softened
1 cup Miracle Whip
½ pint whipping cream, whipped (Cool Whip if desired)
2 (3 ounces each) packages raspberry Jello
2 cups hot water
1 (10 ounce) package frozen raspberries, thawed

Mix lemon Jello with hot water. Drain pineapple well and heat juice to boiling point. Add marshmallows. After it is dissolved, set aside to cool. Then add to lemon Jello. Mix cream cheese until smooth, add salad dressing and crushed pineapple. Add to lemon mixture, fold in whipped cream and put in large pan and let congeal completely. Dissolve raspberry Jello in hot water and cool. Add raspberries. Pour over congealed lemon mixture and return to refrigerator for setting. Top with whipped cream if desired. Serves 20.

Corrine Shaw

☆   ☆   ☆

Blueberry Salad of Many Flavors

SALAD:

2 (3 ounces each) packages black cherry Jello
2 cups boiling water
1 (15 ounce) can blueberries with juice

1 (8 ounce) can crushed pineapple, drained

TOPPING:

1 (8 ounce package) cream cheese, softened
¼ cup sugar

½ pint sour cream
½ teaspoon vanilla
½ cup pecans

SALAD: Dissolve Jello in boiling water. Add blueberries and pineapple. Pour into 9x12 glass baking dish. Refrigerate until set. Serve plain or with topping. Serves 12.

TOPPING: Blend cream cheese and sugar with a mixer. Add sour cream slowly; then add vanilla. Spread over gelatin salad and sprinkle with pecans. Refrigerate until serving time. *Elbie Guindon*

Variation: Substitute 2 packages of raspberry or black raspberry gelatin for the black cherry Jello. Omit cream cheese, sugar, and sour cream and substitute 1 (8 ounce) container Cool Whip or 1 envelope Dream Whip.

Red Hot Jello

½ cup red hots
1 (6 ounce) package raspberry Jello

3 cups applesauce
3 tablespoons lemon juice

Dissolve the red hots in 2 cups of boiling water. Remove from heat. Stir in the Jello until dissolved. Add the applesauce and the lemon juice and mix. Makes a 6 cup mold. Good as a side dish for baked ham or chicken. *Lynda Corbin*

☆   ☆   ☆

Cranberry Christmas Salad

SALAD:

1 (13½ ounce) can crushed pineapple

2 (3 ounces each) packages strawberry Jello

¾ cup cold water

1 (16 ounce) can jellied cranberry sauce

⅓ cup coarsely chopped pecans

1 tablespoon butter or margarine

TOPPING:

1 envelope Dream Whip

½ cup heavy cream

½ cup milk

1 (3 ounce) package cream cheese, softened

SALAD: Drain pineapple juice into measuring cup; add water to equal 1 cup. Bring to boil in saucepan. Remove from heat, add Jello and stir until dissolved. Add cold water. Chill until Jello is consistency of egg whites. In medium bowl mix drained pineapple and cranberry sauce and stir into Jello mixture. Pour into 9 inch square cake pan. Cover and chill until firm. Heat oven to 350°. Put pecans and butter in a shallow pan and bake 8 minutes. Stir occasionally until pecans are toasted. Cool nuts. When Jello mixture is firm add topping.

TOPPING: Prepare Dream Whip according to package directions, but substitute ½ cup heavy cream for milk and ½ cup milk for water. When mixed add cream cheese and blend well. Spread over salad and top with toasted pecans. Serves 8.   *Lynn Trentham*

State Tree — The pecan is the state tree of Texas. The sentiment that led to its official adoption probably grew out of the request of Gov. James Stephen Hogg that a pecan tree be planted at his grave.

☆   ☆   ☆

Cranberry Ring

Worth the Trouble

FIRST LAYER:

1   (3 ounce) package strawberry gelatin

1   cup hot water

1   cup cranberry relish (or whole cranberries)

Salt to taste

SECOND LAYER:

1½ cups canned crushed pineapple

1   (3 ounce) package lemon gelatin

1¼ cups boiling water

2   cups tiny marshmallows

1   (3 ounce) package cream cheese, softened

½   cup mayonnaise

½   cup heavy cream, whipped

FIRST LAYER: Dissolve strawberry gelatin in hot water, add cranberry relish and salt. Pour into 6½ cup ring mold. Chill until firm.

SECOND LAYER: Drain pineapple, reserve liquid, dissolve lemon gelatin in boiling water; add marshmallows and stir until melted; add pineapple juice. Chill until partially set. Blend cream cheese, mayonnaise, salt and add to marshmallow gelatin mixture. Stir in pineapple mixture. If mixture is thin, chill until it mounds slightly when spooned. Fold in whipped cream. Spread over first layer and chill until firm. Serves 10-12.

N. J. Metcalf

Mayonnaise

Perfect Every Time

1   cup vegetable oil, divided

1   egg

½   teaspoon salt

½   teaspoon white pepper or paprika

1   teaspoon dry mustard

2   tablespoons lemon juice

Put ¼ cup oil and the egg into a blender. Add salt, pepper or paprika, mustard and lemon juice. Blend at high speed 15 seconds. Quickly add remaining oil steadily for additional 12 seconds. Stir slightly to give air throughout. Thickens immediately. Makes 1¼ cups.

Tura Bethune

☆   ☆   ☆

Food Processor Mayonnaise

2	egg yolks, room temperature	2	tablespoons lemon juice
1	whole egg, room temperature	1	teaspoon salt
		1	teaspoon Dijon mustard
		1½	cups oil

With the metal blade in place, add the egg yolks, whole egg, lemon juice, salt and mustard to the bowl of the food processor and process for five seconds. Continue processing while slowly pouring the oil through the chute into the food processor, until it thickens. Homemade mayonnaise will keep in the refrigerator for at least two weeks and can be used as a foundation for other salad dressings. Makes about 2 cups. *Liz Willson*

Favorite Italian Dressing

Make Ahead

¼-⅓	cup garlic vinegar or add ½ teaspoon garlic powder to white vinegar	1	teaspoon paprika
		1	teaspoon sugar
1	cup salad oil		Dash of cayenne pepper
2	teaspoons salt	½	teaspoon Beau Monde seasoning
¼	teaspoon pepper		

Combine vinegar, oil, salt, pepper, paprika, sugar, cayenne and Beau Monde. Shake well. Let stand a few hours to allow flavors to blend. Shake well before serving. Makes 1½ cups.   *Eileen MacWithey*

Italian Dressing

1	cup salad oil	¼	teaspoon cayenne
⅓	cup vinegar	1	clove garlic, minced
1	teaspoon sugar		Dash of bottled hot pepper sauce
½	teaspoon salt		
½	teaspoon celery salt		Dash of A-1 sauce
¼	teaspoon dry mustard	⅛	teaspoon paprika

Blend all ingredients in electric blender. Then turn to liquify for a moment to purée garlic. Makes approximately 1⅓ cups.   *Dottie Pinch*

☆   ☆   ☆

Creamy Dressing

1	cup olive oil	1½	teaspoons pepper
¾	cup vegetable oil	⅛	teaspoon garlic
5	teaspoons white or wine vinegar	½	teaspoon dry mustard
		1	teaspoon lemon juice
2	teaspoons salt	3	eggs

Combine all ingredients. Blend thoroughly in blender. This goes very well over tossed salad and especially well on spinach salad. Makes 2 cups.

Martha Brott

Creamy Roquefort Dressing

1	cup sour cream	Roquefort or Blue Cheese, crumbled (according to taste)
¼-¾	cup mayonnaise	
½-1	teaspoon salt	
3	scant tablespoons lemon juice	

Mix all ingredients thoroughly and let stand in refrigerator for several hours. Be sure salad greens are crisp and very dry.   *Dottie Pinch*

Zesty French Dressing

Must Be Made Ahead

¼	cup vinegar	¾	teaspoons sugar
1	cup salad oil	2	tablespoons ketchup
1½	teaspoons salt	1	tablespoon lemon juice
⅛	teaspoon pepper	1½	teaspoons Worcestershire
¼	teaspoon paprika	2	cloves garlic, minced
Dash of celery salt		½	teaspoon curry powder

Blend all ingredients in a blender. Refrigerate overnight. *Tura Bethune*

☆ ☆ ☆

Thousand Island Dressing

Make Ahead

1 cup mayonnaise	3 tablespoons sweet pickle
½ cup chili sauce	relish
⅓ cup finely diced bell	3 hard-cooked eggs,
pepper, optional	chopped
2 tablespoons finely minced	
onion	

Combine all ingredients and refrigerate for at least 3 hours, preferably longer. *Eileen MacWithey*

Avocado and Roquefort Salad Dressing

1 ripe avocado, quartered	2 tablespoons lemon juice
1 cup sour cream	½ teaspoon salt
3 tablespoons milk	1 clove garlic, crushed
1 tablespoon Roquefort	1 teaspoon Worcestershire
cheese	

Mix all ingredients in blender or food processor. Keeps well in refrigerator. *Marilyn Duncan*

Avocado Salad Dressing

1 (6 ounce) can frozen	1 tablespoon lemon juice
avocado dip, thawed	¼ teaspoon pepper
¼ cup salad dressing	¼ teaspoon salt
6 green onions, chopped	¼ teaspoon Tabasco

Combine all ingredients and serve over lettuce. Serves 6.

Variation: Salad may be "spiced-up" by adding cubed ham, swiss cheese, hard-cooked eggs, celery and tomato. *Geri Smith*

☆ ☆ ☆

Tomato Dressing

3   tomatoes, peeled and
     grated
12 ounces olive oil
3   ounces cider vinegar
1   tablespoon Worcestershire
     sauce

1   teaspoon dry mustard
½ teaspoon salt
1   clove garlic

Peeled tomatoes may be grated in a food processor. Place tomatoes in a quart jar. Add all other ingredients and shake well. Refrigerate. Remove garlic clove. Serve over salad greens garnished with sliced hard-cooked egg. Serves 10-12. *Gerry Leftwich*

French Tomato Dressing

1   (10¾ ounce) can tomato
     soup
¾ cup vinegar
1-2 cloves garlic
1   tablespoon salt
½ cup sugar

½ tablespoon Worcestershire
1   tablespoon paprika
1   chopped onion
½ teaspoon dry mustard,
     optional

Combine all ingredients in a bottle; shake and serve. *Paula King*
Dottie Pinch
Ruth Quance

Lemon Dressing

Yummy for Spinach Salad

1   clove garlic, chopped
Rinds of 2 lemons, grated on
     medium grater
3   tablespoons lemon juice
3   tablespoons sour cream

½ teaspoon salt
¼ teaspoon paprika
¼ teaspoon pepper
1   teaspoon sugar
½ cup salad oil

Put garlic, lemon rind, lemon juice, sour cream, salt, paprika, pepper and sugar in a blender or food processor. Blend or process 15 seconds and start adding oil until blended and dressing is a mayonnaise consistency.

This dressing is tart, but very unusual and all you need is the spinach for your salad. *Linda Juba*

☆   ☆   ☆

Parsley Dressing

2	cups parsley tops	2	teaspoons black pepper
2	teaspoons lemon juice	⅛	teaspoon cayenne pepper
1	cup evaporated milk	2	cloves garlic
4	tablespoons tarragon vinegar	1	teaspoon sugar
2	teaspoons salt	1	cup salad oil

Put parsley, lemon juice, milk, vinegar, salt, black pepper, cayenne pepper, garlic and sugar in blender or food processor. Blend for 15 to 20 seconds. Slowly add oil until mixture thickens.

This dressing is wonderful on thick slices of fresh tomatoes in the summer or excellent as a dip for fresh vegetables any time.

Linda Juba

Chef's Salad Dressing

1	clove garlic	½	teaspoon Worcestershire
½	teaspoon salt	1	tablespoon prepared horseradish
Dash of pepper			
3	tablespoons vinegar	½	cup salad oil

Combine all ingredients in a jar. Cover and shake well. This will keep for weeks in the refrigerator. Makes about 1½ cups. *Jere Wagenhals*

Quick and Easy Salad Dressing

1	cup mayonnaise	¼	teaspoon onion powder
½	cup ketchup	¼	teaspoon black or white pepper
¼	teaspoon garlic powder		

Blend all ingredients with a fork. Refrigerate. You may substitute chopped onions for different texture and garlic juice instead of powder. Makes 1½ cups. *Martha Brott*

☆　☆　☆

Dutch Celery Seed Dressing

⅔ cup sugar
1   cup oil
½ cup vinegar
1   teaspoon celery seed

1   teaspoon dry mustard
1   teaspoon salt
1   onion, quartered
1   clove garlic

Combine all ingredients in a blender and blend until smooth. Keeps in refrigerator for a long time. Can be reblended before each use. Great over a tossed salad or spinach salad.   *Shirley Argo*

Mother's Quick Fruit Salad Dressing

4-6 tablespoons sugar
1   tablespoon vinegar
1   teaspoon prepared
     mustard

1   teaspoon vanilla
1   cup Hellmann's
     mayonnaise
1   teaspoon poppy seed

Mix sugar with vinegar, mustard and vanilla. Let stand awhile to dissolve sugar. Add mayonnaise and poppy seed and refrigerate.

Variation: Honey can be used instead of sugar. Use celery seed instead of poppy seed and use in cabbage slaw. Approximately 1½ cups.
          Vivian Jackson

Orange Cream Fruit Salad Sauce

1   (3¾ ounce) package
     instant vanilla pudding
1½ cups milk

½ of a (6 ounce) can frozen
    orange juice, thawed
¾ cup sour cream

In small bowl combine pudding, milk, and orange juice. Beat 1 to 2 minutes with rotary beater; then beat in sour cream. Refrigerate. Makes fruit salad a special treat.   *Anne Eppright*

☆   ☆   ☆

Dip for Fresh Strawberries or Other Fresh Fruit

1	(8 ounce) package cream cheese	1	(7 ounce) jar marshmallow creme

Mix cream cheese and marshmallow. Serve in glass bowl in center of a tray of strawberries. *Clare Bonnett*

Variation: Mix 1 pint sour cream with ½ − 1 cup brown sugar. This is excellent mixed with green grapes or as a dip for fruit.

Sweet Fruit Dressing

½	cup sugar	2	teaspoons grated onion juice
1	teaspoon salt		
1	teaspoon dry mustard	1	cup salad oil
1	teaspoon celery salt	¼	cup vinegar
1	teaspoon paprika		

Mix sugar, salt, mustard, celery salt and paprika. Add onion juice. Add oil and vinegar alternately, with vinegar as last addition. Beat each addition well with a fork. Put on fruit. *Pat Horton.*

Variation: Celery or poppy seeds may be used for added interest.

Use your favorite salad dressing on pita bread sandwiches with your favorite combinations of meats, cheeses and vegetables.

☆   ☆   ☆

Did you ever wonder why Southern women have such a good reputation for their tender, light, fluffy biscuits while yeast breads are more popular in the North and Midwest? The answer is in the type of flour most prevalent in each area.

Winter wheat, which is grown chiefly in the Northern and Midwestern states, yields "hard flour" or bread flour which contains a tough gluten that permits yeast doughs to expand more for a longer period of time without bursting the cells of the dough and causing the dough to fall.

Spring wheat, which is grown in the milder climate of the Southern states, yields a "soft flour" whose gluten is weaker. A dough made with soft wheat flour therefore takes less force to make it rise and the gas formed by baking powder (or buttermilk and soda) is strong enough to make it rise quickly before the heat of the oven stops the rising process.

All purpose flour, which is intended in these recipes, is a mixture of hard and soft wheat flour combined in the right proportion to give good (but not the best) results in both yeast and quick breads. So where soft wheat flour is available, as in the South, it makes superior biscuits and it also requires less shortening for pastry.

Recipes for yeast breads usually call for variable amounts of flour, such as 2 to 3 cups, not a simple amount like 2½ cups. This is because the amount of flour to liquid can vary due to many causes: dryness of flour, age of flour, or humidity. *In yeast breads the smallest ratio of flour to liquid is desired.* Otherwise, the dough can get too stiff and the texture and quality will suffer. To avoid this, you start with the smallest amount of flour given, and add more flour slowly until it reaches the proper consistency.

Mary Cummins

☆   ☆   ☆

Beautiful Bread

2	cakes yeast	2	teaspoons salt
3	tablespoons sugar	1½	cups warm water
¼	cup shortening	1	cup milk, warmed
¼	cup butter	6	cups flour, divided

Directions for this bread are unusual but correct. Dissolve yeast by mixing with sugar. Mix softened shortening, butter with water, salt, milk, yeast mixture and 4 cups flour. Beat thoroughly. Add remainder of flour. Mix. Turn out on floured board. Knead for 6 to 8 minutes. Place in greased bowl; let rise until doubled in warm place. Punch down; let rise until double again. Shape into two loaves. Place in two 5x9 inch loaf pans. Let rise to top of pans. Bake 350⁰ oven for 45 minutes or until done. Brush tops with butter.

I really enjoy this recipe because it makes two loaves. Twice the reward for the work of baking bread.   *Ruth Dirks*

Monkey Bread

Excellent

1	package of yeast	1	teaspoon salt
1	cup milk, scalded and cooled to lukewarm	½	cup melted margarine
			About 3½ cups flour
4	tablespoons sugar		Additional melted margarine

Dissolve yeast in warm milk. Stir in sugar, margarine, and flour. Beat well, cover, and let rise in a warm place until double in bulk. (Takes about 1 hour.) Punch down and roll out on floured board to ¼ inch thickness. Cut into diamond shapes about 2½ inches long. Dip each piece in melted margarine and place in layers in a 9 inch ring mold. The mold should be about half full. Let rise until double in bulk. Bake at 400⁰ for 30 minutes or until golden brown. Serves 12.

At the table, each person pulls off leaves of the warm, tender bread. Do not cut, but serve with butter and a tasty jam.   *Ruth Dirks*

☆   ☆   ☆

Dill Bread

1	package dry yeast	2	teaspoons dried dill weed
¼	cup warm water	2	tablespoons sugar
½	teaspoon salt	½	teaspoon baking soda
1	tablespoon margarine, softened	1	egg, slightly beaten
1	cup sour cream	2¾-3 cups flour	

Soften yeast in warm water in large bowl. Add salt and margarine. Add sour cream, dill, sugar, soda and egg. Mix well. Add half the flour and beat with wooden spoon. Add enough flour to make a stiff dough. Turn on lightly floured board and knead 5-10 turns. Put back in bowl, cover and let rise in a warm place 50 minutes or until doubled. Turn out on board and shape into 2 small balls or loaves. Place each in a greased 9x5x3 pan and let rise 30 to 40 minutes. Bake 350⁰ for 40 minutes. Brush with melted butter and sprinkle lightly with salt after removing from oven. Cover with towel to cool.   *Paula King*

French Bread

In the Food Processor

1	package dry yeast	2	cups flour
1	teaspoon sugar	1	cup unbleached flour
1	cup plus 2 tablespoons warm water	1	teaspoon salt

Dissolve yeast and sugar in warm water for 10 minutes. Put both flours and salt in food processor and pulse lightly. Add yeast with food processor running until dough ball forms. Place in greased bowl and let dough rise until doubled in bulk. Punch down, form into 2 loaves. Place on cookie sheets lightly covered with cornmeal. Let rise. Bake at 350⁰ for 40 minutes until bread sounds hollow when tapped. For a good crust on the bread — put a pan of water on the bottom rack of the oven. Yield: 2 loaves. (May be made in Kitchen Aid mixer also.)

This also makes a good pizza crust.   *Linda Juba*

Microwave Bacon and Cheese English Muffin Bread

Yummy in Your Tummy!

5	cups flour, divided	2	cups milk
2	packages dry yeast	½	cup water
1	tablespoon sugar	1	cup grated Cheddar cheese
2	teaspoons salt	1	cup crumbled bacon
¼	teaspoon baking soda		Cornmeal

In a large bowl combine 3 cups flour, yeast, sugar, salt and soda. Combine milk and water and heat until very warm (120-130⁰). Gradually add to dry ingredients and mix well. Add bacon and cheese and remaining flour. Mix well. Divide between two 9x5x3 inch loaf pans which have been well greased and dusted with cornmeal. Dust tops with cornmeal; cover and let rise until double, about 45 minutes. Follow manufacturer's instructions to let bread rise in microwave. Place rack or inverted saucer in microwave. Bake one loaf at a time on rack. Microwave on FULL POWER 3 minutes and 15 seconds. Turn 90⁰; then bake another 3 minutes and 15 seconds or until bread begins to pull away from the sides of the pans and is no longer sticky. Cool 5 minutes before removing from pan. Slice and toast and use like English Muffins.

Variation: For regular English Muffin bread, omit bacon and cheese and make as directed.

Variation: Omit bacon and cheese and add ¼ cup raisins and 1½ teaspoons cinnamon.

Variation: Omit bacon and cheese and add ½ cup chopped green onion and 2 teaspoons caraway seeds.   *Jean Zinser*

Nonnie Bread

2½	cups milk	1	package dry yeast
4	tablespoons sugar	1	egg
½	teaspoon salt	6½	cups flour
2	tablespoons butter	5-6	tablespoons wheat germ

Scald milk. Remove from heat and add sugar, salt and butter. When lukewarm, add yeast and slightly beaten egg. Add flour and wheat germ gradually. Beat until soft dough. Grease bowl, add dough and let rise until double, about 2 hours. Place on floured board and knead slightly. Divide dough into two buttered loaf pans. Let dough rise until double, about 1 hour. Bake at 350⁰ for 40 minutes. Cool on racks, brushing top of loaves with butter.   *Suzann Deppe*

☆   ☆   ☆

Poppy Seed Egg Bread

Prize Winning Recipe

2	packages dry yeast	¼	cup soft margarine
½	cup warm water	3	eggs
1½	cups warm milk	6	tablespoons poppy seed
1	tablespoon salt		plus a bit extra for
¼	cup sugar		topping
3	eggs	2	tablespoons cold water
7-7½	cups of flour, divided	1	additional egg for topping

Dissolve yeast in warm water. Mix milk, salt and sugar and add 3 cups flour. Beat well. Add yeast and margarine; beat. Beat in 3 eggs one at a time. Add enough of remaining flour to make a soft but workable dough. Turn out on floured board. Knead until smooth and shiny. Place in greased bowl, turning to grease top. Cover; let double in size. Punch down and let rise for 20 minutes more. Turn out on lightly floured board. Divide into 2 portions. Divide each portion into 3 parts; pat each piece into a 3x12 inch strip; sprinkle 1 tablespoon poppy seed down center of each strip. Roll up strip, widthwise in jelly roll fashion; pinch to seal. Smooth strips by rolling back and forth on board. Place strips side by side and beginning at middle, braid to ends. Tuck ends in neatly. Place in greased 9x5x3 inch loaf pan. Repeat with second half of dough. Brush tops with 1 egg beaten with water. Sprinkle with poppy seed. Let double in bulk. Bake at 375⁰ 25 to 30 minutes. Makes 2 loaves.

Ruth Dirks

Melt in Your Mouth Crescent Rolls

1	tablespoon sugar	⅓	cup sugar
1	package yeast	¾	teaspoon salt
½	cup melted butter	4	cups flour, sifted before
1	cup milk		measuring
2	eggs		

Mix sugar and yeast. Heat melted butter and milk until milk is scalded. Cool to warm. Combine with eggs, sugar, salt and flour. Then add yeast mixture. Cover and refrigerate overnight. Dough will rise in refrigerator. Four hours before serving, divide the dough into four parts. Roll each part into the shape of a pie crust. Cut into 10 pie slice shaped pieces. Spread with melted butter. Starting at the wide end roll up in cresent shape. Let rise. Put on greased sheet. Bake for 10 minutes at 350⁰. Makes 40 rolls.

Jere Wagenhals

☆   ☆   ☆

Sixty Minute Rolls

A Favorite Since the Early 1900's

2	yeast cakes	½	teaspoon salt
¼	cup lukewarm water	4	tablespoons vegetable
1¼	cups milk		shortening
3	tablespoons sugar	3	cups flour

Dissolve yeast in lukewarm water. Reserve. Place milk, sugar, salt and shortening in sauce pan and heat to lukewarm. Add yeast and flour, mix well. Cover and let stand in warm place 15 minutes. The dough is very soft and difficult to handle, but do not add more flour. Do not knead or punch down. With greased spoon cut off pieces and shape into balls. Place the balls in well-greased muffin tin; cover. Let stand in warm place 15 minutes. Bake at 450⁰ for 10 minutes. Makes 2 dozen.

Maurine Montgomery

Whole Wheat Rolls

Serve with Raspberry Jam!

2	packages yeast	4	cups whole wheat flour
½	cup warm water	3	cups white flour
1¾	cups warm milk	2	eggs, beaten
½	cup sugar	3	tablespoons margarine,
1	tablespoon salt		softened

Soften yeast in water. Combine milk, sugar and salt. Add 1 cup each white and whole wheat flour; beat well. Add yeast mixture, eggs and margarine; beat. Stir in enough of remaining flours to form a soft dough. Turn out on board and knead about 5 minutes, using flour as needed to keep from sticking to board. Place in greased bowl. At this point dough may be placed in refrigerator for 1 or 2 days or left out to rise until double. Shape into cloverleaf shaped rolls. Place in greased muffin pans. Let double. Bake in 375⁰ oven for 15 minutes. Makes 4 dozen.

Ruth Dirks

☆   ☆   ☆

Basic Sweet Dough

1	package yeast	1½	teaspoons salt
¼	cup warm water	1	cup warm milk
½	cup margarine, softened	About 4 cups flour, divided	
⅓	cup sugar	3 eggs, beaten	

Dissolve yeast in water. Mix softened margarine, sugar and salt with milk. Add 2 cups flour; beat. Add eggs and yeast; beat well. Add remaining flour until soft, firm dough is formed. Turn out on floured surface and knead for about 8 minutes. Cover, let double in bulk and shape into desired rolls. *Ruth Dirks*

Inside Out Cinnamon Rolls
or Old Fashioned Cinnamon Rolls

1	recipe basic sweet dough	¾	cup brown sugar
⅓	cup butter, softened	2	teaspoons cinnamon

For Inside Out Cinnamon Rolls: Roll out dough to 10x24 inch rectangle. Spread with butter and sprinkle with sugar and cinnamon. Cut into strips about 10 inches long and 1 inch wide and roll each separately into snail shape, sugar side out. Place 1 inch apart on greased baking sheet. Let rise until double in bulk. Bake at 365⁰ for 20 minutes.

For Old Fashioned Cinnamon Rolls: Divide dough into two parts. Roll dough into 9x14 inch rectangles. Spread each with butter and sprinkle with sugar and cinnamon. Roll as for jelly roll. Cut into 1½ inch slices. Place in greased 9 inch square pans, 9 rolls to a pan. Let double in bulk and bake at 375⁰ for 25 minutes. Rolls may be brushed with butter after baking and glazed with powdered sugar icing while rolls are warm. Makes 2 dozen medium or 18 large rolls.

Variation: Pour ½ cup whipping cream over rolls just before baking for a crunchy, delicious top crust. *Ruth Dirks*

☆　　☆　　☆

Hot Cross Buns

BUNS:

1	package yeast	¾	teaspoon cinnamon
¼	cup warm water	¼	teaspoon cloves
1	cup warm milk	½	teaspoon nutmeg
1	stick margarine	¾	cup currants
⅓	cup sugar	2	eggs, well beaten
1	teaspoon salt	1	egg yolk plus 1 teaspoon
4	cups flour, divided		water for top

LEMON FROSTING:

1	cup sifted powdered sugar	1	teaspoon water
2	teaspoons lemon juice		

BUNS: Dissolve yeast in water. Mix very warm milk, margarine, sugar and salt together. Cool to lukewarm. Mix 2 cups flour with cinnamon, cloves, nutmeg and currants. Add to milk mixture; beat well. Add yeast, mix; add eggs, beat well. Add remaining flour until very stiff dough is formed. Turn out on floured surface and knead until smooth and elastic. Place in greased bowl, cover and let double in bulk. Punch down and let double again. (A second rising enhances the flavors.) Pinch off pieces of dough and form rounded balls about 1¼ inch in diameter. Place on greased baking sheet, 2 inches apart. Brush with beaten egg yolk and water. Let double (about 30 minutes). Bake at 375⁰ for 12 to 15 minutes. Cool and top each bun with a cross of lemon frosting. Makes 3 dozen.

FROSTING: Mix powdered sugar, lemon juice and water until smooth. Draw cross on bun with icing. *Ruth Dirks*

Easy Cinnamon Rolls

Quick Way to a Special Breakfast!

1	package frozen dinner roll dough (about 2 dozen in package)	2	sticks butter, melted
			Mixture of cinnamon and sugar

Dip frozen rolls, one at a time, in melted butter and then in cinnamon-sugar mixture. Layer rolls in a lightly greased Bundt pan. Pour remaining butter over rolls. Top with a little cinnamon-sugar. Lay a towel over the pan and set out all night to thaw and rise. The next day, bake at 350⁰ for 30 minutes. Invert on cookie sheet. Serves 6.

Valerie McMahan

Variation: Use canned biscuits and bake in greased tube pan according to package directions.

☆　　☆　　☆

Bison Kolaches

4	cups milk, scalded and cooled	8	teaspoons salt
4	packages dry yeast	6	eggs, beaten
½	cup warm water	2	cups sugar
2	cups margarine, melted	8-12	cups flour, sifted

Scald milk, dissolve yeast in water. Add yeast to cooled milk with margarine, salt, eggs, and sugar. Add enough flour to make a soft dough. Let rise until doubled. Punch down and pinch off into walnut size balls. Place in greased pan and let rise. Make an indention in center and put in your choice of fillings. Bake at 375⁰ for 20 minutes. Baste Kolaches with oil lightly as soon as the bread comes out of oven. . .this keeps Kolaches soft. Makes tons.

Poppy Seed Filling

1	pound poppy seed, ground	1	pint heavy cream
¾	quart very thick applesauce	¼-½	cup milk
			Sugar to taste

Cook ground poppy seed with cream and milk very slowly until it boils; it burns very easily, so stir often. Add sugar and thick applesauce and let mixture come to a slow boil and stir often. Boil about 10 minutes. Cool.

Creamed Prune Filling

1	pound prunes	1	tablespoon butter
2½	cups water	1	teaspoon vanilla
1	tablespoon cornstarch	¼	teaspoon cinnamon
1	tablespoon water		Sugar to taste

Soak prunes in water overnight, then cook in the same water 20 minutes. Drain, reserving juice. Remove seeds and mash prunes with a potato masher. Put reserved juice in a saucepan, bring to a boil. Mix cornstarch in water and add to prune juice and cook until it thickens. Remove from heat, add butter, vanilla and cinnamon. Combine juices with mashed prunes and sweeten to taste.

Variation: Cherry or apricot fillings are also very good.

The Cookbook Committee

☆   ☆   ☆

My Neighbor's Coffee Cake

CAKE:
1	package yeast	6	tablespoons warm milk
2	tablespoons warm water	1½	tablespoons sugar
½	cup butter	1	teaspoon salt
2	cups plus 6 tablespoons flour, divided	½	lemon rind, grated
		2	eggs, beaten

FILLING:
½	cup graham cracker crumbs	1	teaspoon cinnamon
¼	cup sugar	1	teaspoon grated lemon rind
¼	cup brown sugar	¼	cup butter

ICING:
1	cup powdered sugar	1	teaspoon cream

CAKE: Dissolve yeast in water. Cut butter into 2 cups of flour with pastry cutter. Blend milk, sugar, salt, lemon rind and eggs and add to flour mixture. Blend well. Dough will be sticky. Sprinkle 6 tablespoons flour on board. Turn out dough and knead until flour is mixed well into dough. Do not use more flour. Place in greased bowl, cover and let rise until double in bulk. Roll into 9x18 rectangle.

FILLING: Mix graham cracker crumbs, sugar, brown sugar, cinnamon and lemon rind. Blend in butter to form rich crumbs. Cover with filling. Roll as for jelly roll. Seal dough and place in greased 9 inch ring mold and let double in bulk. Bake at 375⁰ for 35 minutes.

ICING: Moisten sugar with cream until syrupy consistency. Drizzle over cake while warm. *Ruth Dirks*

Hint: Knead means use a little flour as you knead the dough, stir and work the dough until it shines and is not sticky; if you put a little Crisco on your clean hands the dough will no longer stick to your fingers, when you have kneaded enough.

Hint: A teaspoon of sugar added to dry yeast insures the fermentation process.

☆ ☆ ☆

Raspberry Cream Cheese Coffee Cake

Original Recipe

CAKE:

2	sticks margarine	2	cups flour, sifted
2	cups sugar	1	teaspoon baking powder
2	eggs	1	cup sour cream
¼	teaspoon salt	½	teaspoon vanilla

FILLING:

1	(10 ounce) package frozen raspberries	1	tablespoon flour
		1	egg
1	(3 ounce) package cream cheese	¼	cup sugar

CAKE: Cream margarine and sugar until fluffy. Add eggs one at a time beating well after each egg. Add sifted flour, baking powder, salt. Fold in sour cream and vanilla.

FILLING: Thaw raspberries and drain. Blend cream cheese, egg, sugar and flour. Lightly mix in raspberries. Layer in greased and floured tube pan: ½ batter; filling; ½ batter. Bake at 350⁰ for 60-70 minutes.

Linda Juba

Variation: Filling: ½ cup nuts; 1 teaspoon cinnamon; 2 tablespoons sugar. Layer ½ batter, ½ filling, repeat.　　　　　*Patricia Brott*

Coffee Cake

COFFEE CAKE:

1¾	cups sugar	¾	teaspoon salt
1½	sticks margarine	1⅛	cups milk
3	cups flour	1	teaspoon vanilla
4	teaspoons baking powder	5	egg whites, beaten stiff

TOPPING:

¾	cup margarine	2	teaspoons cinnamon
1⅛	cups brown sugar	1	cup chopped pecans
¾	cup flour		

CAKE: Cream sugar and margarine. Combine flour, baking powder and salt and add to creamed mixture alternately with milk. Add vanilla. Fold in egg whites. Preheat oven to 350⁰. Pour into a greased 9x12 inch cake pan.

TOPPING: Mix all ingredients with a pastry blender to resemble cake crumbs. Sprinkle topping on cake. Bake for 50 minutes.

Millie Fiedorek

☆　　☆　　☆

Apple-Cherry Loaf Bread

Good for Coffee or Committee Meetings

⅔	cup butter	2	teaspoons baking powder
1⅓	cups sugar	1	teaspoon baking soda
4	eggs	1	teaspoon salt
2	cups canned chunky applesauce	1	tablespoon lemon juice
		1⅓	cups chopped nuts
½	cup milk	⅔	cups Maraschino cherries, chopped and drained
4	cups flour		

Cream butter and sugar. Add eggs one at a time, beating after each. Stir in applesauce and milk. Sift baking powder, salt, flour and soda; add and mix well. Add lemon juice, nuts and drained cherries. Grease two 9x3x5 inch loaf pans, don't spray. Bake at 325⁰, 1 hour, 5 minutes. Remove from pans and cool on racks. Freezes well. May spread with cream cheese.   *Ivanette Dennis*

Ruth's Orange Nut Bread

1	orange	2	cups flour
Boiling water		¼	teaspoon salt
1	cup raisins or dates	1	teaspoon baking powder
2	tablespoons melted shortening	½	teaspoon baking soda
		1	cup sugar
1	teaspoon vanilla	½	cup chopped nuts
1	egg, beaten		

Squeeze juice from orange into measuring cup and add enough boiling water to make 1 cup. Remove as much white from orange peel as possible. Put orange peel, raisins or dates through meat chopper and grind. Put into a mixing bowl and add orange juice, shortening, vanilla and egg. Sift flour with salt, baking powder, soda and sugar. Add nuts and mix all ingredients lightly. Place in a 9x5 inch greased loaf pan and bake at 325⁰ for almost an hour.   *Tura Bethune*

☆　　☆　　☆

Date Nut Bread

Richardson Woman's Club Tea Room

1½	cups flour	½	teaspoon salt
1	cup sugar	2	eggs
1	cup chopped pitted dates	¾	cup milk
¾	cup coarsely chopped pecans	3	tablespoons salad oil
2	teaspoons baking powder	1	teaspoon vanilla

Preheat oven to 350⁰. Grease 9x5 inch loaf pan. In large bowl, with fork, mix flour, sugar, dates, pecans, baking powder and salt together. In small bowl, with fork, beat eggs slightly; stir in milk, salad oil and vanilla. Stir into flour mixture just until flour is moistened; pour into pan. Bake 1 hour or until toothpick inserted in center comes out clean. Cool in pan on wire rack 10 minutes; remove from pan and cool completely on rack.

To make Tea Room sandwiches: Mix 1 stick soft margarine and ¼ cup finely chopped dates. Enough for 10-12 slices. *Lynn Karp*

Chocolate Date Nut Bread

Exceptionally Delicious

1	cup boiling water	2	cups flour
1	cup chopped dates	½	teaspoon salt
¼	cup shortening	1	teaspoon baking soda
1	cup sugar	½	cup chopped walnuts (or pecans)
1	egg		
1	teaspoon vanilla		
2	ounces unsweetened chocolate, melted		

Pour boiling water over dates; cool to lukewarm. Cream the shortening and sugar. Add egg and vanilla and beat well. Add chocolate; then add flour which has been sifted with salt and soda, alternately with the dates to the creamed mixture. Beat well after each addition. Stir in nuts. Place in greased 9x5x3 inch loaf pan. Bake at 350⁰ for 1 hour. Cool 10 minutes. Remove from pan and cool on rack. *Ruth Dirks*

☆　　☆　　☆

Blueberry-Orange Bread

Richardson Woman's Club Tea Room

5	cups flour	1½	cups orange juice
1	cup sugar	¼	cup melted butter
2	teaspoons baking powder	2	tablespoons grated orange peel
2	teaspoons salt		
1	teaspoon baking soda	1	(16 ounce) package frozen blueberries, thawed
4	eggs		

Preheat oven to 375⁰. Grease two 9x5 inch loaf pans. In large bowl, with fork, mix flour, sugar, baking powder, salt and baking soda. In medium bowl, with fork, beat eggs; add orange juice, butter and orange peel. Stir into flour mixture just until flour is moistened. Gently fold berries into batter. Pour batter into prepared loaf pans. Bake 50 minutes or until toothpick inserted in center comes out clean. Cool and remove from pans. To make tea sandwiches fill with softened cream cheese.

Lynne Karp

Apricot-Nut Bread

1	cup dried, chopped apricots	½	cup orange juice
1	cup sugar	2	cups sifted flour
2	tablespoons shortening	2	teaspoons baking powder
1	egg, well beaten	½	teaspoon baking soda
¼	cup sugar	1	teaspoon salt
		1	cup chopped nuts

Soak dried apricots for 20 minutes. Meanwhile, cream together 1 cup sugar, shortening and egg. Stir in ¼ cup sugar and orange juice. Add flour, baking powder, soda and salt; blend well. Drain apricots; stir apricots and nuts into batter. Bake in greased and floured 9x5x3 inch loaf pan at 350⁰ for 65 minutes or until done.

Phyllis Roberts

☆　　☆　　☆

Strawberry Bread

BREAD:

3	cups flour	1¼	cups vegetable oil
1	teaspoon salt	1¼	cups chopped pecans
2	cups sugar	1	(16 ounce) package frozen
1	teaspoon baking soda		strawberries (thawed and
1	tablespoon cinnamon		undrained)
4	eggs, beaten		

GLAZE:

1	cup powdered sugar	Red food coloring
2	tablespoons lemon juice	

BREAD: Combine flour, salt, sugar, baking soda and cinnamon. Make a well in the center and add beaten eggs and oil. Mix thoroughly. Add pecans and strawberries and strawberry juice. Pour into greased and floured loaf pans. Bake at 350⁰ for 40 minutes for small loaves or 60 minutes for large loaves.

GLAZE: Mix sugar and lemon juice. Add enough food coloring for strawberry pink. Makes 6 small loaves or 2 large loaves.

Sharon Odell

Healthful Banana Bread

2	cups whole wheat flour	⅔	cup brown sugar
1	teaspoon baking powder	2	eggs
½	teaspoon baking soda	2	bananas (ripe or over-ripe)
½	teaspoon salt	3	tablespoons sour cream or
⅓	cup salad oil		buttermilk

Measure flour, baking powder, soda and salt into a mixing bowl. Place salad oil, brown sugar, eggs, bananas and cream or buttermilk in blender and blend well. Pour blended ingredients over dry ingredients and mix well with mixer. Pour batter into 2 small or 1 large well greased loaf pan. Bake at 350⁰ until done, from 30 to 45 minutes, depending on the pan size.

Peggy Jones

☆   ☆   ☆

Strawberry Preserves Bread

3	cups flour	1	teaspoon vanilla
½	teaspoon baking soda	¼	teaspoon lemon extract
1	teaspoon salt	4	eggs
¼	teaspoon cream of tartar	1	cup strawberry preserves
1	cup shortening	½	cup sour cream
1½	cups sugar	½	cup chopped nuts

Sift together flour, soda, salt and cream of tartar. Set aside. Cream shortening, sugar, vanilla and lemon extract. Add eggs, one at a time, beating well after each addition. Alternate adding ½ the preserves, sour cream, nuts and reserved dry ingredients. Repeat. Pour into 2 large loaf pans. Bake at 350° for 50 minutes. Cool 10 minutes before removing from the pans.   *Carolyn Stanphill*

Banana Nut Bread

1	stick margarine	2	cups flour
1½	cups sugar	2	bananas, mashed
2	eggs	½	cup chopped pecans
1	cup buttermilk	1	teaspoon vanilla
1½	teaspoons baking soda		

Cream margarine; add sugar and beat well. Then, add eggs and beat well again. Mix buttermilk with soda and add alternately with flour. Add bananas, pecans and vanilla. Line a 7x3 inch loaf pan with wax paper; pour in batter and bake at 350° for approximately 1 hour. Do not under bake. Loaf should be golden brown. Recipe will fill 4 individual loaf pans. Reduce baking time accordingly.   *Kay Wunderlich*

Hint: Very ripe bananas can be frozen whole or lightly puréed, and measured; then kept on hand for banana breads and cakes.

☆   ☆   ☆

Lemon Bread

A Tour of Homes Favorite

BREAD:

2	sticks margarine	3	cups flour, sifted
2	cups sugar	1	cup buttermilk
4	eggs		Grated rind of one lemon
½	teaspoon salt	1	cup nuts, chopped
½	teaspoon baking soda		

GLAZE:

2	lemons	1	cup powdered sugar

BREAD: Cream margarine and sugar. Blend in eggs. Sift together salt, soda and flour and add alternately with buttermilk. Add lemon rind and nuts. Grease two 7x3 loaf pans. Line bottom of pans with wax paper. Bake at 350° for 40 minutes. Bread is done when straw poked in center comes out clean. If not, done, reduce oven temperature and cook until done.

GLAZE: Mix lemon juice and powdered sugar. Punch holes in bread with toothpick and pour glaze over bread while still warm.   *Ann Long*

Avocado Bread

3 eggs				
1	cup oil	¼	teaspoon baking powder
1¾	cups sugar	1	teaspoon salt
2	cups mashed avocado	1	teaspoon baking soda
3	teaspoons vanilla	3	teaspoons cinnamon
3	cups plus 2 tablespoons flour	1	cup (may use less) chopped nuts

Beat eggs until light and creamy. Add oil, sugar, avocado and vanilla. Mix lightly. Add flour, baking powder, salt, soda and cinnamon. Blend. Add nuts. Grease two 7x3x2 loaf pans. Bake at 350⁰ for 55 to 60 minutes.
Vivian Jackson

☆　　☆　　☆

Mother's Gingerbread Cupcakes

A Tour of Homes Recipe

2	sticks butter	2	teaspoons baking soda
1	cup sugar	4	cups flour
4	eggs	¼	teaspoon cinnamon
1	cup light molasses	¼	teaspoon allspice, optional
1	cup buttermilk	2	teaspoons ginger

Cream butter and sugar. Add eggs, one at a time, beating well after each egg. Add molasses and beat well. Add buttermilk with soda dissolved in it; then flour sifted with cinnamon, allspice and ginger. Bake at 350⁰ about 15 minutes for regular muffins, for small muffins (Gem pans) bake at 350⁰ for 10 minutes. Dough keeps for 2 or 3 weeks in refrigerator. Makes 4-5 dozen large muffins or 6-8 dozen small muffins.

Ivanette Dennis

Grandma Sargent's Graham Loaf

This Recipe is at Least 100 Years Old.

2	cups whole wheat flour	1	teaspoon baking soda
1	cup white flour	1	teaspoon baking powder
1½	cups sour milk or buttermilk	1	teaspoon salt
		½	cup sugar
1	egg		Additional sugar

Combine whole wheat and white flours with soda, baking powder, salt and sugar and stir well. Beat egg and add milk. Add to dry ingredients and stir just until flour mixture is dampened. Do *not* beat. Pour batter into greased 9x5x3 inch loaf pan. Generously coat top of batter with sugar. Bake at 350⁰ for 45 minutes or until bread tests done with cake tester or a straw. Serve warm with butter and jam. This bread has the nutty sweet flavor of a yeast baked bread. *Ruth Dirks*

Hint: Milk may be soured by pouring 1 tablespoon vinegar in a cup, fill cup to 1½ cup mark with milk and let set for 10 minutes.

☆   ☆   ☆

Zucchini-Pineapple Bread

3	cups flour	2	cups sugar
½	teaspoon salt	1	cup vegetable oil
½	teaspoon baking powder	2	teaspoons vanilla
2	teaspoons baking soda	2	cups coarsely shredded
2	teaspoons cinnamon		zucchini
¾	cup chopped walnuts	1	(8 ounce) can crushed
3	eggs		pineapple, drained

Combine flour, salt, baking powder, soda, cinnamon and walnuts and set aside. Beat eggs lightly in large mixing bowl. Add sugar, oil and vanilla. Beat until creamy. Stir in zucchini and pineapple. Add dry ingredients, stirring only until moist. Spoon into 2 well-greased and floured 9x5x3 inch loaf pans. Bake at 350° for 1 hour then test for doneness. Cool 10 minutes and remove from pan. Freezes well.   *Vivian Brotherton*

Zucchini Walnut Bread

Yum!

4	eggs		
1½	cups brown sugar, packed	¾	teaspoon salt
¾	cup vegetable oil	2	teaspoons cinnamon
3	cups unsifted unbleached flour	2	cups unpeeled grated zucchini, (2-3 zucchini)
1½	teaspoons baking soda	1	cup coarsely chopped walnuts
¾	teaspoon baking powder	1	teaspoon vanilla

Beat eggs. Gradually beat in sugar; then oil. Combine flour, baking soda, baking powder, salt and cinnamon. Add to egg mixture alternately with zucchini. Stir in walnuts and vanilla. Turn into greased and floured 9 inch tube pan. Bake at 350° for 50 minutes. Let stand 10 minutes; turn out, cool.   *Marge Grogg*

Variation: Substitute 2 cups granulated sugar for brown sugar, omit cinnamon and add ½ cup grated coconut. Bake in 2 greased 9x5 loaf pans for 1 hour at 350°. Good spread with cream cheese. *Meredith Marston*

☆   ☆   ☆

Zucchini Tea Bread

2½	cups whole wheat flour	1	cup honey
½	teaspoon baking powder	2	teaspoons vanilla
2	teaspoons baking soda	2	cups unpared and coarsely
1	teaspoon salt		grated zucchini (not
3	teaspoons cinnamon		packed down)
3	eggs	2	cups coarsely chopped
1	cup vegetable oil		walnuts

On wax paper mix flour, baking powder, soda, salt and cinnamon. Beat together eggs, vegetable oil, honey and vanilla in large bowl. Stir in zucchini. Gradually stir in the flour mixture keeping smooth. Stir in walnuts. Pour into oiled and floured 12 cup fluted pan or Bundt pan. Bake at 350⁰ for 55 to 60 minutes. (If cake is browning too much the last 10 minutes, cover with foil.) Cool on wire rack 10 minutes. Loosen edges and turn out on rack. Cool completely.   *Lynn Trentham*

Holiday Pumpkin Bread

3	cups sugar	3	tablespoons brandy
4	eggs	3	tablespoons rum or Sherry
1	cup oil		add water to liquor to
1	(1 pound) can pumpkin		total ⅔ cup
3⅓	cups flour, divided	1	cup candied cherries
1	tablespoon nutmeg	1	cup candied pineapple
1	tablespoon cinnamon	1	cup candied mixed fruit
2	tablespoons baking soda	1	cup raisins
1	tablespoon salt	1	cup nuts

Beat eggs and sugar. Add oil; beat well. Add pumpkin and beat again. Blend flour with nutmeg, cinnamon, soda, salt and add alternately with water mixture. Add candied fruits and nuts that have been dredged with some of the flour. Mix well. Grease and flour four 1 pound coffee cans. Fill half full. Bake at 350⁰ 1 hour to 1 hour-15 minutes. Refrigerate 24 hours before slicing. Freezes well. Cool thoroughly before turning out on rack.   *Virginia Hager*

☆   ☆   ☆

Pumpkin-Pecan Bread

Yum-Yum

3½	cups flour	2	cups cooked pumpkin
2	teaspoons baking soda	4	eggs, beaten
1½	teaspoons salt	1	cup oil
3	cups sugar	⅔	cup water
2	teaspoons cinnamon	½	cup chopped pecans
2	teaspoons nutmeg	1	cup dates or raisins
1	teaspoon allspice		

Combine flour, soda, salt, sugar, cinnamon, nutmeg and allspice in large mixing bowl. Make a deep well in center. Add pumpkin, eggs, oil, water, pecans and raisins; mix just enough to moisten all ingredients. Pour into 3 greased 9x5 inch loaf pans. Bake at 350⁰ for 1 hour. Cool 10 minutes before removing from pan. Continue cooling on rack. Wrap and store in refrigerator or freezer. Serves 28-30.   *Mary Rode*

Variation: Decrease flour to 2½ cups and oil to ¾ cup. Add ½ cup orange juice and ½ of a (28 ounce) jar Borden's minced meat with brandy and rum. Bake in 2 large loaf pans, 1 Bundt pan, or 5 small loaf pans that are well greased. Bake at 325⁰ for 1½ hours, or until done.

Dolores Spence

Buttermilk Pancakes

2	cups sifted flour	2	tablespoons sugar
2	teaspoons baking powder	⅓	cup oil
½	teaspoon baking soda	2	eggs
1	teaspoon salt	1½-2	cups buttermilk

Sift flour, baking powder, soda, salt and sugar together and put in mixing bowl. Make a well in flour mixture. Beat eggs and oil together and pour into well. Slowly blend together and add buttermilk. Do not over mix. Batter will be lumpy.   *The Cookbook Committee*

☆　　☆　　☆

Waffles With Club Soda

Light and Crispy

1	egg, beaten	1⅓	cups club soda
½	cup oil	2	cups Bisquick

Mix beaten egg, oil and club soda and add slowly to Bisquick and mix by hand. Bake according to waffle iron directions. This batter can not be saved. Bake all waffles, wrap in foil and freeze. Pop in toaster to reheat. Makes four 7 inch waffles. *Marilyn Duncan*

Surprise Sandwiches

Prepare the Day Before

12	slices bread, crusts removed	1	meat of your choice: 1 (16 ounce) can ham, chicken, turkey, tuna or salmon
¼	cup butter		
¼	cup mustard, or less	4	eggs, beaten
½-1	pound grated Cheddar cheese	3½	cups milk
		½	teaspoon salt

Grease 9x13 inch glass dish. Place 6 slices of bread spread with butter-mustard mixture in bottom of dish. Cover bread with one half the grated cheese. Reserve remaining half of cheese for topping. Layer with choice of meat. Spread remaining 6 slices of bread with butter-mustard mixture and place on top of meat, buttered side up. Mix eggs with milk and salt and pour over bread. Top with remaining cheese. Let stand overnight in refrigerator. Bake at 300⁰ for 1½ hours. Serves 12-14.

Variation: May omit meat in center. Great for leftovers.

Jonelle Jordan

☆　　☆　　☆

Hot Cheese Sandwiches

Must Be Frozen

4	(5 ounces each) jars Kraft Old English cheese	1½	teaspoons Worcestershire
1	pound margarine, softened		Dash of cayenne pepper
1	teaspoon Tabasco	1½	teaspoons dill weed
1	teaspoon onion powder	3	loaves Pepperidge Farm Sandwich Bread

Blend all ingredients except bread. Cut crusts off bread. Take 3 slices and spread cheese between. Cut into 3 rectangular pieces. Ice all around sides and top, but not bottom, with cheese spread. Repeat. Place on wax paper on a cookie sheet and freeze. When frozen put in plastic bags and store in freezer. Do not defrost. At serving time place on cookie sheet with uniced side down and bake 350⁰ for 15 to 20 minutes. Makes 54 finger sandwiches. Good with coffee or drinks. *Pat Bailey*

Herbed Bread Thins

2	cloves crushed pressed garlic	2	teaspoons chopped parsley
2	sticks butter, softened	2	loaves French bread, approximately 2½ inches in diameter
2	teaspoons basil		
1	teaspoon tarragon	Oil	
1	teaspoon chervil		

Blend garlic, butter, basil, tarragon, chervil and parsley until smooth. Refrigerate mixture overnight. Bring butter mixture to room temperature the next day. Slice French bread thinly; brush bread rounds with oil. Spread thinly with butter mixture. Bake flat on cookie sheet at 325⁰ until slightly brown and bubbly. Watch closely. Store in plastic bags, secured with a tie. *Nancy Parker*

☆　　☆　　☆

Virg's Hot Pepperoni Bread

1	loaf frozen bread dough	1	(6 ounce) package
12	ounces pepperoni, sliced		Provolone cheese, sliced
2	eggs		Parmesan cheese, grated or
1	(6 ounce) package		Romano cheese, grated
	Mozzarella cheese, sliced		

Thaw bread dough and let rise in a large oiled bowl. Cover. Let double (4 to 5 hours). Roll out in a rectangle ⅛ to ¼ inch thick on a floured board. (The thinner the better.) Place pepperoni slices, slices of Mozzarella and Provolone cheese on rectangle. Pieces should touch or lap, but not be stacked. Sprinkle with one beaten egg. Sprinkle with grated Parmesan or Romano cheese. Roll like jelly roll and place seam side down on oiled cookie sheet, either straight, in a circle or horseshoe shape. Pinch ends shut. Rub one beaten egg on sides and top. Place oiled waxed paper and two dish towels on loaf and let rise 30 to 40 minutes. Bake at 400⁰ for 20 minutes, then 350⁰ for 10 minutes or until dark brown. Cool slightly and slice.

Good as an hors d'oeuvre or as a main dish with a green salad.
Jean Zinser

Variation: Substitute cooked sausage or baked ham for pepperoni.

Easy Cheese Blintzes

Must Be Frozen

1	(2 pound) loaf thin sliced sandwich bread, crusts removed	2	egg yolks
		½	cup sugar
		¾	cup melted butter
1	pound cream cheese, softened	½	cup sugar
		2-3	teaspoons cinnamon

Cream egg yolks, sugar and cream cheese. Set aside. Mix cinnamon and sugar. Set aside. Roll one slice of bread at a time with rolling pin until fairly flat. Spread cheese mixture over bread and roll jelly-roll fashion. Dip in melted butter, then in sugar and cinnamon mixture. Place on waxed paper lined cookie sheet and freeze. Take out of freezer ½ hour before cooking. Thaw 15 minutes; then cut in half. Put on ungreased cookie sheet or wire rack and bake at 400⁰ for 15 minutes. Makes about 40.

Great for a coffee or special breakfast.
Elbie Guindon and Sharon Odell

☆   ☆   ☆

Poppy Seed Twists

1   (10 ounce) can refrigerated   Melted butter
     flaky buttermilk biscuits   Poppy seeds or sesame seeds
     (do not substitute)

Separate biscuits. Dip in melted butter; then in poppy seeds which have
been spread thinly on wax paper. Pull each biscuit about 3 inches long
and twist in opposite directions. Place on cookie sheet and bake at 450°
10 to 12 minutes. Serves 4.   *Betty Stripling*

Hot Dog Bun Bread Sticks

Try These!

Hot dog buns   Canned grated Parmesan cheese
Melted butter

Quarter hot dog buns and dredge in melted butter. Cover with Parmesan
cheese. Bake in 200° oven for several hours. Store in covered container.
Serve with Soccer Soup (see index) or green salad.   *Carole Price*

Orange Biscuits

1   stick margarine   1½   cups sugar
1   cup orange juice   ¼   cup chopped pecans
1   teaspoon grated orange   24 biscuits (flaky buttermilk
     rind   biscuits or homemade)
3   tablespoons lemon juice

Melt margarine and add orange juice, orange rind, lemon juice and sugar.
Bring to boil and boil 2 minutes. Pour in bottom of 8x12 inch pan.
Sprinkle with pecans. Place biscuits in pan and bake at 450° 15 to 20
minutes. Do not overbake.

Variation: To make pinwheels, roll out biscuit dough and sprinkle with
1 teaspoon cinnamon mixed with ¼ cup sugar. Roll and slice and place
in pan and bake as above.   *Ruth Becker*

☆   ☆   ☆

Honey Butter

Stephenson's Apple Orchard Farm Restaurant near Kansas City

1 stick butter	¼ cup honey
1 stick margarine	¼ cup half and half

Cream butter and margarine together in an electric mixer at medium speed until well blended. Beat in honey, a tablespoon at a time, until blended thoroughly. Beat in half and half, a tablespoon at a time, until smooth and fluffy. Makes about 1½ cups.

Seasoned Butter for Breads

Quick and Easy

1 stick butter, softened	1 teaspoon oregano
½ cup grated Parmesan cheese	¼ teaspoon garlic salt
4 teaspoons chopped parsley	1 (12 count) package brown and serve rolls

Combine butter with seasonings. Split rolls and butter the insides. Put back together and spread more herb butter on top. Bake according to package directions or until slightly brown on top. *Katie Marks*

Variation: Substitute 2 cloves garlic, crushed, for garlic salt, add ¼ teaspoon marjoram and ¼ teaspoon oregano. Slice a loaf of French bread and spread both sides of the slices with butter, place on a cookie sheet and bake for 10 minutes in 375⁰ oven. *Dottie Pinch*

Poppy Seed Surprises

Sauce:

½ cup melted butter	¼ cup mustard
½ cup grated onion	1 tablespoon poppy seed
18 small buns	½ pound Baby Swiss cheese, thinly sliced
1 pound boiled ham, thinly sliced	

Slice small round buns and spread sauce on top and bottom. Place 1 slice of cheese between 2 slices of ham. Wrap in foil and bake 15 to 20 minutes at 350⁰. May be prepared the day before or may be frozen.
VirGinia Talley

☆　　☆　　☆

Mama Jones' Chili Sauce

1	gallon tomatoes, peeled and sliced	½	teaspoon allspice
1	cup finely chopped onions	½	teaspoon ground cloves
1	cup finely chopped green bell peppers	1	teaspoon cinnamon
		1	teaspoon nutmeg
1	cup finely chopped red bell peppers	1	teaspoon cayenne pepper
		1	teaspoon celery seed
1	cup sugar	1	teaspoon mustard seed
1	pint vinegar	2	tablespoons uniodized salt

Mix all ingredients in large stainless steel or enamel pan. Simmer, uncovered, stirring frequently until desired thickness. Ladle into 6-7 hot pint jars, filling to within ⅛ inch of jar top. Wipe rims and adjust lids. Process in boiling water bath 15 minutes.

Sunshine Dill Pickles

Very Crisp Pickles

1	cup salt	1½	cloves garlic, divided
5	cups water	3	red hot peppers, divided (optional)
6	cups vinegar		
Cucumbers			
6	sprigs fresh dill or 3 tablespoons dill seed, divided		

Bring salt and water to a boil to dissolve salt; let cool. Add vinegar. In each of 3 quart jars place clean cucumbers, fresh dill, garlic and pepper. Pour prepared liquid to ½ inch of jar top, covering all cucumbers. Wipe jar top clean and seal, using new jar tops. SEAL TIGHTLY: No water bath necessary. Set jars in sunshine for 8 days. After this time, bring inside and store in a dark cool place. They are ready to eat after eight days, but are better after a longer period.   *Dolores Spence*

☆   ☆   ☆

Pickled Beets or Green Beans

4 cups sugar	8 pints or 8 (16 ounces each) cans sliced, whole or quartered beets
4 cups vinegar	
4 cups water	
3 sticks cinnamon and/or 2 dozen whole cloves	

Combine sugar, vinegar, water, cinnamon and/or cloves in large pan and simmer until well blended. Pour over cooked beets and seal. One-eighth of the recipe is just right for 1 (16 ounce) can of beets. Will keep in refrigerator.

Variation: Can also be used for whole green beans.   *Mary Cummins*

Green Tomato Pickles

Crisp!

7 pounds green tomatoes, sliced medium thick	3 pints vinegar
	1 tablespoon salt
4 cups slacked lime (builders' hydrated lime)	1 tablespoon whole cloves
	1 tablespoon allspice
4-5 pounds of sugar	1 cinnamon stick

Soak tomatoes in lime dissolved in about 3 quarts water (use enough to cover) 24 hours. Use enamel, crockery or stainless steel container. Drain. Soak in cold water to cover for 4 hours, changing water every hour. Drain well; let stand several hours or overnight. Make syrup of sugar, vinegar and salt. Let come to rolling boil, add spices tied in cloth bag. Pour over tomatoes. Let stand about 12 hours or overnight. Cook for 40 minutes. Pack in sterilized jars, cover with syrup and seal.

Eileen MacWithey

☆   ☆   ☆

Summer Corn Relish

2	cups sugar	2	cups chopped onions
2	cups vinegar	2	cups chopped tomato
1½	teaspoons salt	2	cups chopped cucumber
1½	teaspoons celery seed	2	cups corn, cut from cob
½	teaspoon tumeric	2	cups chopped cabbage

In large Dutch oven, combine sugar, vinegar, salt, celery seed and tumeric. Heat to boiling. Add onions, tomatoes, cucumbers, corn and cabbage. Cook, uncovered, 25 minutes, stirring occasionally. Pack in hot, scalded jars and seal. Makes 3 pints. *Marge Grogg*

Garden Tomato Sauce

1	gallon tomatoes, chopped	2	cups white vinegar
5	bell peppers, chopped	2	tablespoons salt
5	onions, chopped	2-3	pods hot pepper
2	cups sugar		

Combine all ingredients in a large stainless steel pan and simmer for 1½ hours. Freezes well. Makes 6-8 pints. *Myra Harris*

Tomato-Peach (or Mango) Chutney

2-3	cups chopped fresh or canned tomatoes	1	cup brown sugar
2-3	cups chopped peaches or mangoes	¾	cup white vinegar
		1	teaspoon canning salt
½	cup white seedless raisins	½	teaspoon ground ginger
1	cup chopped bell pepper	½	teaspoon dry mustard
½	cup chopped onions	⅛	teaspoon cayenne pepper
		1	teaspoon curry powder

Remove skins from fresh tomatoes, peaches or mangoes. Include juice if using canned tomatoes. Combine all ingredients. Cook slowly until thickened (about 1 hour). Pack boiling hot in sterilized jars and seal tightly. Process in boiling water bath 5 minutes for ½ pints and 10 minutes for pints. *Novella Bailey*

☆   ☆   ☆

Egg and Sausage Brunch Casserole

Prepare the Day Before

8	slices Peppridge Farm White Bread	¼	teaspoon Spice Island Beau Monde
2	cups grated Cheddar cheese	1	(10¾ ounce) can cream of mushroom soup
1	pound sausage links	½	cup milk
4	eggs, beaten	1	(2 ounce) jar of mushrooms, drained
2½	cups milk	2	dashes of garlic powder
½	teaspoon salt		
¾	teaspoon dry mustard		

Butter bread, cut off crusts and cut the bread into cubes. Grate cheese. Cut sausage into 1 inch pieces and brown. Put the bread in the bottom of a greased 9x13 baking dish. Cover with cheese and add the sausage. Mix eggs, 2½ cups milk, salt, mustard and Beau Monde and pour over bread, cheese and sausage mixture. Cover and refrigerate overnight.

The next morning blend the soup, ½ cup milk, mushrooms and garlic powder. Pour over the casserole and bake uncovered at 350⁰ for 1½ hours. Serves 6. *Carol Garrigues*

George's Egg Casserole

½	pound sharp cheese, grated, divided	½-1	cup sour cream
½	teaspoon dry mustard	1	pound sausage, cooked, drained, crumbled
½	teaspoon paprika	10	eggs, beaten
1	teaspoon salt		

Spray 3 quart casserole or 9x13 baking dish with Pam. Cover bottom of dish with ½ cheese. Mix mustard, paprika, salt and sour cream and pour half of it over cheese. Cover with sausage. Beat eggs and pour over casserole. Spoon remaining sour cream mixture over this and top with other ½ of cheese. Bake at 325⁰ for 20 to 25 minutes. Serves 6-8. *Dot McCalpin*

☆   ☆   ☆

Sausage and Eggs Casserole

Make Ahead

1 pound sausage	⅓ can milk
18 eggs	Monterey Jack or Cheddar
1 (10¾ ounce) can cream of	cheese, grated
mushroom soup	

Brown sausage and drain. Scramble eggs in drippings until not quite done. Put browned sausage in 9x12 casserole, cover with eggs. Dilute mushroom soup with the milk. Pour over eggs. Cover and refrigerate. Before serving, sprinkle generously with cheese (can be Cheddar or your favorite) and bake at 375⁰ until bubbly and browned lightly. Serves 8-12.

Martha Clem

Jo's Arlington Brunch

Chill Overnight

14 slices sandwich bread, crusts removed	½ teaspoon salt
1 pound shaved ham	½ teaspoon seasoned salt
¾ pound sharp Cheddar cheese, grated	Dash of Worcestershire
3 eggs	Dash of nutmeg
3 cups milk	½ cup crushed cornflakes
½ teaspoon dry mustard	4 tablespoons margarine, melted

In greased 10x14 inch glass dish, layer ½ of bread, ham and cheese. Repeat. Mix eggs, milk, mustard, salt, seasoned salt, Worcestershire and nutmeg, and pour over casserole. Cover and refrigerate overnight. Stir crushed corn flakes together with margarine and sprinkle over top of casserole. Bake uncovered 1 hour at 325⁰. Serves 8-10 people.

Jean Zinser

☆   ☆   ☆

Overnight Egg and Cheese Strata with Variations

Good for Lunch or Brunch!

8	slices bread, trimmed and buttered	1	tablespoon Worcestershire
6	eggs, beaten	10	ounces shredded Cheddar cheese
2	cups milk	1	tablespoon bell pepper
Salt to taste		1	(10¾ ounce) can cream of mushroom soup
Pepper to taste			

Place bread in the bottom of a buttered 9x13 baking dish. Combine eggs, milk, salt, pepper, Worcestershire, cheese and bell pepper. Pour over buttered bread. Refrigerate, covered, overnight. Next day bake at 350° for 45 minutes. Before serving pour heated mushroom soup over each serving. *Mary Rode*

Variation: Replace bread with 2 cups seasoned croutons. Omit bell pepper and add ½ pound cooked, crumbled bacon. *Jean Zinser*

Variation: Omit bell pepper. Add 1 pound cooked, drained, cooled sausage and 1 teaspoon dry mustard. *Carolyn Stanphill*

Variation: Omit bell pepper. Add 1 teaspoon dry mustard and 2 cups cubed ham. Before baking combine mushroom soup, 1 (5.33 ounce) can Pet milk and 1 (4 ounce) can mushrooms, drained. Bake at 300° per 1½ hours. This freezes well. *Jean Zinser*

Egg and Ham Brunch

8-10	hard-cooked eggs, chopped	¼	cup milk
1-2	pounds ham, diced	½	pound Velveeta, cubed
½	onion, chopped	1	teaspoon dry mustard
4	tablespoons margarine	1	tablespoon Worcestershire
¼	cup flour	1	tablespoon dried parsley flakes

Place ham and eggs in 2 quart casserole. Sauté onion in margarine. Remove from heat and add flour. Cook over low heat and add milk and cheese until you have a thick sauce and the cheese is melted. Add mustard, Worcestershire and parsley. Pour over egg and ham mixture. (May be prepared the day before to this point). Heat in 350° oven, stirring once or twice until heated through. Serve over warm buttered English Muffins. *Jean Zinser*

☆   ☆   ☆

Sunday Nite Scrambled Eggs

½	pound bulk sausage	1	cup grated Velveeta
1	onion, chopped	4	eggs, beaten
½	bell pepper, chopped	¼	cup milk
1	(17 ounce) can cream style corn		

Brown sausage; pour off grease. Add remaining ingredients and stir until eggs are set and cheese melted. If desired, sauté onion and pepper slightly before adding other ingredients. Serves 4-6. Leftovers may be reheated in the microwave the next day. *Barbara England*

Curried Eggs in Shrimp Sauce

EGGS:

8	eggs, hard-cooked	¼	teaspoon curry powder
⅓	cup mayonnaise	½	teaspoon paprika
½	teaspoon salt	¼	teaspoon dry mustard

SAUCE:

2	tablespoons margarine	1	soup can of milk
2	tablespoons flour	½	cup shredded sharp Cheddar cheese
1	(10¾ ounce) can condensed cream of shrimp soup	1	cup soft bread crumbs
		1	tablespoon butter

EGGS: Prepare and fill egg whites as for deviled eggs. Arrange in 8x8x2 inch pan.

SAUCE: Melt 2 tablespoons margarine and stir in flour. Add soup and milk. Stir until bubbles and thickens. Add cheese. Pour sauce over eggs. Cover with bread crumbs and butter. Bake at 350° for 15 to 20 minutes. Serves 6-8. *Claire Hine*

Quiche aux Fruits de Mer

¾	cup crab meat (frozen or fresh) about ½ pound	1	(9 inch) unbaked pie shell
¾	cup cooked, deveined shrimp	½	cup mayonnaise
		2	tablespoons flour
½	cup grated Swiss cheese	½	cup dry white wine
¼	cup cooked, diced celery	2	eggs, slightly beaten
¼	cup chopped green onions		Dash of salt

Combine crab, shrimp, cheese, celery and green onions. Place in unbaked 8 or 9 inch pie shell. Combine mayonnaise, flour, wine and eggs. Pour over seafood mixture. Bake at 375° for 25 to 30 minutes. Or freeze to bake later at 350° for 50 minutes. Serves 6. *Adele Hutton*

☆   ☆   ☆

Ham and Broccoli Quiche

1 cup Bisquick baking mix
¼ cup cold water
1 cup chopped broccoli
  (slightly undercooked)
1 cup shredded natural
  Swiss cheese

½ cup chopped ham
4 eggs
2 cups whipping cream
Salt to taste
Pepper to taste

Preheat oven to 425⁰. Mix Bisquick and water until soft dough forms and beat about 20 strokes. Knead about 5 times. Roll dough 2 inches larger than 9 inch pie plate, or use a quiche pan. Flute edge if desired. Sprinkle broccoli, cheese and ham into crust. Beat eggs, whipping cream, salt and pepper and pour over ham mixture. Bake 1 minute. Reduce oven temperature to 300⁰. Bake until knife inserted 1 inch from edge comes out clean, about 35 minutes. Let stand 10 minutes before cutting. Serves 6.

Myra Harris

Variation: Substitute, for the broccoli, 1 (10 ounce) package frozen chopped spinach which has been cooked only to defrost the icy particles and then well drained. Or sauté 1 (4 ounce) jar marinated artichokes in the oil from the marinade with 4 tablespoons chopped onion.

Zucchini Quiche

Salt to taste
1 pound zucchini, chopped
1 tablespoon fresh lemon
  juice
¼ teaspoon pepper
3 tablespoons chopped
  parsley

1 9-inch baked pastry shell
  with high fluted edge
¼ cup grated Swiss cheese
3 eggs, beaten
¼ cup half and half cream

Salt zucchini lightly and let stand in a colander 45 minutes to draw out moisture. Press down to remove most of moisture and pat dry with towel. Combine zucchini with lemon juice, pepper and parsley and place in the baked pastry shell. Smooth evenly and top with cheese. Mix eggs with cream and pour over the zucchini mixture. Bake at 350⁰ for 40 to 45 minutes. Let stand for 15 minutes before cutting.

Zucchini Quiche can be served as a main dish by cutting in pie-shaped pieces or it can be cut into small pieces and served as a hot appetizer.

Jane Thomas

☆ ☆ ☆

Quick Onion-Cheese Quiche

1	cup thinly sliced or chopped onions	3	eggs
2	tablespoons margarine	1½	tablespoons flour
1	9-inch unbaked pie shell	2	teaspoons prepared mustard
¾	cup grated cheese, American, Cheddar or Swiss	1	(10¾ ounce) can cream of mushroom soup, undiluted
		½	cup milk

Sauté onions in margarine and spread in bottom of pie shell. Sprinkle with cheese. Blend together eggs, flour, mustard, soup and milk, and pour into pie shell. Bake 45 to 60 minutes at 350⁰. Wait 10 minutes before serving. Serves 6.

Variation: May add ham, bacon, chicken, shrimp, mushrooms, etc. to egg mixture as desired.   *Lee Williams*

Quiche Pizza Rustica

CRUST:

1½	sticks softened margarine	2	eggs, slightly beaten
3	cups unsifted flour		Dash of salt

FILLING:

2½	cups cottage cheese	4	eggs, slightly beaten
⅓	pound Provolone Cheese, diced	½	pound smoked, hard salami, diced
½	pound Mozzarella cheese, diced	¼	cup chopped parsley
1⅔	cups grated Parmesan cheese	1	egg yolk

CRUST: Cut margarine into flour. Add eggs and salt. Quickly work mixture together until dough holds together. Cover with damp cloth and let stand 30 minutes.

FILLING: Combine cottage cheese, Provolone, Mozzarella and Parmesan cheeses. Add eggs, salami, and parsley. Mix well. Divide dough into 2 portions. Roll out one portion between pieces of waxed paper and cover bottom and sides of shallow 9x13 casserole. Spoon cheese filling into casserole. Make latticed pastry with remaing dough to cover top. Brush pastry with an egg yolk which has been beaten with 1 tablespoon water. Bake in preheated oven at 375⁰ for 1 hour. Serves 8-10.

Anna Wade Pierson

☆   ☆   ☆

Sausage Lasagna

Delicious!

1	pound Italian bulk sausage	1	(6 ounce) can tomato
1	pound ground beef		paste
2	(1.5 ounces each) packages	1	pound Mozzarella cheese
	Lawry's spaghetti sauce	2	eggs
	mix	3	cups Ricotta cheese
1	(16 ounce) can tomatoes	1	(16 ounce) box lasagna
1	(8 ounce) can tomato		noodles
	sauce	½	cup Parmesan cheese

Brown meat, drain off all fat. Add spaghetti sauce mix, tomatoes, tomato sauce, tomato paste. Simmer covered 1 hour stirring occasionally. Slice Mozzarella cheese. Beat eggs and mix into Ricotta cheese adding a little Parmesan cheese. Cook lasagna noodles (add 2 tablespoons oil to water) as directed on package. In a 9x13 casserole layer noodles, Ricotta and Mozzarella cheese and sauce. Repeat layers and top with ½ cup Parmesan cheese. Bake 350⁰ for 35 to 40 minutes, or until bubbly and heated through. Serves 12. *Brenda Chattaway*

Lasagna

1	pound ground beef	½	teaspoon oregano
2	cloves garlic	1	(8 ounce) package lasagna
1	teaspoon hot fat		noodles
1	(6 ounce) can tomato	1	(8 ounce) package
	paste		Mozzarella cheese, grated
2½	cups tomatoes	1	(12 ounce) carton cottage
1	teaspoon salt		cheese
¼	teaspoon pepper		

Brown beef and garlic in hot fat. Add tomato paste, tomatoes, salt, pepper and oregano and simmer 20 minutes covered. Layer cooked noodles, Mozzarella cheese, cottage cheese and meat in baking dish. Bake 20 minutes at 350⁰. Serves 4-6. *Jane Oxley*

Variation: Add 1 tablespoon basil and ½ cup chopped bell pepper to meat mixture. Add ½ cup grated Parmesan cheese, 2 beaten eggs, 2 table-spoons parsley flakes and 2 tablespoons flour to cottage cheese. Increase baking time to 375⁰ for 30 minutes. Let stand 10 minutes before cutting. *Ute Schnetzinger*

☆   ☆   ☆

Broccoli Lasagna Roll-Ups

12	lasagna noodles	⅛	teaspoon oregano
¾	cup chopped onion	1	cup Parmesan cheese,
2	tablespoons butter		divided
1¼	cups cottage cheese	1	tablespoon flour
1½	cups shredded Cheddar cheese	1	(32 ounce) jar Ragu Italian Cooking sauce
1	(10 ounce) package frozen chopped broccoli, cooked, well drained	1	(8 ounce) can tomato sauce
¼	teaspoon salt	1	(8 ounce) can sliced mushrooms
⅛	teaspoon seasoned salt		Ripe olives, sliced as desired
⅛	teaspoon garlic powder		for garnish
⅛	teaspoon Italian seasoning		

Cook noodles; cool in cold water. Sauté onion in butter. Beat cottage cheese until smooth; add Cheddar cheese. Mix in broccoli, onion, salt, seasoned salt, garlic powder, Italian seasoning and oregano. Combine ½ cup Parmesan and flour. Preheat oven to 350⁰. Remove noodles from water singly; pat dry. Spread with ¼ cup cheese filling. Sprinkle with Parmesan mixture. Roll up. Spread a little of the Italian sauce in the bottom of a 2 quart rectangular baking dish. Arrange roll-ups in dish. Cover with sauce; add mushrooms, olives and ½ cup Parmesan cheese. Bake 30 minutes. Serves 4.   *Danna Almon*

Pasta with Carrots and Ham

½	pound tagliatelle	Salt to taste
2	carrots, sliced	Grated Parmesan cheese
2	tablespoons butter	Freshly ground pepper
½	cup finely diced ham	
2	tablespoons chopped parsley	

Cook pasta according to package directions. Meanwhile, slice carrots and cook in salted water until tender but still firm. Reserve cooking water. In medium saucepan heat butter and ham. Add cooked carrots, 4 tablespoons cooking water from carrots, and parsley. Heat thoroughly. Mix with drained pasta. Serve with Parmesan cheese and pepper. Serves 2.

You can use spaghetti, but it is fun to try something else. This makes a nice lunch with ice tea, green salad, and fruit for dessert.

Marian Rose

☆   ☆   ☆

Pastitso

Greek Macaroni and Beef Casserole

MEAT SAUCE:

1	onion, chopped	1	cinnamon stick
2	tablespoons butter	1	bay leaf
1½	pounds ground beef	¼	cup red cooking wine or Sherry
1	(8 ounce) can tomato sauce	Salt to taste
1	teaspoon instant beef bouillon	Pepper to taste

MACARONI:

1	pound long macaroni	3	eggs, slightly beaten
4	tablespoons butter		
½	cup fresh grated Parmesan cheese		

WHITE SAUCE:

⅓	cup butter	1	egg, slightly beaten
½	cup flour	Salt to taste
2	cups milk	Pepper to taste
1	cup chicken broth	

Butter
Cracker or bread crumbs

1½ cups grated Parmesan cheese

MEAT SAUCE: Sauté onion in butter. Cook until soft; add ground beef and cook slightly. Add tomato sauce, bouillon, cinnamon stick, bay leaf, salt and pepper. Simmer 45 minutes, covered. Add wine last 10 minutes. If too juicy, remove cover. Remove spices. Set aside.

MACARONI: Boil macaroni according to package directions for casserole dishes. Strain. Melt butter in pan. Return macaroni to pan with ½ cup Parmesan cheese and beaten eggs.

WHITE SAUCE: Make a white sauce (see index) with butter, flour, milk and broth. Cook over low heat. As it thickens, add egg. Cook until creamy. Season with salt and pepper.

Butter 9x13 casserole. Sprinkle cracker crumbs or bread crumbs on bottom of pan. Pour in ⅔ of macaroni mixture. Add all of meat sauce. Layer remaining macaroni on top. Pour white sauce over all. Top with 1½ cups Parmesan cheese. Bake 350⁰ for 45 minutes. Cut in squares to serve. Can be baked for 35 minutes day before. Reheat, covered with foil, for 30 minutes. Serves 10.

☆   ☆   ☆

Turkey "Tet"

Elegant Enough for a Dinner Party!

4	cups chopped turkey or chicken
½	pound short cut spaghetti, cooked
2	(4 ounces each) cans mushrooms and liquid
2	sticks butter or margarine, divided
1	bell pepper, chopped
1	onion, chopped
1	quart whole milk (do not substitute)
¾	cup flour
½	pound grated Deluxe Kraft American cheese (do not substitute)
½	pound grated Old English cheese (do not substitute)
1	(2 or 4 ounce) jar chopped pimientos, as desired

Place turkey and cooked spaghetti in a very large mixing bowl. Add mushrooms and liquid. In a Dutch oven melt 4 tablespoons of butter, sauté the bell pepper and onion. Add to turkey. Stir gently. Melt the remaining butter and make a white sauce with the flour and milk. After sauce thickens, add grated cheeses and continue stirring until melted. Pour over turkey mixture. Add pimientos. Freezes well. Bake in a 3 quart casserole or 8x11 baking dish. Cover with bread crumbs if desired. Bake 325⁰ for 45 minutes. If frozen, bake 1½ hours. Stir often. Serves 8.

Ivanette Dennis

Chicken Spaghetti

1	(4-6 pound) hen
1	(12 ounce) package spaghetti
1	(15 ounce) can stewed tomatoes
1	(10¾ ounce) can tomato soup
2	cups chopped celery
1	onion, minced
2	(2 ounces each) jars sliced pimientos
2	(4 ounces each) cans mushrooms, stems and pieces
½	teaspoon garlic powder
2	teaspoons ground cumin
1	teaspoon salt
1	teaspoon pepper
1	pound American cheese, grated

Cook hen until tender. Reserve broth. Bone and dice chicken into bite-size pieces. Add to the broth the stewed tomatoes, soup, celery, onion, pimientos, mushrooms, garlic powder, cumin, salt and pepper. Simmer for 30 minutes. Add spaghetti and cook for 7 to 8 minutes. Add chicken and cheese. Place in 2 greased 3 quart casseroles. Can be frozen at this point or bake for 1 hour at 325⁰. Serves 20.

Linda Juba

☆　　☆　　☆

Chicken Tetrazzini

Progressive Dinner Favorite

2	(3 pounds each) chickens or 1 (6 pound) turkey	1	(4 ounce) jar chopped pimiento
1	(8 ounce) package green noodles		Garlic powder to taste
1	(8 ounce) package white noodles	1	tablespoon lemon pepper
1	stick margarine	½	cup white wine, divided
1	onion, chopped	1	pound Velveeta
¾	tablespoon flour	1	(4½ ounce) can chopped ripe olives
2	(10¾ ounces each) cans undiluted cream of mushroom soup	1	(8 ounce) can sliced water chestnuts
½	cup milk	1	(8 ounce) can mushrooms with liquid

Cook and bone chicken. Reserve broth. Cook noodles in chicken broth and drain. In large skillet, melt margarine, sauté onion, add flour, soup, milk, pimientos, garlic powder, lemon pepper, ¼ cup white wine and half mushroom liquid. Cut Velveeta in small cubes, for easy melting, and add to sauce above. Do not melt completely. To chicken add ripe olives, water chestnuts and mushrooms. Combine with sauce. In large casserole, layer noodles and chicken sauce. Pour ¼ cup white wine over, or mix all together and add ¼ cup white wine. Bake at 350⁰ for 30 minutes or until bubbly. *Tura Bethune*

Virginia's Noodle Kugel

Good with Baked Ham

1	(16 ounce) package wide noodles	1	(20 ounce) can crushed pineapple
1	(8 ounce) package cream cheese	3	eggs, slightly beaten
1	carton Ricotta cheese	¼	cup sugar and 1 teaspoon cinnamon mixed together
4	tablespoons margarine, melted		

Cook noodles according to package directions. Drain. Cut in smaller pieces. Blend with a fork the cream cheese, Ricotta and margarine. Add pineapple to eggs. Fill 9x13 inch buttered casserole with alternating layers of noodles, cheeses and pineapple. Sprinkle cinnamon mixture on top. Bake at 375⁰ for 1 hour. Serves 12. *Tura Bethune*

☆　　☆　　☆

Sour Cream and Macaroni

Use to Stuff Peppers or Tomatoes

1	egg	1	tablespoon grated onion
1	cup sour cream	2	cups cooked elbow
2	teaspoons prepared		macaroni, divided
	mustard	1	cup grated sharp Cheddar
¼	teaspoon salt		cheese, divided

Beat egg slightly; then mix with sour cream, mustard, salt and onion. Put ½ the macaroni in the bottom of a greased 1 quart casserole. Pour ½ of the sour cream mixture over macaroni and sprinkle with ½ of the shredded cheese. Add remaining macaroni, pour remaining sour cream mixture over it and sprinkle with the remaining cheese. Bake at 350° for 30 minutes. Serves 6.

Variation: May be served stuffed in bell peppers. Cut the tops off 6 bell peppers, remove seeds; parboil in salted water for 3 minutes. Drain. Stand green peppers in casserole; then stuff with ½ macaroni and proceed as above. *Anna Wade Pierson*

Variation: Scoop centers out of 8 tomatoes and proceed as above, but reduce baking time to 20 minutes.

Mushroom Noodles

3	cups uncooked egg noodles	½	teaspoon garlic salt
2	cups quartered fresh	1	tablespoon flour
	mushrooms	⅔	cup milk
½	cup bell pepper, diced	½	teaspoon seasoned salt
¼	cup green onion, chopped	⅓	cup dry white wine,
3	tablespoons butter, melted		optional
	and divided	2	cups grated Monterey Jack cheese, divided

Cook noodles as directed. Drain and set aside. Sauté mushrooms, bell pepper and onion in 2 tablespoons butter in large skillet. Sprinkle with garlic salt. Remove vegetables. Set aside. Combine 1 tablespoon butter and flour in skillet. Gradually add milk, stirring and cooking until smooth and thickened. Blend in salt, wine and 1 cup cheese. Cook until cheese melts, stirring constantly. Stir in noodles and vegetables. Spoon mixture into lightly greased 1½ quart casserole. Top with remaining 1 cup of cheese. Bake at 350° for 20 minutes. Serves 4-6.

Mildred Phillips

Variation: Add ham, chicken, shrimp or crabmeat for a 1 dish meal.

☆   ☆   ☆

Spaghetti with Fresh Tomato Sauce

6 ripe tomatoes, about 2
pounds (Beef Steak variety
is excellent)
½ teaspoon crumbled dried
basil
1 clove garlic, minced
3 tablespoons chopped fresh
parsley

Salt to taste
Freshly ground black pepper
to taste
1 tablespoon olive oil
12 ounces linguini
⅓ cup grated Parmesan or
Romano cheese

Scald tomatoes in boiling water to facilitate peeling. Peel and chop finely (don't use blender) into large mixing bowl. Add basil, garlic, parsley,
salt, pepper and olive oil. Mix well, and let stand at room temperature.
Meanwhile, cook linguini in boiling salted water until al dente; drain.
Serve sauce over linguini with Parmesan or Romano cheese. This is very
good with cold tuna, crusty hard rolls and a dry red wine. Serves 4.

Excellent summertime meal, when good tomatoes are plentiful.
Ruth Becker

Variation: Use corkscrew or elbow macaroni instead of linguini and serve
as a cold salad.

Southern Rice Delight

1 cup rice (don't use instant)
½ stick butter, melted
2 (10½ ounces each) cans
beef bouillon

¼ cup chopped onions
1 (8 ounce) can sliced
mushrooms

Combine all ingredients in a 2 quart casserole and bake uncovered at
325⁰ for 1 hour and 15 minutes or until liquid is absorbed.
Carol Garrigues

Variation: Add 1 teaspoon oregano. Substitute 2 cups beef consommé
for bouillon. Bake at 400⁰ for 45 minutes.   *Mildred Phillips*

☆   ☆   ☆

Rice with Mushroom Almond Sauce

4	cups cooked rice, kept warm	4	tablespoons butter or margarine
½	cup chopped onion	4	tablespoons flour
½	cup chopped celery		Salt to taste
½	cup sliced mushrooms		Pepper to taste
½	cup sliced almonds	2	cups chicken broth

Put rice in casserole. Sauté onions, celery, mushrooms and almonds in butter. Add flour, salt and pepper, cook until lightly brown. Add chicken broth and cook until thick. Pour over rice. Bake at 325° for 30 minutes. May be made ahead and frozen.

Variation: Use brown or white rice mixed with wild rice.

Dorthy Watkins

Real Cajun Red Beans and Rice

1	pound dried red beans	1	teaspoon black pepper
½	pound salt pork	3	generous dashes of Tabasco
2	quarts water	1	tablespoon Worcestershire
3	cups chopped bermuda onions	1	(4 ounce) can tomato sauce
1	bunch green onions, chopped	¼	teaspoon oregano
1	cup chopped parsley	¾	teaspoon dried thyme
1	cup chopped bell pepper	1	pound bulk sausage made into 8-10 little balls, optional
2	cloves garlic, crushed		
1	tablespoon salt		
1	teaspoon cayenne pepper		

Soak beans overnight. Cook beans and pork in water slowly 45 minutes. Add onions, parsley, bell pepper, garlic, salt, cayenne pepper, black pepper, Tabasco, Worcestershire, tomato sauce, oregano and thyme. Cook slowly another hour, and 45 minutes stirring occasionally. Add sausage (if used) for the last 45 minutes. Cool, let stand. Add salt if needed. Reheat and bring to a boil, then lower heat and simmer 30 to 40 minutes. Serve over boiled rice. Serves 6-8.

Louise Propps

☆   ☆   ☆

Alpine Rice

1	cup brown rice	⅔	cup grated Swiss cheese
4	tablespoons butter	½	cup sesame seeds roasted
⅔	cup grated Parmesan		and ground
	cheese	1	cup hot milk

Cook rice according to package directions. Immediately add butter, Parmesan and Swiss cheeses and sesame seeds. When cheese melts, add hot milk and toss again. Serve at once. Serves 4.

The Cookbook Committee

Hereford House Potatoes

6	baking potatoes, peeled	Parmesan cheese, grated
1	cup melted butter (do not	Paprika, if desired
	substitute)	

Peel and thinly slice (not quite through) potatoes. Press tightly together to form the natural shape of the potato. Use a pan small enough to press potatoes close together. Fill the pan ½ full of water and add melted butter. Sprinkle the potatoes with plenty of Parmesan cheese. Bake at 350° for about 1½ hours, basting frequently with own juice. It is most important to keep the potatoes moist and not allow them to dry out. Serves 6.

Virginia Steenson

Potatoes Chantilly

4	baking potatoes	Pepper to taste
½	cup heavy cream	Chopped parsley
3	tablespoons butter	½ cup grated sharp cheese
Salt to taste		

Peel and cut potatoes into thin strips, as for French fries. Place potatoes in center of large sheet of heavy duty foil and pour cream over them. Dot with butter, then sprinkle with salt, pepper, parsley and cheese. Fold foil over, making a tight package. Place on shallow pan in 425° oven for 40 minutes. Serves 4.

Ruth Becker

☆   ☆   ☆

Potatoes Delicious

Quick and Easy!

2	pounds frozen hash brown potatoes, thawed	1	(10¾ ounce) can cream of chicken soup
2	cups grated cheese, optional	1	teaspoon pepper
1	pint sour cream	1-2	cups crushed corn flakes or bread crumbs
2	teaspoons salt	½	cup melted margarine
½	cup grated onion		

Mix potatoes, cheese, sour cream, salt, onion, soup and pepper. Pour into a 2 quart casserole. Top with crushed corn flakes mixed with melted margarine. Bake at 350⁰ for 1 hour 20 minutes. May be frozen, but don't add cornflakes until baking time.

Variation: Use potato or celery soup. May add pimientos or substitute chopped green onions for grated onions.

Variation: Reduce sour cream to ½ pint and add 1 (10¾ ounce) can mushroom soup.   *Diane Iacoponelli and Colleen Pumpelly*

Sweet Potato Casserole

CASSROLE:

3	cups cooked, mashed sweet potatoes	4	tablespoons margarine, melted
½	cup sugar	½	cup milk
2	eggs, well beaten	1½	teaspoons vanilla

TOPPING:

1	cup brown sugar	1	cup chopped nuts
⅓	cup flour	⅓	cup melted margarine

CASSEROLE: Mix sweet potatoes, sugar, eggs, margarine, milk and vanilla. Put in a greased 2 quart casserole. Cover with topping.

TOPPING: Mix sugar, flour, nuts and margarine.

Bake at 350⁰ for 35 minutes. Serves 6-8.   *Martha Aldridge*

☆   ☆   ☆

Richardson Woman's Club

THE TEXAS EXPERIENCE *reflects the true meaning of the Richardson Woman's Club. Volunteering time for community projects, sharing good food and promoting friendship are of great importance to the women of this organization.*

Organized in 1955, members of RWC, as the club is called, soon became well-known for their annual Holiday Tour of Homes held in November. Featured were the Country Store with its arts and crafts, the Bake Sale, the Tea Room and beautiful homes decorated for the Christmas Season. Today this event draws over 3,000 people. Many arrive early, standing in line, to be first in the Bake Shop. They fill their baskets with an assortment of homemade pies, cakes, cookies, candies and breads to be enjoyed during the Holidays. Requests for sharing the Tea Room recipes and the recipes for the Bake Sale favorites were one of the reasons for writing this cookbook.

RWC participates in civic, social, cultural and philanthropic activities promoting the development of skills and enrichment of its members' lives. The club awards college scholarships to young women and men and educational grants to displaced homemakers or women needing other educational assistance. Financial support is given to local and national non-profit organizations on the basis of existing needs.

The Clubhouse

Nestled under stately pecan and red oaks in a picturesque enclave of northeast Richardson is the home of Richardson Woman's Club, a blend of past and present.

An aura of bygone days surrounds the old farm house where small meetings and luncheons are held. The "new" is Founders Hall which accommodates larger gatherings. The structures are connected by porches, decks, terraces and walkways. Painted a soft yellow, spanning the hilly terrain, the buildings create a sense of tranquillity. A winding drive passes an historic old stone well, favored by brides as a wedding site, and meanders down to the beautiful old house. The sun porch shown in the photograph has a scenic view of the sun-dappled grounds and is popular for intimate dinner parties and receptions.

The Clubhouse and Founders Hall are in demand throughout the year for weddings, recitals, receptions, parties, meetings and other social functions.

The historic site is part of the Peters Colony land grant claimed in the mid-1800's by Anthony Leake and sold to Bob Huguley in 1868. Philanthropist Alger Meadows used the property as a country retreat in the 1950's and 1960's. The City of Richardson became the owner in 1971 and built the adjacent golf course.

Today's luncheon features:

Spinach Salad, Creamy Dressing,
French Bread and Butter for Breads

Patrician Potatoes

6 potatoes	1½ tablespoons minced onion
Milk	2½ teaspoons salt
3 cups creamed cottage cheese	⅓ teaspoon white pepper
	Butter
¾ cup sour cream	Chopped toasted almonds

Boil potatoes, peel and mash with a little milk. Add cottage cheese, sour cream, onion, salt and pepper. Pour in a 2 quart greased casserole. Dot with butter and sprinkle with almonds. Bake at 350⁰ for 30 minutes. Serves 8-10.   *N. J. Metcalf*

Hot Lump Crabmeat a la Chateaubriand

ROUX:

1 pound flour	1 cup Crisco oil

CRABMEAT:

1½ pounds fresh mushrooms, sliced	Salt to taste
5 green onions, chopped	Pepper to taste
Salad oil	Accent to taste
2 teaspoons flour	Chicken stock to taste
2 quarts heavy cream	1 pound Romano cheese, grated
½ gallon milk	5 pounds lump crabmeat
1 cup Cream Sherry	

ROUX: Cook flour and oil over a double boiler 30 minutes until flour browns. Keep hot until thick.

CRABMEAT: Sauté mushrooms and onions in oil until brown. Add 2 teaspoons flour to absorb mixture. Blend well. Add heavy cream and milk and cook until very hot. Blend slowly with equal amounts of roux. Whip well with metal whip. Blend with Sherry, salt, pepper, Accent and chicken stock. Gently add ¾ grated cheese and fold in lump crabmeat. Pour into 2½ quart baking dish and top with remaining cheese. Brown under broiler. Serves 20.   *Marge Veerman*

☆   ☆   ☆

Crabmeat Casserole

1   cup cream of mushroom
    soup
1   (5.3 ounce) can evaporated
    milk
1   (6-7 ounce) can crabmeat
2   tablespoons lemon juice
1   (3 ounce) package slivered
    almonds

1   (2 ounce) can black olives
1   (6 ounce) can water
    chestnuts
Fresh mushrooms (optional)
2   cups Pepperidge Farm
    dressing (may use plain or
    herb dressing)

TOPPING:
½   cup chopped green onion
½   cup chopped bell pepper

½   cup chopped celery
1   cup mayonnaise

Combine soup and milk. Flake crabmeat and add to soup mixture. Add lemon juice, almonds, olives, water chestnuts, mushrooms and dressing. Bake at 350⁰ for 30 minutes.

TOPPING: Mix onion, pepper and celery with mayonnaise. Spread over casserole and bake 10 minutes longer.   *Mildred Phillips*

Baked Crab in Sea Shells

1½ cups mayonnaise
1   cup cream
1   tablespoon minced parsley
1   teaspoon minced onion
½   teaspoon salt
⅛   teaspoon pepper

Dash of red pepper
6   hard-cooked eggs, diced
1   cup soft bread crumbs
1   cup flaked crabmeat
½   cup buttered bread crumbs

Blend mayonnaise and cream. Add parsley, onion, salt, pepper, and red pepper, eggs and soft bread crumbs. Fold in crab. Place in greased shells. Sprinkle with buttered crumbs. Bake at 350⁰ about 20 minutes or until crumbs are golden brown. Serves 8.   *Dot McCalpin*

☆   ☆   ☆

Deviled Crab Meat

1   (6-7 ounce) can or ½
    pound fresh crab meat
1   tablespoon lemon juice
2   tablespoons butter
2   tablespoons flour
½   teaspoon dry mustard
½   teaspoon salt
1   cup milk

1   tablespoon minced parsley
1   tablespoon minced green
    onions
¼   teaspoon Tabasco or to
    taste
1   cup soft bread crumbs
2   tablespoons butter

Drain and shred canned crab or pick fresh crab. Sprinkle with lemon juice. Melt butter; add flour, mustard, and salt, stirring to a smooth paste. Add milk and cook until it thickens and comes to a boil. Add crab, parsley, green onions and Tabasco. Bake individual servings in shells or small casseroles. Sprinkle with bread crumbs that have been tossed with melted butter. Bake at 350⁰ for 20 to 25 minutes. Serves 3-4.

Tura Bethune

Crab Louis

DRESSING:
1   cup mayonnaise
¼   cup heavy cream
¼   cup chili sauce
¼   cup chopped bell pepper

¼   cup chopped green onion
    and tops
1   teaspoon lemon juice

SALAD:
Lettuce torn into bite-sized
    pieces
2-3 cups cooked crab meat

2   hard-cooked eggs, sliced
2   tomatoes, cut in wedges

DRESSING: Combine mayonnaise, cream, chili sauce, bell pepper, onion and lemon juice for dressing. Refrigerate until ready to serve.

SALAD: On a large plate, arrange lettuce (enough to serve 6 people); then add crab meat, eggs and tomatoes. Serve with dressing.

Valerie McMahan

☆   ☆   ☆

Ham and Crab Creole

1	bell pepper, diced	1	(4 ounce) can button
1	onion, chopped		mushrooms
½	clove garlic, minced	Pinch of sugar	
4	tablespoons butter	Pinch of nutmeg	
1	(16 ounce) can tomatoes	Worcestershire to taste	
Pinch of baking soda		1	tablespoon flour
Salt to taste		¾	cup cream
Pepper to taste		1	pound crab, flaked
1	(2 ounce) jar pimientos	1	pound ham, diced

Sauté pepper, onion and garlic in butter. Add tomatoes, soda, salt, pepper, pimientos, mushrooms, sugar, nutmeg, and Worcestershire. Mix flour with cream. Gradually stir into first mixture. Add crab and ham. Cook 10 to 15 minutes. Serve over cooked rice. Serves 6-8.

Tura Bethune

Crabmeat Au Gratin

1	cup finely chopped onion	1	teaspoon salt
1	celery rib finely chopped	½	teaspoon red pepper
1	stick margerine or butter	¼	teaspoon black pepper
½	cup flour	1	pound white crabmeat
1	(13 ounce) can evaporated	½	pound Cheddar cheese,
	milk		grated
2	egg yolks		

Sauté onions and celery in butter until wilted. Blend flour in well with this mixture. Pour in milk gradually, stirring constantly. Add egg yolks, salt, red and black pepper. Cook for 5 minutes. Put crabmeat in a bowl suitable for mixing and pour cooked sauce over crabmeat. Blend well and transfer into a lightly greased 9x9 inch casserole. Sprinkle with cheese. Bake at 375⁰ for 10 to 15 minutes. Serves 6.

Hint: Since crab is so rich, less may be used. Fresh, frozen or canned crab is suitable.

Thecia Faulkner

☆   ☆   ☆

Ginger's Crab Eleganté

6   slices of pineapple
¾   pound fresh crabmeat or 2
     (6-7 ounces each) cans
1   cup medium white sauce
     (see index)

6   mushroom caps (as large
     as possible)
1   recipe Hollandaise sauce
     (see index)

Place pineapple ring on cookie sheet. Mix crabmeat with just enough white sauce to stick mixture together. (All of the sauce may not be needed.) Stuff in the largest mushroom caps possible, place filling side up on top of pineapple slice. Bake at 300⁰ about 20 minutes. Place on plate and garnish with Hollandaise sauce. Serves 6.   *Linda Juba*

Salmon Soufflé

½   stick plus ¼ teaspoon
     butter, divided
½   cup plus 1 tablespoon
     Swiss cheese, divided
¼   cup flour
1⅓   cups boiling milk and
     salmon liquid

¾   teaspoon salt
¼   teaspoon pepper
¼   teaspoon oregano
½   teaspoon onion powder
6   eggs
1   cup canned salmon,
     reserve liquid

Preheat oven to 400⁰. Butter soufflé dish with teaspoon butter and sprinkle with 1 tablespoon cheese. Melt remaining butter in saucepan; stir in flour and cook over medium heat until mixture foams. Add milk to salmon liquid to total 1⅓ cups. Slowly add boiling liquid beating constantly. Add salt, pepper, oregano and onion powder. Cook over medium heat until very thick, about 1 minute, stirring constantly. Separate eggs and put whites in mixing bowl. Beat yolks and add to hot sauce very slowly, beating well. Beat egg whites until stiff, but not dry. Add cheese and salmon to sauce. Stir large spoonful of egg whites into sauce and then slowly pour sauce into egg white mixture folding whites into sauce. Pour soufflé into prepared dish. Place in center of preheated 400⁰ oven and immediately turn oven to 375⁰. Bake 35 to 45 minutes. Serve immediately. Serves 5-6.   *The Cookbook Committee*

☆   ☆   ☆

Salmon Fritters

1 (7¾ ounce) can salmon
Milk
1 cup biscuit mix
1 egg, slightly beaten
1 teaspoon lemon juice
¼ cup finely chopped celery

3 tablespoons finely chopped bell pepper
3 tablespoons finely chopped onion
1 tablespoon minced parsley
½ teaspoon seasoned salt

Drain, reserve liquid and flake can of salmon. Add milk to salmon liquid to equal ½ cup. Add to biscuit mix along with egg and lemon juice. Blend in salmon, celery, bell pepper, onion, parsley and seasoned salt. Drop batter by spoonfuls into 375⁰ deep fat. Fry until golden brown on both sides, about 3 minutes. Drain. Serve fritters with lemon wedges and tartar sauce. Serves 4.   *Danna Almon*

Salmon-Shrimp Casserole

2 tablespoons butter or margarine
2 tablespoons flour
1 (10½ ounce) can Cheddar cheese soup
1 cup milk
2 ounces sharp cheese, shredded
1 (15½ ounce) can Red Sockeye Salmon, drained, boned and broken into large pieces

1 (4½ ounce) can shrimp, drained
½ of a (10 ounce) package frozen peas
1 cup packaged biscuit mix

In saucepan melt butter; stir in flour. Add soup and milk. Cook and stir until thickened and bubbly. Remove from heat. Add cheese, stirring until melted. Stir in salmon, shrimp and peas. Turn into a 1 quart baking dish. Bake at 425⁰ until bubbly and heated through, about 30 minutes. Prepare biscuit mix according to package directions for drop biscuits. Spoon 10 biscuits around edge of hot casserole. Bake until golden about 15 minutes longer. Serves 4.   *Betsy Halford*

☆   ☆   ☆

Trout in Garlic Butter

2	whole trout, cleaned and drained, heads and tails intact	2	cloves garlic
		¼	cup margarine
		1	lemon, quartered
Olive oil		Parsley	

Wash fish with cold water and dry with paper towels. Brush cooking sheet or casserole with oil. Brush both sides of fish well with oil. Measure thickness of fish at its thickest part and allow 10 minutes broiling time per inch, and divide total time by 2 and cook each side that length of time. (Example: 2 inch fish = 20 minutes; divided by 2 = 10 minutes per side). While fish broils, crush garlic and sauté in margarine. After fish is broiled, place on board and bone. (Cut straight down to bone, just behind gills and lift up flesh; then lift bone out). Pour garlic butter over fish and garnish with parsley. Serve with lemon.   *Ruth Becker*

Butter and Herb Baked Fish

½	cup butter	½	teaspoon oregano leaves
⅔	cup crushed saltine crackers	½	teaspoon salt
		¼	teaspoon garlic powder
¼	cup grated Parmesan cheese	1	pound frozen sole or perch fillets, thawed and drained
½	teaspoon basil leaves		

In 9x13 inch baking dish melt butter in preheated 350⁰ oven 5 to 7 minutes. Meanwhile, in 9 inch pan combine cracker crumbs. Parmesan cheese, basil, oregano, salt and garlic powder. Dip fish fillets in butter and then in crumb mixture. Arrange fish fillets in baking pan. Bake uncovered near center of oven for 25 to 30 minutes or until fish is tender and flakes with a fork. Serve immediately. Serves 4.   *Cathy Martin*

Onion Baked Fish Fillets

2	pounds flounder or sole	1	(1 ounce) package Original Ranch Salad Dressing Mix
1	teaspoon salt		
1	cup sour cream	1	(3 ounce) can French fried onions, crushed
1	cup mayonnaise		

Cut fillets in serving sized pieces and sprinkle with salt. Combine sour cream, mayonnaise and salad dressing mix. Dip fish into 1 cup of the mixture; then place in well-greased dish. Sprinkle crushed onions on top of fillets. Bake at 350⁰ for 20 minutes or until done. Serve with remaining sauce. Serves 6.   *Valerie McMahan*

☆   ☆   ☆

Quick Baked Fish (Spencer Method)

2	pounds fish filets	2	cups fine dry bread
¼	cup evaporated milk		crumbs
¼	cup water		Salad oil
2	teaspoons salt		

Dip fish in mixture of milk, water and salt, then into bread crumbs. Place on oiled cookie sheet. Sprinkle fish with oil. Bake at 500°-600° for 10 minutes, until brown and fish flakes easily. Garnish with lemon slices and chopped parsley. Serves 6.   *Ellen Tippit*

Fish Fillets Tarragon

1	teaspoon instant minced onion	2	teaspoons warm water
½	teaspoon dry mustard	2	teaspoons lemon juice
¼	teaspoon tarragon leaves	½	cup mayonnaise
¼	teaspoon black pepper	1½	pounds fish fillets

Mix onion, mustard, tarragon and pepper with water. Let stand 10 minutes. Add lemon juice and mayonnaise. Lightly salt to taste. Wipe fish dry; sprinkle with salt and spread mixture on top of fish. Bake in preheated oven at 425° for 25 to 30 minutes. Garnish with paprika and lemon. Serves 4-6.   *Linda Juba*

Batter for Deep Frying Fish or Onion Rings

½	cup flour	½	cup milk or flat beer
1	egg	1-2	tablespoons butter, melted
	Salt to taste		

Beat egg white stiff and fold into other ingredients. Add more flour if batter looks too thin. Dip fish or onion rings in this and deep fat fry.

During the last 10 years over 3,000,000 Texans fished 1½ million acres of lakes and 80,000 miles of rivers, streams and bayous. The favorite catches of these sportsmen are largemouth bass, crappie, sunfish, white bass and various species of catfish.

☆   ☆   ☆

Oriental Frying Batter

½   cup unsifted flour
⅓   cup cornstarch
½-⅔ cup cold water
1   teaspoon soy sauce
1   pint corn oil

2   teaspoons baking powder
Shrimp, raw
Pork, raw cut in bite-sized
     pieces
Chicken, raw cut in bite-sized
     pieces

In medium bowl, stir together flour and cornstarch. Gradually stir in ½ cup of water and soy sauce until batter is smooth. Add additional water, 1 tablespoon at a time until batter is just thick enough to coat pieces.

TO FRY SHRIMP: Heat oil to 375⁰. Stir 1 tablespoon hot oil into batter. Stir in baking powder. Dip shrimp in batter. Fry 3 minutes. Drain. Serve with mustard.

FOR PORK AND CHICKEN, proceed as above. Fry 8 minutes.

Dottie Pinch

Baked Shrimp or Crab Sandwiches

8   slices of bread, crusts
     trimmed, divided
2   cups shrimp or crab or
     1 cup each
1   onion, diced
1   bell pepper, diced
1   cup diced celery
½   cup mayonnaise

4   eggs, beaten
2   cups milk
1   (10¾ ounce) can cream of
     mushroom soup, undiluted
1   cup grated American
     cheese
Dash of paprika

Put 4 slices of bread in the bottom of a buttered pan or dish. Mix crab or shrimp with onion, bell pepper, celery, mayonnaise and spread on bread. Top with remaining slices of bread. Combine eggs with milk and pour over the sandwiches. Let stand overnight in the refrigerator. Bake at 325⁰ for 15 minutes. Remove from oven, cover with soup, cheese and paprika. Continue baking 1 hour. Serves 4.   *Tura Bethune*

☆   ☆   ☆

Shrimp Creole

¼	cup oil	½-1	teaspoon chili powder
½	cup chopped onion	1	tablespoon Worcestershire
½	cup chopped celery		Dash of Tabasco
1	clove garlic, minced	1	teaspoon cornstarch
1	(16 ounce) can tomatoes	2	teaspoons cold water
1	(15 ounce) can herb seasoned tomato sauce	¾	pound raw, deveined shrimp
1½	teaspoons salt	½	cup chopped bell pepper
1	teaspoon sugar		

Sauté onion, celery and garlic in oil until tender. Add tomatoes, tomato sauce, salt, sugar, chili powder, Worcestershire and Tabasco. Simmer uncovered for 45 minutes. Mix cornstarch with water and stir into mixture. Continue stirring until the mixture thickens. Add shrimp and bell pepper. Cover and simmer about 5 minutes. Serve over rice. Serves 5-6.

To prepare in advance, make sauce and refrigerate. Reheat and add shrimp and bell pepper the last 5 minutes before serving. Cooked rice may be reheated in microwave.   *Valerie McMahan*

Super Shrimp Supper

SHRIMP:

6	pounds raw shrimp	1	tablespoon pickling spices
½	gallon water	1	teaspoon dry mustard
1	tablespoon carraway seeds	8	teaspoons salt
1	tablespoon whole peppercorns		Leaves from one stalk celery

SAUCE:

	Juice of 2 lemons	7-8	dashes Tabasco
1	tablespoon tarragon vinegar	1	teaspoon salt
1	tablespoon Worcestershire	½	pound butter, do not substitute
2	tablespoons soy sauce		

SHRIMP: Cook shrimp in ½ gallon water with carraway seeds, peppercorns, pickling spice, mustard, salt and celery leaves. Serve in shells and let guests peel and dip their own shrimp in the sauce.

SAUCE: Heat to blend lemon juice, vinegar, Worcestershire, soy sauce, Tabasco, salt and butter and serve hot in individual dishes. Serves 6.
                                        Nancy Brown

☆   ☆   ☆

Barbequed Shrimp

¼ cup olive oil
2¾ cups corn oil
2 tablespoons red wine vinegar
1 tablespoon tomato paste
1 (8 ounce) can tomato sauce

1 tablespoon oregano
1 tablespoon minced garlic
3 tablespoons finely chopped fresh parsley
1 teaspoon salt
Freshly ground pepper
16-18 shrimp

Combine olive oil, corn oil, vinegar, tomato paste, tomato sauce, oregano, garlic, parsley, salt and pepper in mixing bowl; add shrimp and mix until well coated. Marinate for 2 hours, turning every 30 minutes. Put in shallow pan. Place under broiler 3 inches from heat for 5 minutes. Turn with tongs. Broil 5 minutes or until lightly browned and firm to the touch. Serve with a small dish of drippings for French bread dip. Excellent with tossed salad and twice baked potatoes.   *Dottie Pinch*

Yvonne's Shrimp Curry

2 (10¾ ounces each) cans cream of mushroom soup
3 (10¾ ounces each) cans of cream of celery soup
1 tablespoon curry powder
1 teaspoon Worcestershire
Salt to taste
Pepper to taste

Dash of cayenne pepper
1 (2 ounce) can mushroom buttons
3 tablespoons butter
1 onion, chopped
1½ cup chopped celery
1 bell pepper, chopped
3 pounds cooked shrimp

Put all soups in pan and heat; then add curry powder, Worcestershire, salt, pepper, cayenne pepper and mushrooms. Sauté in butter the onion, celery and bell pepper until the vegetables are soft. Add to soup mixture. Add shrimp and heat over low heat until hot. Serve over rice. Serves 10-12.   *Carole Price*

☆   ☆   ☆

Italian Broiled Shrimp

2	pounds jumbo or large shrimp	¼	cup olive oil
¼	cup flour	¼	cup melted butter
		1	cup drawn butter sauce

DRAWN BUTTER SAUCE:

⅔	cup butter		Lemon juice if desired
⅔	cup water	2	tablespoons minced garlic
4	tablespoons minced parsley		

Shell shrimp, leaving tails on. Dry, dust with flour. Stir oil and butter into flat baking dish (about 8x10 or 8x12). Put shrimp in dish, broil at medium heat for 8 minutes. Make drawn butter sauce. Pour over shrimp and stir until shrimp are coated. Broil for 2 minutes. Serve immediately. Serve with leftover butter sauce. Serves 6.

BUTTER SAUCE: Melt butter in water. Add parsley, lemon juice and garlic. Let stand. Pour clear yellow liquid off top and add to shrimp. Discard water.   *Joan Pesce*

Shrimp Cajun

1	onion, chopped	1	clove garlic, minced
1	bell pepper, chopped	2	tablespoons parsley
4	ribs celery, chopped	⅛	teaspoon cloves
3	tablespoons bacon drippings	¼	teaspoon thyme
1½	cups diced cooked ham	½	teaspoon chili powder
1	(10¾ ounce) can tomato soup	⅛	teaspoon cayenne
¼	soup can water		Salt to taste
1	bay leaf		Pepper to taste
		1	pound cooked shrimp

Sauté onion, bell pepper and celery in bacon drippings until almost tender, but do not brown. Add ham, soup, water, bay leaf, garlic, parsley, cloves, thyme, chili powder, cayenne, salt and pepper to taste and simmer for one hour. Add shrimp and cook just long enough for them to heat through. Serve over rice. Serves 4.   *Tura Bethune*

☆   ☆   ☆

Shrimp with Yellow Rice

½	cup olive oil		1	tablespoon salt
2	cloves garlic, chopped		½	teaspoon yellow food
1	Spanish onion, chopped			coloring
1	bell pepper, chopped		2	cups seafood broth or
1	pound peeled and			water
	deveined raw shrimp		1	cup valencia rice,
⅔	cup whole tomatoes			uncooked
1	pinch saffron			

Heat oil, sauté the garlic, onion and bell pepper; when half done add the raw shrimp. When shrimp turns pink, add the tomtoes, saffron, salt, coloring and liquid. When mixture starts boiling, add rice. Bake in 350⁰ oven for 15 minutes. Garnish with peas, pimiento and parsley. Serves 4.

Tura Bethune

Northwest Seafood Stew

1	pound halibut or any white fish		1	(8 ounce) can tomato sauce
½	pound sole		1	cup water
½	pound red snapper		3	potatoes, diced
¼	pound raw shrimp		1½	teaspoons salt
6	slices bacon		⅛	teaspoon pepper
¾	cup chopped onions		¼	teaspoon oregano
1	clove garlic, minced		¼	teaspoon basil
¾	cup bias-cut celery		1	tablespoon chopped parsley
¼	cup chopped bell pepper			
2	(16 ounces each) cans whole tomatoes, chopped			

Cut fish into bite-sized pieces. Peel the shrimp. Fry bacon in large saucepan; dice. Add onion, garlic, celery and bell pepper. Sauté until vegetables are translucent. Add cut-up tomatoes, tomato sauce, water, potatoes, salt, pepper, oregano and basil. Cover and simmer 15 minutes. Add fish and shrimp. Cover and continue cooking 5 to 8 minutes. Sprinkle with parsley. Serve with green salad and crusty French bread for dunking. Serves 6.

Shirley Rind

☆   ☆   ☆

Seafood Stew

¼ cup oil or margarine
2 tablespoons flour
2 onions, chopped
1-2 cloves of garlic, chopped
3 cups water
1 (16 ounce) can tomatoes
1 teaspoon chili powder
1 teaspoon salt
¼ teaspoon pepper

Dash hot pepper sauce
1 (16 ounce) package frozen shrimp
1 (6 ounce) package frozen crab
1 (5 ounce) can oysters, drained
2 tablespoons chopped parsley

Heat oil or margarine in Dutch oven and stir in flour. Add onions and garlic and cook until tender. Stir in 3 cups water, tomatoes, chili powder, salt, pepper and hot pepper sauce. Cook covered 10 minutes. Stir in seafood and parsley and cook 10 minutes longer. Serve over rice. May be made in microwave. Follow manufacturer's instructions for seafood. Serves 8.   *Ellen Tippit*

Marinated Fish in Sour Cream Sauce

1½ pounds cod, sole or white fish

MARINADE:
1 cup vermouth or white wine

Chopped parsley
Celery salt as desired

SAUCE:
8 ounces sour cream
1 tablespoon Parmesan cheese
1 tablespoon mayonnaise

1 teaspoon tarragon
1 clove garlic, crushed
1 teaspoon lemon juice
Freshly ground pepper

3 tablespoons buttered bread crumbs

Paprika

MARINADE: Mix vermouth, parsley and celery salt. Marinate fish for 1 hour. Remove and drain and put in oiled dish. Cover with sauce.

SAUCE: Combine sour cream, Parmesan cheese, mayonnaise, tarragon, garlic, lemon juice and pepper. Spread on fish. Sprinkle with buttered bread crumbs and paprika. Bake at 350⁰ for 25 minutes. Serves 4-6.
                                                Helen Grieve

☆   ☆   ☆

Deviled Seafood Special

Good Luncheon Dish

1	(6 ounce) can tuna, drained	1	teaspoon finely chopped onion
1	(4½ ounce) can shrimp, rinsed and drained	1	teaspoon dry mustard
½	cup finely chopped bell pepper	1	teaspoon Worcestershire
		½	teaspoon salt
1	cup finely chopped celery	⅛	teaspoon pepper
		1	cup mayonnaise

TOPPING:
1   cup soft bread cubes
2   tablespoons melted margarine

Combine all ingredients in a 1 quart casserole. Toss bread cubes with margarine and sprinkle on top. Bake at 350° for 30 minutes. Garnish with lemon and parsley. Serves 4. *Frances Falkner*

Scallops Sauté

1½	pounds scallops	1	clove garlic, minced
¼	cup butter, divided	4	tablespoons lemon juice
½	teaspoon salt	4	tablespoons white wine
⅛	teaspoon white pepper	1	tablespoon minced parsley
¼	teaspoon paprika	1	tablespoon flour

Wash and dry scallops. If the scallops are large cut in 3rds or 4ths. Heat 2 tablespoons butter in large skillet and add salt, pepper, paprika and garlic. Add scallops to cover pan, do not crowd them. Cook quickly over high heat, stirring until golden brown, 5 to 10 minutes. Remove scallops and place on platter or individual serving plates. In same skillet, add rest of butter and melt. Then add lemon juice and wine mixed with parsley and 1 tablespoon flour. Simmer slightly. Pour over scallops. Serves 4. *Lee Williams*

☆　　☆　　☆

Wild Rice and Oyster Casserole

2   cups wild rice
1   stick butter, melted
4   dozen raw oysters, drained
Salt to taste
Pepper to taste
Hot pepper sauce to taste
1   (10¾ ounce) can cream of
    chicken soup

1   cup light cream
1½ tablespoons onion powder
¾   teaspoon thyme
1½ tablespoons curry powder
¼   cup hot milk

Cook and drain wild rice according to package directions. Add melted butter and toss with the rice until well mixed. Place half the rice in the bottom of a 9x13 baking dish. Cover the rice with oysters. Sprinkle with salt, pepper and hot pepper sauce. Top with the rest of the rice. In a saucepan, heat soup and cream. Dissolve onion powder, thyme and curry in hot milk. Pour this mixture over the layers of rice and oysters. Bake at 300⁰ for 45 minutes. Garnish with parsley. Serves 10-12.

Tura Bethune

Oysters Benedict with Capers

OYSTERS:

2   (12 ounces each) packages
    fresh or frozen oysters
6   slices white bread

6   ounces sliced Canadian
    bacon

CAPER HOLLANDAISE:

¾   cup Hollandaise, canned
    or homemade

2   tablespoons light cream
1   tablespoon capers

OYSTERS: Thaw frozen oysters. Toast bread. Place toast on a warm serving platter or individual serving dishes. Keep warm. Fry Canadian bacon in a skillet and drain on absorbent paper. Place bacon on toast. Pour oysters and liquid into skillet. Simmer 3 to 5 minutes or until edges curl. Remove oysters with a slotted spoon and place on bacon. Pour hot caper Hollandaise over oysters. Serve immediately. Serves 6.

CAPER HOLLANDAISE: Combine Hollandaise, cream and capers. Heat, stirring occasionally. Do not boil.

Tura Bethune

☆   ☆   ☆

Sea Shelf Dinner

1 cup cream of celery soup
2 dashes of Tabasco
1 teaspoon Worcestershire
1 tablespoon lemon juice
½ cup light cream
1 (4 ounce) can sliced
  mushrooms

1 cup shrimp (frozen or
  canned)
1 (6-7 ounce) can crab meat
  (may use frozen)
1 cup pitted ripe olives
1 (2 ounce) jar chopped
  pimientos

Combine soup, Tabasco, Worcestershire, lemon juice and cream. Heat slowly to blend. Add mushrooms, shrimp and crab. Top with olives (may be halved) and pimientos. Garnish with toasted almonds. Serve with rice or chow mein noodles. Serves 8. *Anne Eppright*

Chicken and Broccoli Casserole

2 (10 ounces each) packages
  frozen broccoli spears
8-10 chicken breasts, cooked
  and cut in bite-sized pieces
1 (10¾ ounce) can cream of
  chicken soup
1 (10¾ ounce) can cream of
  celery soup
1 cup Hellmann's
  mayonnaise

1 teaspoon lemon juice
¼ teaspoon curry powder
Salt to taste
1 cup grated Cheddar cheese
½ cup bread crumbs
1 tablespoon butter
Parmesan cheese

Cook broccoli and drain. Arrange in a buttered 2 quart rectangular glass dish. Place chicken on top of broccoli. Combine soups, mayonnaise, lemon juice and curry powder. Salt to taste. Pour over the chicken and sprinkle with Cheddar cheese. Combine bread crumbs and butter and sprinkle over all. Dust lightly with Parmesan cheese. Bake in 350⁰ oven 25 to 30 minutes. Serves 8. *Carol Garrigues*

Good with Southern Rice Delight (see index).

Variation: May use 2 cans cream of chicken soup instead of 1 can cream of chicken soup and 1 can cream of celery soup. Increase curry to 1-2 teaspoons. *Clare Bonnett*

☆ ☆ ☆

Saffron Chicken

½   cup salad oil
¼   teaspoon black pepper
4   tablespoons minced onion
1   clove garlic, minced
1   cup converted rice, uncooked
2   cups chicken stock

½   teaspoon saffron
2   teaspoons salt
1   teaspoon paprika
3-4   cups cooked, chopped chicken
1   (17 ounce) can Leseur young sweet peas

Heat salad oil and pepper in large frying pan; add onion, garlic and rice and cook over low heat until yellow. Add stock, saffron, salt and paprika. Cover tightly and cook over low heat until rice is cooked, about 15 minutes. Add chicken and peas. Heat thoroughly.

Variation: Add 1 cup chopped ham.

Almond Chicken Casserole

6   whole chicken breasts
8   cups uncooked noodles
2   cups mayonnaise
2   (10¾ ounce each) cans cream of chicken soup
1   (10¾ ounce) can cream of mushroom soup
1   (10¾ ounce) can cream of
·   celery soup

8   tablespoons dried, minced onion
2   cups slivered, toasted almonds
¾   cup milk
1   bell pepper, diced
1   teaspoon curry powder
1   (1 pound) bag potato chips, crushed

Cook chicken breasts. Cut in chunks. Cook noodles until just tender. Mix mayonnaise, soups, onion, almonds, milk, noodles, bell pepper, curry powder and chicken. Put in two 9x13 inch pans. Cover with crushed potato chips. Bake 20 minutes at 425⁰ or until hot through. Serves 24.

Jean Wallace

☆   ☆   ☆

Dinner Party Chicken

8	chicken breasts, boned		Mushroom slices
2	(10¾ ounces each) cans cream of chicken soup	1	teaspoon paprika
			Dash of pepper
6	tablespoons brandy	½	cup cashew nuts
⅔	cup sour cream		Parsley
4	green onions, chopped		

Place chicken in single layer in ungreased 2½ quart baking dish. Bake at 400⁰ for 35 minutes. Meanwhile, combine undiluted soup, brandy, sour cream, onions, mushrooms, paprika and pepper and blend well. Pour over chicken, cover and continue baking another 20 minutes or until chicken is tender. Garnish with nuts and parsley. Serves 8.

Martha Crowley

Chicken Breast with Asparagus

A Testing Luncheon Favorite

8	chicken breasts, boned	½	cup white wine
1	stick butter	1	cup freshly grated Parmesan cheese, divided
2	cups sour cream		
2	(10¾ ounces each) cans cream of asparagus soup	1½	pounds fresh asparagus, partially cooked
1	(3 ounce) can mushrooms, drained		

Sauté chicken breasts in butter until browned. Remove breasts to a 10 inch square baking dish. Combine the sour cream, soup, mushrooms and white wine. Pour ¼ of this sauce over chicken. Sprinkle ½ cup cheese over sauce. Layer the asparagus over cheese and add remaining sauce. Top with remaining cheese and bake at 350⁰ uncovered for about 1 hour or until chicken is tender. Serves 6.

Valerie McMahan

☆   ☆   ☆

Chicken Piccata

A Testing Luncheon Favorite

4	chicken breasts, boned	1	chicken bouillon cube
Salt to taste		¼	cup boiling water
Pepper to taste		2	tablespoons lemon juice
Flour		1	tablespoon butter
1	tablespoon butter	4	lemon slices
1	tablespoon vegetable oil		

With a meat cleaver pound the chicken breasts until very thin. Sprinkle with salt and pepper and dredge in flour. In a skillet heat the oil and melt the butter; then cook chicken 3 to 4 minutes on each side until golden brown. Dissolve bouillon in boiling water, add lemon juice and combine with the pan drippings. Cook until all the browned bits are dissolved and add 1 tablespoon butter. Return the chicken to the skillet and heat. Garnish the top of each chicken breast with a lemon slice. Serves 4.

Carole Price

Parmesan Chicken Breast

A Testing Luncheon Favorite

¾	pounds chicken breast, boned	¾	cup grated Parmesan cheese
1	egg, beaten with 2 tablespoons water		Margarine
¾	cup unseasoned bread crumbs		

Pound chicken very thin and cut into serving size pieces. Dip chicken in egg mixture. Then dip in a mixture of bread crumbs and Parmesan cheese. Sauté in melted margarine in electric skillet (about 400⁰) until tender, about 5 minutes on each side. Serves 2. *Valerie McMahan*

Variation: Cut chicken into bite-sized pieces and use as hot hors d'oeuvres. Serve immediately.

☆　　☆　　☆

Chicken in Pineapple Half

6 boneless chicken breasts,
   cut into bite-sized pieces
Salt to taste
Pepper to taste
Dash of tarragon
1 cup pineapple juice
½ cup white wine
1 tablespoon flour
2 pineapples
¼ cup orange marmalade
Dash of paprika

Sprinkle chicken with salt and pepper. Sauté seasoned chicken pieces in butter. Add tarragon, pineapple juice, wine and flour. Cut pineapple in half lengthwise and scoop out the inside. Spoon chicken mixture into pineapple halves and top with marmalade. Sprinkle with paprika. Bake at 400° for 50 to 60 minutes or until chicken is cooked. Serves 4.

Dot McCalpin

Chicken Bayou Teche

6 slices dry toast
2½ cups chicken broth,
   divided
2 white onions, chopped
1 bell pepper, chopped
6 ribs celery, chopped
1 (8 ounce) can mushroom
   stems and pieces
3 cloves garlic, pressed
4 tablespoons bacon
   drippings
1 tablespoon Worcestershire
1 teaspoon salt
½ teaspoon freshly ground
   black pepper
½ teaspoon celery salt
1 teaspoon crushed oregano
Dash of hot sauce
¾ cup chopped parsley
1 (3 pound) chicken, stewed
   and boned
¾ cup cracker crumbs
3-4 tablespoons butter
Paprika

Crumble toast and allow to soak in 1¼ cups of chicken broth. Sauté onions, bell pepper, celery, mushrooms and garlic in bacon drippings until tender. Add Worcestershire, salt, pepper, celery salt, oregano and hot sauce and simmer in skillet until well blended. Add parsley and remaining 1¼ cups chicken broth to moisten. Finally, add boned chicken, blend thoroughly and turn into buttered 3 quart casserole. Cover with cracker crumbs, dot with butter and sprinkle with paprika. Bake at 350° for 25 to 30 minutes. If casserole is made ahead and refrigerated, bake 40 to 60 minutes. Serves 8.

Variation: This casserole is delicious made with crabmeat instead of chicken.

Danna Almon

☆   ☆   ☆

Chicken Vol Au Vent

2	tablespoons butter	¼	teaspoon pepper
2	tablespoons salad oil	2	cups diced cooked chicken
½	cup sliced green onions	1	(2 ounce) jar sliced
1	cup sliced fresh		pimientos
	mushrooms	¼	cup mayonnaise
4	tablespoons flour	2	tablespoons dry Sherry
2	cups water	6	frozen puff pastry shells
2	tablespoons chicken stock		
	base		

Melt butter with salad oil. Sauté green onions. Remove onions and sauté mushrooms. Return onions to skillet and blend in flour. Add water and stir until smooth and thickened. Add chicken stock base, pepper, chicken, pimientos, mayonnaise and Sherry. Bake pastry shells as directed on package. Fill shells with chicken. Nice with a fruit salad and English peas sautéed with celery.

Marge Hurt

Chicken Deluxe

1	cup white rice	1	bell pepper, chopped
1	cup wild rice	2	(10¾ ounces each) cans
2	cups diced celery		mushroom soup
1	onion, minced	2	(4 ounces each) cans
3	cups chicken broth		whole mushrooms
2	chickens stewed, boned		Buttered crumbs
	and diced	2	cups blanched almonds
1 .	(2 ounce) jar chopped		
	pimiento		

Cook rice until starch is removed, about 10 minutes. Drain. Mix semi-cooked rice, celery, onions and chicken broth and cook until tender. Stir constantly as mixture will be thick. Layer ½ each of diced chicken, rice, pimiento, bell pepper, mushrooms and soup in 4-5 quart casserole dish. Repeat to form second layer. Sprinkle with buttered crumbs. Bake at 350⁰ for 45 minutes. Add almonds last 15 minutes of baking time. May be frozen. Serves 12.

Florence Whiting

☆　☆　☆

West Indies Chicken Curry

1/3	cup butter or margarine	1	bay leaf
1	onion, chopped	3	whole cloves
2	ribs celery, chopped	2	teaspoons instant chicken bouillon
1	tart apple, peeled and diced	2½	cups chicken stock
5	tablespoons flour	4	cups bite-sized cooked chicken breast
1½	tablespoons curry powder	¼	cup cream or milk
¼	teaspoon dry mustard	2	tablespoons chopped chutney
Salt to taste			
Pepper to taste		3	Papayas or avocados
1	teaspoon M.S.G.		

In a 3 quart saucepan melt butter, add onion, celery and apple and cook about 10 minutes stirring occasionally. Mix together flour, curry powder, dry mustard, salt, pepper, and M.S.G. Stir into apple mixture along with bay leaf and cloves. Dissolve seasoned stock base in stock and stir into apple mixture. Cook, stirring until sauce thickens. Reduce heat and simmer 30 minutes. Add chicken, cream and chutney and cook 5 minutes longer. Cut papayas in half. Carefully remove seeds and fill papaya halves with curried chicken. Arrange in baking dish and bake in 350⁰ oven 25 minutes. Serve with rice and chutney. If avocados are used slice into thin wedges and sprinkle with lemon juice. Serves 8.   *Tura Bethune*

Chicken Italiano

1	(8 ounce) bottle Kraft's Creamy Italian Dressing	1	bay leaf
1	package onion soup mix	1	teaspoon oregano
1	(4 ounce) can mushrooms, drained	1	(2½-3 pound) fryer, cut up

Combine Creamy Italian Dressing, onion soup mix, mushrooms, bay leaf and oregano and pour over chicken. Bake covered at 350⁰ for 1 hour and 10 minutes. Serves 4.   *Mildred Phillips*

☆   ☆   ☆

Scalloped Chicken and Oysters

1	(5 pound) stewing chicken	3	tablespoons flour
2	(8 ounces each) cans or 1 pint raw oysters, cut up if preferred.	2	cups reserved chicken stock
1	cup chopped celery	1	cup milk
1	bell pepper, diced	½	teaspoon salt
2	pimientos, cut up	½-¾	teaspoon mace
3	tablespoons butter	1½	cups bread crumbs

Stew chicken. Remove meat from bones and reserve stock. Mix cut up chicken pieces with oysters, celery, bell pepper and pimientos. Make white sauce (see index) using butter, flour, chicken stock and milk. Season with salt and mace. In a deep 3 quart casserole, alternate layers of chicken mixture, white sauce and bread crumbs. Top layer should be crumbs. Bake in 400⁰ oven for 30 minutes. Serves 10. *Virginia Steenson*

Wine Bar-B-Que Chicken

A Sure Way to a Man's Heart

½	cup Sauterne (do not substitute)	1	teaspoon Worcestershire
½	cup Heinz chili sauce		Salt to taste
1	tablespoon salad oil		Pepper to taste
3	tablespoons wine vinegar	3	pounds chicken pieces, boned breasts or cup-up fryer
1	clove garlic, chopped		
1	tablespoon chopped onion		

Combine Sauterne and chili sauce. Add oil, wine vinegar, garlic, onion, Worcestershire, salt and pepper and stir well. Marinate chicken in the sauce in the refrigerator for 2 or 3 days, turning chicken once or twice a day. Cover and bake at 375° for 1½ hours. Serve remaining sauce over white or brown rice. Excellent when reheated the second day. Doubles or triples well. Serves 4. *Ivanette Dennis*

☆　　☆　　☆

Sweet and Sour Chicken

2	sticks butter	1	onion, cut into rings
1	frying chicken cut into pieces or 2 cups cooked chicken or turkey	1	bell pepper, cut into rings
		1	(3 ounce) jar stuffed green olives
½	cup flour	1	cup cooked, cleaned shrimp or 1 (7 ounce) can shrimp
2	tablespoons sesame seeds, optional		
1½	teaspoons salt	1	(10¾ ounce) can tomato soup
¼	teaspoon pepper		
1	(15 ounce) can pineapple chunks	¼	cup chili sauce

Melt butter in large electric skillet with temperature set at 350⁰. Coat chicken with flour, sesame seeds, salt and pepper. Brown in skillet. Cover and continue frying with unit set at 250⁰ for 25 minutes, or until tender. Turn chicken skin side up. May be refrigerated at this point. Drain pineapple, reserving ¼ cup syrup. Top chicken with onions, bell pepper, olives, pineapple and shrimp. Combine tomato soup, chili sauce and pineapple syrup. Pour over chicken. Cover and heat at 300⁰ for 15 minutes. Serves 6.   *Irma O'Malley*

Chicken with Champagne Sauce

1	(3-4 pound) chicken	1	pint dry Champagne or Brut, divided
½	stick unsalted butter		
Salt to taste		½	pint heavy cream
Pepper to taste		1	tablespoon tomato paste
4	ounces brandy	1	truffle
½	cup chicken bouillon		

Cut chicken in serving size pieces. In large skillet, cook slowly in butter without browning. Salt and pepper lightly. When chicken is half cooked, pour off butter from pan and set aside. Add brandy and ignite. Add bouillon and all but 4 ounces of Champagne. Simmer until cooking juices are reduced to half. Add heavy cream and tomato paste and continue to simmer until chicken is tender. Arrange chicken on serving platter. Whisk butter in reduced sauce, add remaining Champagne, pour sauce over chicken and garnish dish with sliced truffle. Serves 8.

Novella Bailey

☆　☆　☆

Chicken Paprika

1	cup plus 1 tablespoon flour	2	tablespoons cooking oil
1	teaspoon salt	1	onion, sliced
¼	teaspoon pepper	3	tablespoons paprika
2	(3 pounds each) frying chickens, disjointed	1½	cups water
		2	cups sour cream

Combine 1 cup flour, salt and pepper. Dredge chicken in seasoned flour. Heat oil in Dutch oven or heavy frying pan; then brown chicken in oil. Add onion, paprika and water; simmer for about 30 minutes. Blend in sour cream; thicken with remaining flour. Heat through; serve on buttered noodles. Poppy seeds are good on noodles. Serves 6-8.

Eileen MacWithey

Crêpes de Pollo

CRÊPES:

1	cup flour	½	cup water
½	teaspoon salt	4	tablespoons melted butter
½	cup skim milk	2	eggs, well beaten

FILLING:

1 (5 pound) chicken	Pepper to taste
Jalapeños to taste	4-6 ounces grated Swiss cheese, divided
3-6 whole pimientos	
1 teaspoon grated onion	½ pint heavy cream, divided
Salt to taste	Paprika, optional

CRÊPES: Mix flour and salt. Add milk, water, butter and eggs and beat until no lumps appear. Batter will be consistency of thin cream. Makes 18 crêpes.

FILLING: Cook and bone the chicken and cut the meat in small pieces. Add Jalapeños, pimientos, onion, salt, pepper and most of the Swiss cheese. Mix well and place on crêpes, rolling like an enchilada. To make a moist dish, add 1 tablespoon heavy cream to the mixture as you roll the crêpes. Place rolled crêpes in a baking dish and sprinkle more Swiss cheese over the top. Pour cream over all. Sprinkle with paprika if desired. Bake at 350⁰ for 30 minutes. Makes 18 crêpes. *Tura Bethune*

☆　　☆　　☆

Crunchy Fried Chicken

1	chicken, cut into serving pieces	1-2	teaspoons salt
		1-2	teaspoons freshly ground black pepper
Milk to cover			
¼	teaspoon Tabasco	1	pound lard
1	cup flour	1	stick butter

Put chicken pieces in a bowl and add milk to cover. Add Tabasco and stir. Refrigerate an hour or longer. Coat chicken with seasoned flour. Deep fry in lard. Drizzle with butter. Put in preheated 350⁰ oven for 10 minutes.

Hint: Secret to crunchiness is soaking the chicken in milk.

Dottie Pinch

Poultry Loaf

1	cup cooked rice	½	teaspoon salt
2	cups bread crumbs	¼	cup diced pimiento
1	cup milk	4-5	cups chicken or turkey, cooked, boned and chopped
2	cups chicken broth		
4	eggs, beaten		

Combine rice and crumbs and put in the bottom of a greased 9x4 inch loaf pan. Blend milk and broth and pour over rice and crumbs. Add eggs, salt, pimiento. Add poultry and press into loaf pan. Bake at 350⁰ for 45 minutes to 1 hour. Serve with giblet gravy. Serves 6-8.

Good for left-over turkey!   *Janna Pickering*

State Motto — The state motto of Texas is "Friendship". The word Texas, or Tejas, was the Spanish pronunciation of a Caddo Indian word meaning "friends" or "allies".

☆   ☆   ☆

Chicken Avocado

Luscious Luncheon Dish

6	boned chicken breasts	1¼	tablespoons curry powder
6	tablespoons butter	2-3	ripe avocados
2	cups mayonnaise	2	cups Cheddar or Swiss cheese, grated
2	(10¾ ounces each) cans cream of chicken soup		
½	teaspoon Spice Islands chicken stock base		

Pound chicken breasts thin and sauté for 5 minutes on each side in butter. Mix mayonnaise, soup, chicken stock base and curry powder. Heat until bubbly over low heat. Watch carefully. Slice ripe avocados on bottom of buttered casserole, lay chicken breast on top, add sauce and sprinkle with cheese. Bake at 350⁰ for 20 minutes. Serves 6.

Linda Juba

Tarragon Chicken

1	(3 pound) chicken or an equal amount of thighs or breasts	1	cup chicken stock (canned is fine)
2	teaspoons salt	1	bay leaf
1	onion, peeled and sliced	1¼	teaspoon tarragon leaves
2	tablespoons shortening	¼	teaspoon ground black pepper
3	tablespoons flour	1	cup sour cream

Wash chicken and cut into serving pieces. Season with salt. Brown chicken and onion in shortening in a Dutch oven or large heavy saucepan. Blend flour with a little of the chicken stock and add to chicken along with the remaining stock and bay leaf. Cover and simmer 25 minutes or until chicken is tender. Add tarragon leaves and black pepper and continue cooking 5 or more minutes. Stir in sour cream. Cook only until hot. Do not boil after sour cream has been added. Serve with fine noodles or rice. Citrus Avocado Salad is a good accompaniment. To make ahead, prepare up to the point of adding sour cream. Can be made the day before. Re-heat to very hot then add sour cream. Serves 4.

Lynn Townsend

☆　　☆　　☆

Herbed Chicken

Quick and Easy

2   pounds chicken thighs
    and/or breasts
½   teaspoon paprika
½   teaspoon thyme
½   teaspoon marjoram

1   teaspoon dried parsley
1   teaspoon dried onions
1   teaspoon salt
2   tablespoons lemon juice

Place chicken pieces in baking dish. Sprinkle pieces with paprika, thyme, marjoram, parsley, onions and salt. Pour lemon juice on each piece. Bake at 350⁰ approximately 45 minutes. Cover with foil for jucier chicken, or bake uncovered for crispier chicken. Serves 4.   *Peggy Jones*

Chicken in Sherry Sauce

3   whole chicken breasts,
    boned
1   teaspoon salt, divided
1   pint sour cream
1   (10¾ ounce) can cream of
    mushroom soup

3   tablespoons flour
¼   cup dry Sherry
½   cup sliced almonds

Cut chicken breasts in half after boning. Sprinkle with ½ the salt and roll each loosely. Arrange in glass casserole. Mix sour cream, flour, soup and remaining salt. Blend in Sherry and pour over the chicken. Sprinkle with almonds and paprika. Bake in preheated oven at 325⁰ for 1½ hours. Serve over hot rice. Serves 6.   *Eileen MacWithey*

Microwave Mock Fried Chicken Breasts

½   cup butter or margarine,
    melted
4   chicken breasts, boned
1   cup crushed Cheddar
    cheese crackers

1   teaspoon M.S.G., optional
1½ tablespoons taco
    seasoning mix

Melt margarine or butter for 45 seconds on FULL POWER in 8 inch round glass dish. Dip chicken in melted butter. Coat with cheese crackers, M.S.G. and taco seasoning mixture. Cook covered for 8 minutes on FULL POWER. For chicken breasts with bone-in, increase cooking time to 14 to 15 minutes. Serves 4.   *Charlye Conrey*

☆   ☆   ☆

Chicken in Orange Sauce

1 (3 pound) chicken, or equivalent in chicken breasts	⅛ teaspoon pepper
	2 tablespoons brown sugar
	½ teaspoon ginger
¼ teaspoon salt	2 cups orange juice
Paprika	2 tablespoons grated orange
1 cup butter	rind
3 tablespoons flour	

Wash chicken and dust with salt and paprika. Brown in butter. Remove and set aside. Add flour, pepper, brown sugar and ginger to make paste in leftover butter in skillet. Stir well. Add orange juice and rind and cook until thick. Pour over chicken in 9x13 baking dish. Bake at 375⁰ for 1 hour, basting occasionally. Serve over favorite rice and spoon extra orange sauce over both. To freeze reduce the baking time by ½. Cool and freeze up to a week before serving. To serve, thaw and continue baking. Serves 4.   *Vivian Brotherton*

Diet Chicken Breasts

Doesn't Taste Like Diet Food!

4 chicken breasts	¼ teaspoon curry powder or
1 (4 ounce) can mushrooms	oregano
1 chicken bouillon cube	Dash of pepper
¼ cup Sauterne	
½ teaspoon instant minced onion	

Skin chicken breasts and sprinkle with salt and paprika. Put in 9x13 inch baking pan. Drain liquid from mushrooms into saucepan. Add chicken bouillon cube. Heat and stir until dissolved. To the liquid add mushrooms, Sauterne, onion, curry or oregano and pepper. Pour over chicken. Cover with foil and bake 350⁰ for 40 minutes. Uncover and bake 20 minutes longer. Serve with juice. Serves 4.   *Barbara Eveleth*

☆   ☆   ☆

Apricot Chicken Breasts

4	whole chicken breasts	1	cup apricot preserves
4	ounces grated Swiss cheese	3	tablespoons Worcestershire
¼	cup toasted chopped almonds	1	teaspoon dry mustard, or more to taste

Skin, bone and halve chicken breasts. Cut pockets in chicken breasts with sharp knife. Combine cheese and almonds and stuff into pockets. Top with sauce made from preserves, Worcestershire and dry mustard. Bake at 325⁰ covered, 30 minutes. Uncover and bake about 30 minutes longer, basting as needed. Garnish with almonds if desired. Low calorie apricot preserves are very good. Serves 4.   *Barbara Israel*

Chicken Delight

Served at Spring Bridge Festival

3	chicken breasts, cooked and cut in small pieces	¼	teaspoon celery salt
		⅛	teaspoon pepper
1	(2 ounce) jar pimientos	2	tablespoons lemon juice
1	(8 ounce) can sliced water chestnuts	1	cup mayonnaise
		1	cup cream of chicken soup
½	cup slivered almonds	1	(3 ounce) can onion rings

Dash of M.S.G.

Mix chicken, pimiento, water chestnuts, almonds, M.S.G., celery salt, pepper, lemon juice, mayonnaise and chicken soup. Bake at 350⁰ for 30 minutes. Sprinkle with onion rings and bake another 20 minutes. Serves 4.   *Roberta Madden*

☆   ☆   ☆

Menu

RENDEZVOUS ON THE PLAZA

Pizza Fruit Platter

Chutney Cheese Ball   Assorted Crackers

Simply Super Salad

Baked Crab in Seashells

Ham Mousse   Monkey Bread

Lucy's Praline Apricot Torte

City Hall Park Plaza

Cosmopolitan dining in Texas? It's possible; it's probable. Six flags have flown over Texas; Spain, France, Mexico, The Republic of Texas, The Confederacy and The United States, and each group has contributed its culinary customs. Native Texans spice their cooking with the favorite flavors of their German, Italian, Greek, Czech, Irish and Asian neighbors. Cultures blend here in Texas where southern forests merge into midwestern plains.

At City Hall Park Plaza in downtown Dallas, you may take a lunch break and watch the peoples of the world walk by. Shown is a 27,000 pound bronze by British sculptor, Henry Moore, a bold contrast to the cantilevered façade of the unique City Hall, designed by New York architect, I. M. Pei.

In the background is Reunion Tower, named for La Reunion, the 1850's colony of French, Swiss and Belgian craftsmen who brought their arts to frontier Dallas.

Today's Metroplex residents celebrate their ethnic heritages at the Dallas International Bazaar in April and Cityfest in October at this plaza. Nearby are the Dallas Public Library, Dallas Convention Center and Memorial Auditorium, and Pioneer Cemetery, where one may stroll among the tree-shaded headstones of early Dallas settlers.

Photography
Donna Rogers

Turkey in the Bag

Cooking Oil
1   brown grocery bag
½   cup Bourbon
1   teaspoon salt
1   teaspoon pepper

1   teaspocn thyme
1   teaspoon sage
1   teaspoon paprika
1   (10 pound) turkey

Oil inside of grocery bag with cooking oil. Mix Bourbon, salt, pepper, thyme, sage and paprika. Rub mixture on turkey. Put turkey in bag and tie closed with string. Place in roasting pan and bake at 325⁰ for 2½ hours for a 10 pound bird. Bag will not hold turkey larger than 12 pounds. Serves 8.   *Pat Wilkins*

Beef Tenderloin Madeira

TENDERLOIN:
1   (5-6 pound) beef
     tenderloin
Butter as desired, melted
Salt to taste

Pepper to taste
Thyme
5-6 strips of bacon

SAUCE MADEIRA:
1   (10½ ounce) can beef
     gravy
¼   cup Madeira wine

Lemon juice, if desired

TENDERLOIN: Trim fat off tenderloin and rub well with melted butter, salt, pepper and a little thyme. Top with strips of bacon. Place on rack in roasting pan and roast at 450⁰ about 20 minutes. Remove bacon and discard. Brush with more melted butter. Reduce oven temperature to 350⁰ and return tenderloin to oven until it reaches an internal temperature of 130-135⁰. Tenderloin is best rare. Serve with Sauce Madeira.

SAUCE MADEIRA: Combine pan juices with beef gravy. Add Madeira and simmer 2 or 3 minutes. Adjust seasonings. You may add a dash of fresh lemon juice.   *Yvonne Prevo*

☆   ☆   ☆

Baked Tenderloin

1	large beef tenderloin, well skinned	1	cup red wine
2	sticks margarine	1	pound fresh mushrooms, sliced, optional
1	beef bouillon cube		

Place tenderloin in long pan (jelly-roll pan works well) and cover top and sides with softened margarine. Bake at 400° for 50 minutes. *No longer.* During last 20 minutes baste with wine with bouillon cube dissolved in it. If using mushrooms add these at last 20 minute interval also. Serve pan juices with meat. Serves 8-10.

Hint: Use meat thermometer to assure desired doneness.

Lee Williams

Beef Tenderloin a la Nancy

1	onion, chopped	¼	cup fresh parsley, finely chopped
1	clove garlic, minced		Dry red wine (preferably Burgundy)
1	stick butter		
1½	cups finely chopped fresh mushrooms	1	(4½ pound) beef tenderloin
1	(6 ounce) box seasoned croutons		

Sauté onion and garlic in butter for 3 minutes. Add mushrooms and cook for five minutes over low heat. Crush croutons in food processor or blender. Add parsley mixed with onion, garlic and mushrooms. Add enough wine to mixture to make a paste. Pat on tenderloin. Pack well around tenderloin. Preheat oven to 450°. Cook tenderloin for 30 minutes and turn off. *Don't open oven!* Let sit 30 more minutes.   *Linda Juba*

Rare Rib Roast

1   beef rib roast, any size

Let roast stand at room temperature for at least 30 minutes per pound before baking. Season with salt and pepper. Transfer the roast to a shallow baking pan, fat side up. Preheat oven. Bake uncovered 5 minutes per pound at 500° and turn off the heat. Leave the meat in the unopened oven for at least 2 hours. Roast will be crusty on the outside and rare inside (the roast may remain in the closed oven for up to 3 hours).

Elbie Guindon

☆   ☆   ☆

On and Off Prime Rib

May Be Started Several Hours Ahead.

Any size prime rib roast   Pepper to taste
Salt to taste

Remove the roast from the refrigerator 2 to 4 hours before cooking time. Place the roast in a shallow roasting pan, fat side up. Preheat oven to 375⁰. Salt and pepper roast and put in oven, uncovered, for 1 hour.

Turn off the oven, but do not open the oven door!

For rare roast beef:
    45 minutes before serving time, turn oven on at 300⁰.

For medium roast beef:
    50 minutes before serving time, turn oven on to 300⁰.

For medium well done roast beef:
    55 minutes before serving time, turn oven on to 300⁰.

That's all. But don't ever peek!   Freddi Thomson

Eye of Round

1	eye of round	1	tablespoon Accent
½	stick butter	1	cup water
1	pound carrots, sliced	2	beef bouillon cubes
4	ribs celery, sliced	1	cup white wine
2	onions, sliced	2	cups sliced fresh
1	cup Cognac or brandy		mushrooms
1	teaspoon garlic salt	½	pound Swiss cheese,
2	teaspoons Kitchen Bouquet		grated

In a large pan sear the beef in butter. Add carrots, celery and onions. Add Cognac, garlic salt, Kitchen Bouquet, Accent and water. Bake covered at 350⁰ for 3 hours. (If roast is small, 2 hours.) Remove meat. Strain juices from vegetables and add bouillon cubes. Add wine and mushrooms. Slice beef and return to pan. Cover with gravy and top with grated cheese. Bake at 350⁰ for 1 hour. Uncover pan after the first 35 minutes.

                                                              Tura Bethune

☆   ☆   ☆

Vicky's Pot Roast

A Testing Luncheon Favorite

4	pound rump or bottom round roast	2	bay leaves
Salt to taste		6	tablespoons cider vinegar
Pepper to taste		6	tablespoons dark corn syrup or 5 tablespoons molasses
Allspice to taste			
3	tablespoons salad oil	1¼	cups water, divided
2	onions, sliced	2	tablespoons flour
3	anchovy filets	1	cup whipping cream

About 3 hours before serving, sprinkle meat very generously with salt, pepper and allspice (pat on). In Dutch oven over medium-high heat, brown meat well in hot oil. Add onions, anchovy filets, bay leaves, cider vinegar, corn syrup or molasses and 1 cup water. Simmer, covered, over low heat for 2 hours or until meat is fork tender. Place meat on warm platter. Skim off excess fat and remove bay leaves. Heat liquid to boiling over medium heat. Mix ¼ cup water with flour; gradually stir into liquid; cook until smooth and thickened. Stir in cream and heat thoroughly. Do not boil. Return meat to gravy and serve. Serves 6.

Linda Cummings

Fake Charcoal Steak or Hamburger Patties

THIS REQUIRES AN IRON SKILLET. Sprinkle a thin layer of salt and some coarsley ground black pepper in skillet. Heat until salt is dark brown and skillet is smoking. Using 1 inch thick strip sirloin, T-Bone, or your choice of steak, let cook 7 minutes on one side, turn, lower heat and cook 7 to 10 minutes on other side for medium rare. Remove steak and remove skillet from heat, add ¼ cup water for delicious au jus gravy. For steaks about ½ to ¾ inch thick cook on high heat 2 minutes on each side for medium rare, 3 minutes if you desire steak "just pink."

Novella Bailey

Variation: For hamburger patties cook 4 minutes on each side. Omit au jus gravy if using on buns.

☆　　☆　　☆

Rouladen

Grey Poupon mustard
8   beef round thin sandwich
    steaks
8   slices bacon
Dill pickles
Salt to taste
Pepper to taste
Chopped onions

Margarine
Flour
Approximately ½ cup
    whipping cream
Dash of sugar
Paprika

Spread mustard on inside of steaks. Add bacon and pickles (cut in strips). Roll up and hold together with toothpick. Season with salt and pepper on outside. Slightly sauté onion in skillet, using margarine. Add meat rolls and brown uncovered for 10 minutes. Then cover and cook for about 1½ hours, until nice and brown, adding water if necessary. Thicken drippings with flour, add whipping cream, sugar, paprika and more salt and pepper to taste. Serve with potato dumplings or spaetzle and almond carrots (buttered carrots with parsley and slivered almonds). Serves 4.

Ute Schnetzinger

Pepper Steak

1   pound sirloin or round ¼
    inch thick
2   tablespoons fat
¼   cup chopped onion
1   clove garlic, halved
1   teaspoon salt
Dash of pepper
1   beef bouillon cube

1   cup hot water
1   (1 pound) can tomatoes
1   bell pepper, cut in thin
    rings
2   tablespoons cornstarch
¼   cup cold water
2   tablespoons soy sauce

Cut meat in finger sized pieces and brown slowly in hot fat, about 15 minutes. Add onion and garlic last few minutes. Season with salt and pepper. Dissolve bouillon cube in hot water; add to meat. Cover and simmer until meat is tender, 20 to 25 minutes. This may be done early in day, and refrigerated. Add tomatoes and bell pepper to meat mixture; cook 10 minutes longer. Combine cornstarch, water and soy sauce; stir into meat mixture. Bring to boil. Cook, stirring constantly, 5 minutes longer. Remove garlic and serve over hot noodles. Serves 4.

Ruth Becker

☆   ☆   ☆

Gourmet Beef Ragout

2 pounds beef chuck, shank, or round, cut in 1 inch cubes
¼ cup flour
Salt to taste
1½ teaspoons pepper
Shortening or oil to brown meat
1 clove garlic, minced
3 cups boiling water
2 cans (8 ounces each) tomato sauce
4 sprigs fresh parsley
2 bay leaves
½ teaspoon dried marjoram
½ teaspoon dried rosemary
½ teaspoon dried thyme
3 tablespoons butter or margarine
2 tablespoons sugar
8 white boiling onions
4 carrots, scraped and cut into bite-sized pieces
4 baking potatoes, pared and cut into bite-sized pieces
1 cup cooked or canned green peas, drained

Trim fat from meat and shake in a bag containing flour, salt and pepper. Cover the bottom of a Dutch oven with ¼ inch shortening, heat, and brown meat on all sides. Drain on absorbent paper. Discard any fat remaining in pan. Return meat to pan and add garlic, water and tomato sauce. Simmer, covered, 1½ to 2 hours or until meat is almost tender. Tie parsley, bay leaves and marjoram loosely in a cheese cloth bag and place in pan with meat. Melt butter or margarine and sugar in medium frying pan. Add onions and carrots and heat, stirring often until vegetables are well glazed. Add to meat mixture. Add diced potatoes; cover and cook 30 minutes longer. Add peas 5 minutes before serving. Serves 8.

Tura Bethune

Texas provides more beef than any other state, providing 12% of the national yield. Cattle herds can be seen grazing in almost all of Texas' 254 counties. Raising beef is the largest agricultural operation in the state.

☆   ☆   ☆

Parsley Steak Rolls

½ pound fresh mushrooms
2 pounds top round steak, pounded to tenderize and cut into 6 pieces, ¼ inch thick
1 cup chopped parsley
¾ cup chopped onion
1 cup grated Parmesan cheese

Salt to taste
Pepper to taste
2 tablespoons vegetable cooking oil
1 beef bouillon cube
½ cup water
2 tablespoons cornstarch
½ cup water

Reserve mushroom crowns, chop stems and sprinkle over steak together with parsley, onions and cheese. Roll and fasten with toothpicks and lace with string. Brown slowly in oil. Add mushroom crowns. Dissolve bouillon cube in water. Add to steak. Bake at 350⁰ for 1 hour and 15 minutes. Remove meat rolls. Combine cornstarch and water and add to gravy. Cook until thick. Remove string and toothpicks. Pour gravy over meat and serve. Garnish with parsley. Serves 6. *Novella Bailey*

Beef and Brew Pie

STEW:
2 pounds stew meat
¼ cup flour
¼ cup oil
1 (12 ounce) can beer
2½ teaspoons salt
¼ teaspoon pepper
2 cloves garlic

1 bay leaf
1 (20 ounce) bag frozen onions
1 (10 ounce) package frozen lima beans
1 egg yolk

PASTRY:
5 cups flour
2½ teaspoons salt

2¼ cups shortening
¾-1 cup water

STEW: Coat beef with flour and brown in oil. Return all meat to skillet. Add beer, salt, pepper, garlic and bay leaf. Simmer covered 2 hours. Discard bay leaf. Add onions and beans. Spoon into 2 quart casserole. Preheat oven to 400⁰. Fit pastry loosely over meat. Trim and make a rope edge. Beat egg yolk with 1 teaspoon water. Brush pastry and slit crust. Bake 40 minutes.

PASTRY: Stir flour with salt. Cut in shortening until coarse crumbs. Sprinkle with water, 1 tablespoon at a time. Mix with fork until it holds together. Form ball; then roll 2 inches larger than dish. Serves 6-8.
Susann Deppe

Baked Beef and Beer

⅓	cup butter	3	tablespoons brown sugar
3	pounds chuck steak, cut into 1 inch cubes	1½	tablespoons minced parsley
3	cups chopped onion	2	bay leaves
1½	cloves garlic, minced	1½	teaspoons thyme
½	cup flour		Salt to taste
1	(12 ounce can) beer		Pepper to taste
1½	cups beef consommé		

Melt butter in large skillet. Add steak, onions and garlic and brown. Add flour, mixing well to coat all ingredients. Pour beer and consommé over meat mixture. Add brown sugar, parsley, bay leaves, thyme, salt and pepper. Cook covered in 300° oven until meat is tender; about 3 hours. If sauce becomes too thick dissolve a bouillon cube in cup of water and add as needed. Serves 6. May be prepared ahead and frozen. Bring to room temperature and reheat on top of stove. Good served with buttered noodles. Serves 6. *Vivian Jackson*

Ruben Casserole

1	(11 ounce) can sauerkraut	8	ounces Swiss cheese, shredded
2	tomatoes, sliced		
2	tablespoons butter	12	slices small party rye bread
2	tablespoons Thousand Island Dressing		
1	(8 ounce) can corned beef, shredded		

Spread drained sauerkraut in 8x12 dish. Top with tomato slices. Dot with butter and dressing. Cover with corned beef. Sprinkle with cheese. Bake at 425° for 15 minutes. Remove casserole from oven. Butter rye bread and place buttered side up over top of pan. Return to oven and bake for 15 to 20 minutes longer. Serves 6-8. *Virginia Suttle*

☆　　☆　　☆

Beef Tips on Rice

1½ pounds boneless round or
stew meat, cut in small
cubes
Flour to dredge meat
6 tablespoons shortening
¼ cup flour
1 (4 ounce) can mushrooms

2 cups boiling water or
stock
Salt to taste
Pepper to taste
Worcestershire, optional
1 cup sour cream, optional

Flour meat and brown in hot shortening. Remove meat. Reserve ¼ cup drippings and make a roux with ¼ cup flour. Add mushrooms and liquid, stock, salt, pepper and Worcestershire. Cook until thick. Stir constantly. Return meat to skillet and simmer, covered until fork tender or bake in covered casserole at 300⁰. If gravy is too thin, remove cover and cook down. Serve over fluffy rice. Add sour cream just before serving. Serves 6.

We also like this with cooked noodles with toasted sesame seeds.
Irene Howland

Beef Stroganoff

12 pounds Sirloin
Flour
Salt to taste
Pepper to taste
2 pounds mushrooms
2 onions

2 pounds margarine
4 (10 ounces each) cans
bouillon
Tabasco
2 quarts sour cream
½ cup lemon juice

Cut beef in desired bite size, dredge in flour, salt, and pepper. Brown meat in margarine reserving one stick. Sauté onions and mushrooms in a separate skillet beginning with onions and cooking until light golden color adding mushrooms for the last 3 minutes. Add bouillon, salt, pepper, Tabasco, and simmer for 30 minutes. Add meat and sour cream, the amount used is a matter of individual taste. If the mixture becomes too thick, add more bouillon. Five minutes before serving add the lemon juice. Serves 32-36.
Tura Bethune

☆   ☆   ☆

Cheesy Ground Beef Casserole

1	(8 ounce) package medium egg noodles	1	teaspoon salt
½	cup chopped green onion, divided	⅛	teaspoon pepper
		1	cup small curd cottage cheese
2	tablespoons butter or margarine	1	(8 ounce) carton sour cream
1½	pounds ground beef	3	ounces grated sharp cheese, about ¾ cup
2	(8 ounces each) cans tomato sauce		

Cook noodles according to package directions; rinse well and set aside. Sauté ¼ cup onion in butter in a large skillet until tender. Add beef and cook until browned. Drain well. Add tomato sauce, salt and pepper. Stir well and simmer 20 minutes. Combine cottage cheese, sour cream and remaining onion. Mix well and set aside. Place noodles in lightly greased 2½ quart casserole. Spoon cottage cheese mixture over noodles. Pour meat mixture over cheese mixture and sprinkle with grated cheese. Bake at 350⁰ for 25 minutes. Serves 4-6.

I cook a 12 ounce package of noodles, double the rest of this recipe and make three 2 quart casseroles. Cook one and freeze the other two. Thaw completely before baking. This size serves 4. Charleye Conrey

Bavarian Meat Loaf

MEAT LOAF:

1	pound ground pork	1	cup sour cream
1	pound ground beef (2 pounds beef)	1	teaspoon salt
			Pepper to taste
1	cup shredded carrots		Onion salt to taste
1	cup crushed saltine crackers (about 22)		

SAUCE:

1	bouillon cube	1	(3 ounce) can mushrooms
½	cup sour cream	1	tablespoon flour

Mix meats with carrots, crackers, sour cream, salt, pepper and onion salt. Put in a 9x5x3 inch loaf pan and bake 1½ hours at 350⁰. Let stand 10 minutes before serving. Meanwhile, pour the meat dripping into a saucepan and add bouillon cube, sour cream, mushrooms and liquid. Blend with flour. Heat sauce and pour over meat loaf or serve on side. Serves 6. Ute Schnetzinger

☆　　☆　　☆

Company Meat Loaf

Expensive, but worth it

MEAT LOAF:

1	pound ground sirloin	2	green onions, finely chopped
1	pound ground beef		
1	pound ground veal	6	soda crackers, crumbled
2	teaspoons salt	1	teaspoon soy sauce
¼	teaspoon black pepper	1	teaspoon Worcestershire
Dash of garlic powder		2	eggs, lightly beaten
¼	cup chopped parsley	1¼	cups milk
2	ribs celery, finely chopped		

TOPPING:

Ketchup   3-4 slices bacon

VEGETABLES:

6-8 potatoes   1   bell pepper

MEAT LOAF: Combine meats, salt, pepper, garlic powder, parsley, celery, onions, soda crackers, soy sauce, Worcestershire, eggs and milk. Add more milk if texture is too stiff. Shape into loaf. Place in 9x13x2 inch glass pan.

TOPPING: Cover top with ketchup and 3-4 slices of bacon.

VEGETABLES: Surround meat loaf with 6-8 pared whole potatoes and 1 sliced bell pepper. Cover with foil. Bake at 325° for 1½ hours. Serves 8.

Marge Veerman

Meat Loaf

6	slices of bread, divided	2	teaspoons Worcestershire
½	cup milk	1	onion, chopped
2	pounds lean hamburger	1	(8 ounce) can tomato
2	eggs, beaten		sauce
1	teaspoon salt		

Soak 4 bread slices in the milk in a large mixing bowl. Add more milk if necessary to make the bread rather soggy. Tear the bread apart into small pieces. Add meat, eggs, salt, Worcestershire and onion and mix well with your hands, as in making bread. Line an ovenproof skillet with foil. Place two slices of bread end-to-end in the center of the pan. Shape meat loaf to fit over the bread slices. Depress the loaf slightly at top along the center. Pour tomato sauce over the top. Bakes at 350° about 1 hour. Serve with potatoes baked in the oven with with the meat loaf. Serves 6.

Peggy Jones

☆   ☆   ☆

Italian Meat Loaf

2	slices rye bread	1	teaspoon salt
2	slices white bread	¼	teaspoon pepper
1	pound ground beef	2	tablespoons butter
1	onion, chopped	1	(8 ounce) can tomato
4	sprigs parsley		sauce
3	tablespoons Parmesan	1	teaspoon oregano
	cheese, grated		(optional)
1	egg, slightly beaten		

Put both kinds of bread in mixing bowl. Pour 1 cup water over and let soak a few minutes; then mash fine with fork. Add meat to bread along with onion, parsley, cheese, egg, salt and pepper. Mix together and shape into loaf and put into 8½ inch loaf pan. Put dots of butter over top and bake for 30 minutes at 375⁰. Pour tomato sauce over loaf and sprinkle with oregano. Bake 20 minutes longer. Serves 4.   *Dorothy Carr*

Pizza Meat Loaf

Children and Adults Love This!

1	onion, chopped	1	egg, slightly beaten
1	tablespoon butter	1	teaspoon salt
½	cup Pepperidge Farm herb	1	teaspoon pepper
	stuffing mix	1	tablespoon butter
½	cup bouillon	1	(8 ounce) can tomato
1	pound lean ground beef		sauce
4	sprigs chopped parsley	1	teaspoon oregano
3	tablespoons grated		
	Parmesan cheese		

Sauté onion in butter. In large bowl mix herb stuffing and bouillon. Add onion, beef, parsley, cheese, egg, salt and pepper. Blend: form a loaf. Dot with butter. Bake 30 minutes at 375⁰. Drain. Pour tomato sauce over meat and sprinkle with oregano. Bake 20 minutes longer. Serves 4.

Microwave 20 minutes at ⅔ POWER. Drain. Add tomato sauce and oregano. Microwave 3 minutes at ⅔ POWER. Let stand 5 to 10 minutes.
          Ivanette Dennis

☆   ☆   ☆

Stuffed Peppers with Cheese Sauce

1	pound ground chuck	1	(10¾ ounce) can condensed cream of chicken soup
2	bell peppers		
2	tablespoons butter or margarine	½	soup can water
1	onion, chopped	1	cup grated American or mild Cheddar cheese
½	cup chopped celery		
¾	cup cooked rice	1	teaspoon Worcestershire
1	teaspoon salt	1	teaspoon curry powder or more to taste
¼	teaspoon pepper		

Cut bell peppers in half, remove seeds. Place in boiling water, remove from fire, let poach for 5 minutes. Drain. Place in buttered 7½x12x1¾ inch casserole. Heat butter in heavy skillet; add meat, onions, celery. Stir with fork, breaking meat in small pieces. Cook until brown. Add rice, salt and pepper. Spoon over pepper halves in buttered casserole. Heat soup with ½ soup can water. Stir until smooth. Add cheese, Worcestershire and curry powder. Stir over low heat until cheese melts. Pour cheese sauce over meat and peppers. Bake at 350⁰ for 30 to 40 minutes. Serves 4. *Dorthy Watkins*

Pizza Burger

1½-2 pounds ground beef		2	teaspoons oregano
1	pound Velveeta cheese, cubed	½	teaspoon salt or onion salt
1	(10¾ ounce) can tomato soup		

Brown ground beef and drain well. Add cheese, soup, oregano and salt. Spread thinly on hamburger buns and broil until bubbly. Meat mixture freezes well. *Kay Wunderlich*

☆   ☆   ☆

Beef Bologna

2	pounds ground beef	1½	teaspoons liquid smoke
1	cup water	½	teaspoon onion powder
2	tablespoons Morton Tender Quick	1½	teaspoons garlic salt

Mix all ingredients. Roll into 2 rolls. Wrap in Saran, wax paper, or foil and refrigerate for 24 hours. Bake on broiler pan at 350° for 1½ hours. Top with barbecue sauce before baking. Recipe doubles easily. Freezes well. *Anne Eppright*

Beef Salami

5	pounds hamburger meat (do not use extra lean)	2½	teaspoons black pepper
5	teaspoons curing salt	2½	teaspoons garlic salt
2½	teaspoons mustard seed	1	teaspoon hickory smoke sauce

Mix all ingredients. Let stand covered in refrigerator for 3 days. Mix well with hands once or twice. Form into 5 rolls. Bake on broiler pan for 5 hours at 225°. Turn once after 2½ hours. Freezes well.
Anne Eppright

Beer Marinade for Steaks

1	(12 ounce) can beer	1	tablespoon parsley
⅓	cup peanut oil	1	tablespoon basil
1	onion, chopped	½	teaspoon salt
1	clove garlic, crushed	½	teaspoon pepper
3	tablespoons honey		

Combine all ingredients in a glass dish large enough to hold the steak. Score the meat and marinate 12 hours. Use for round steak, flank steak or brisket. Serves 4-6. *Martee Bethune Benton*

☆　　☆　　☆

Beef Shish Kebab Marinade

⅓ cup red wine vinegar
½ cup soy sauce
3 tablespoons oil

1 tablespoon instant minced onions

Marinate meat in above mixture for several hours or overnight.
Maggie Pearce

Coe's Steak Marinade

1 jigger vodka
½ cup soy sauce
½ cup salad oil
½ cup water
½ teaspoon ginger

½ teaspoon sugar
½ teaspoon Accent
2 cloves garlic, slightly bruised
Pepper to taste

Combine all ingredients together and shake well. Marinate several hours or overnight. If desired, baste with marinade the last few minutes of cooking time.
Tura Bethune

Country Pork Chops

6 pork chops 1 inch thick
Salt to taste
Pepper to taste
½ cup finely diced carrot
½ cup finely diced celery
¼ cup finely diced onion

½ cup beef stock
½ cup tomato sauce
2 tablespoons mustard
2 teaspoons Worcestershire
Chopped parsley

Season chops with salt and pepper and brown on both sides. Sprinkle carrot, celery and onion in a shallow 2 quart casserole. Arrange pork chops on top. Pour off excess fat from skillet. Add stock, tomato sauce, mustard and Worcestershire to skillet. Blend. Pour over chops; cover. Bake 50 minutes at 350⁰. Remove cover and continue baking 15 minutes. Sprinkle with chopped parsley. Serves 4-6.
Betty Gibson

☆　　☆　　☆

Sausage Crêpes

CRÊPES:

3	eggs, beaten	1	cup flour
1	cup milk	1	tablespoon fines herbes
1	tablespoon cooking oil	½	teaspoon salt

SAUSAGE FILLING:

1	pound bulk sausage	1	(3 ounce) package cream
¼	cup chopped onion		cheese
½	cup shredded cheese	¼	teaspoon marjoram

TOPPING:

Cream of mushroom soup, undiluted   Sour cream

CRÊPES: Combine eggs, milk and oil. Add flour, fines herbes and salt. Beat until smooth. Pour 2 tablespoons batter in greased 6 inch skillet (or dip in crêpe pan). Cook on 1 side. Cool between paper toweling.

FILLING: Brown sausage and onion and drain. Add cheese, cream cheese and marjoram.

Place 2 tablespoons sausage filling on unbrowned center of each crêpe; roll up. Freeze or place in baking dish. Cover and chill. Top with equal parts cream of mushroom soup and sour cream. Bake uncovered at 350⁰ for approximately 40 minutes. Serves 8-10.   *Jean Zinser*

Sausage Bake

Tour of Homes Recipe

1	pound bulk sausage	¾	cup sugar
1-2	tart apples, peeled and sliced	1	tablespoon butter
		1	tablespoon flour

Put layer of sausage in baking dish. Cover with layer of apples. Blend sugar, butter and flour together to make crumb mixture and cover apples. Bake about 1 hour at 375⁰. Drain the juice several times during baking. This is a yummy winter time dish for brunch.

☆   ☆   ☆

Basic Italian Tomato Sauce

1	onion, chopped	1	cup sugar
3	ribs of celery, diced	1	rounded tablespoon
4	cloves of garlic, minced		baking soda
2	tablespoons oil	Water	
Salt to taste		6	lean pork chops
Pepper to taste		6	hard-cooked eggs,
2	(12 ounces each) cans		chopped
	tomato paste		

In a large pan sauté onion, celery and garlic in oil. Add salt and pepper to taste. When vegetables are brown, add the tomato paste, blend well and continue cooking at medium heat. Add sugar and soda (the soda will make the paste bubble and neutralize the acid in the tomato) and allow the mixture to cook for 20 minutes. In large pot add 4 cans (from the tomato paste) of water and add salt and pepper to taste. Blend the vegetable mixture with the water, bring to a boil and then reduce to medium heat. In a separate skillet brown the pork chops, drain well and add to the sauce. Add the eggs after the sauce has thickened and continue cooking on medium-low heat for 1½ to 2 hours. Cook pasta, add sauce and serve the pork and eggs on the side.

Variation: Any browned meat or poultry can be added to the basic sauce recipe.   *Debra MacWithey*

HINTS FOR PASTA:
Add 1 tablespoon oil to pasta while cooking to prevent sticking.

Adding cold water to pot after pasta is done will stop cooking process plus reduce starchiness. (Stir in with boiling water.)

After pasta is cooked and drained return to pot and add 1 or 2 cups sauce and mix. This will make pasta less sticky and keep until ready to serve.

In some Italian families very fine browned breadcrumbs mixed with sugar are sprinkled on top of pasta instead of grated cheese.

Debra MacWithey

☆   ☆   ☆

Wild Rice Pork Chops

1	cup wild rice	1	teaspoon sage
1	onion, chopped, divided	1	teaspoon parsley
6	pork chops	1	teaspoon sugar
½	bell pepper, diced		Salt to taste
4	slices bacon, diced		Pepper to taste
1	(10¾ ounce) can cream of chicken soup		

Cook rice and ½ onion. Cover with water 1 inch above rice in pan. Cover and bring to boil; simmer 20 minutes. Brown pork chops and set aside. Sauté ½ onion, bell pepper and bacon. Add undrained rice and mix. Place in greased 9x13 pan. Add soup, sage, parsley, sugar, salt and pepper. Place pork chops on top. Bake 1 hour at 325⁰. Add water if needed. Serves 6.   *Marjo Jeanes*

Pork and Sauerkraut Casserole

2	pounds pork shoulder, cut in 1½ inch pieces	1	(27 ounce) can sauerkraut, well drained
2	tablespoons oil	2	red apples, cut in 1½ inch pieces
1	cup water	½	cup apple juice
1	cup sliced carrots	2	tablespoons chopped parsley
1	onion, chopped		
1	tablespoon salt	1	tablespoon light brown sugar
1	bay leaf		
¼	teaspoon pepper		

Heat oil in Dutch oven over medium high heat. Brown pork well on all sides; then add water, carrots, onion, salt, bay leaf and pepper. Reduce heat to low; simmer, covered, 1½ hours or until meat is fork tender. Add sauerkraut, apples, apple juice, chopped parsley and brown sugar. Cook covered, 15 minutes more or until apples are tender and sauerkraut is heated through. Serve on warm, large platter. Serves 6-8.

Ruth Holzschuh

☆   ☆   ☆

Clark Gable's Pork Tenderloin

1   (32 ounce) bottle ketchup
½   cup mustard
½   cup brown sugar

4   (1 foot long) pork
     tenderloins

Mix ketchup, brown sugar and mustard. Pour over tenderloins, wrap in foil and bake at 275° for 2½ hours. Cool and slice very thin. Serve with small rolls or biscuits. Good party fare. Serves 50 or more for a cocktail buffet.   *Marge Grogg*

Roast Pork Loin Dijon

4   pound pork loin or rib
     roast
Syrup from spiced apples

Garnish: hot spiced apples
Parsley

DIJON SPREAD:
3   tablespoons lemon juice
2   tablespoons Dijon mustard
1   teaspoon salt

½   teaspoon powdered ginger
½   teaspoon onion salt or
     garlic salt

Place meat in open shallow roaster, fat side up. Combine lemon juice, Dijon mustard, salt, ginger, and garlic salt and spoon Dijon spread over meat. Roast at 325° for 40 minutes per pound. After first hour of roasting, baste frequently with apple syrup. Garnish with hot sliced apples and fresh parsley. Serves 6.   *Lynn Trenthan*

Ham and Green Noodle Casserole

2   cups (6 ounces) green
     noodles
1   (10¾ ounce) can cheese
     soup
1   cup sour cream
1½   cups diced ham

1   (2 ounce) can sliced
     mushrooms, drained
½   teaspoon dry mustard
½   teaspoon pepper
1   cup sharp Cheddar cheese,
     grated

Cook noodles slightly and drain. Heat soup and blend with sour cream. Add noodles, ham, mushrooms, dry mustard and pepper. Place in shallow, 2½ quart baking dish. Sprinkle cheese over top. Bake at 350° for about 25 minutes. Serves 10. Especially good with Flora's Slaw. (see index)   *Flora Anderson*

☆   ☆   ☆

Ham Rolls with Mornay Sauce

HAM ROLLS:

2   (6 ounces each) boxes
    Uncle Ben's long grain and
    wild rice with seasoning
    mix

1   cup sliced celery
1   cup seedless raisins
2   eggs, beaten
24-36 slices Danish ham

MORNAY SAUCE:

1   stick butter
1   cup flour
½   can beer

4   cups milk
1   pound Velveeta cheese or
    more if desired

HAM ROLLS: Cook both packages of rice, but use only one package of seasoning mix. Cool until warm. Add celery, raisins and eggs. Stir. Place 3 tablespoons mixture on each slice of ham. Roll. Place seam side down. (May be frozen at this point). About 30 minutes before baking (ham rolls should be at room temperature) cover with Mornay sauce. Bake at 350⁰ for 30 minutes or until bubbly. Serves 12.

MORNAY SAUCE: Melt butter. Add flour, beer and milk. Stir until thick. Add cheese and heat until cheese is melted. Serves 12.

Jean Zinser

Cecilia's Croquettes

1½ cups cooked white fish,
    ham, chicken, tuna or
    pork
1   stick of butter or
    margarine
1   onion, finely chopped
1   cup of milk

5   tablespoons flour
2   eggs, divided
Salt to taste
Pepper to taste
Finely chopped hot peppers
    or Tabasco to taste
Bread crumbs

Sauté onion in butter; add flour and slowly pour in milk, stirring constantly. Remove from heat. Cool; then add egg and fish mixture. Chill for 2 or 3 hours; then form croquettes. Dip in beaten egg and roll in bread crumbs. Fry immediately or freeze. Serves 6.

Variation: Make into small balls; then fry and serve hot as an hors d'oeuvre.

Tura Bethune

☆   ☆   ☆

Ham Noodle Bake

3   cups cooked noodles
1½ cups diced cooked ham
1   (1¼ ounce) package sour
     cream mix
1   cup milk

1½ cup chopped olives, ripe
     or green
⅓   cup dry wine
Bread crumbs

Cook noodles as package directs, drain and mix well with ham, sour cream mix, milk, olives and wine. Pour into 1½ quart baking dish. Sprinkle with bread crumbs. Bake at 350⁰ for 30 minutes.

Chris Norman

Party Ham Dinner

10 pounds potatoes
4-5 pounds cooked ham

1   pound processed cheese
1½ pints whipping cream

Boil potatoes in jackets until tender. Cool. Peel and dice. Dice ham and cheese. Arrange in large buttered pan or roaster alternating layers of potatoes, ham and cheese. Pour cream over all. Bake 1½ to 2 hours in 325⁰ oven. Stir occasionally. Serves 35.

Florence Whiting

Veal Veronese

2   pounds veal scallopine (cut
     in 2 inch square scallops)
¼   cup flour
¾   teaspoon salt
⅛   teaspoon white pepper
6   tablespoons butter

1   clove garlic, minced
½   pound fresh mushrooms,
     sliced
¾   cup white wine
1   teaspoon parsley, chopped

Dredge veal in flour seasoned with salt and white pepper. Heat butter in skillet; add veal and garlic and brown lightly on both sides. Reduce heat; add mushrooms and wine, mixing well with pan juices. Cover and simmer 5 minutes. Season to taste and sprinkle with parsley. Serve with lemon wedges. Serves 6.

Lynn Trentham

☆   ☆   ☆

Veal and Bell Peppers

1	onion, chopped	1	(16 ounce) can tomatoes
2-3	bell peppers, seeded and		and liquid
	sliced	½	cup dry white wine
1	tablespoon margarine		Salt to taste
1	pound veal stew meat		White pepper if desired
1	tablespoon bacon		
	drippings or oil		

Sauté onion and sliced peppers in margarine until soft. Remove from skillet and set aside. Brown veal in bacon drippings. Return onion and peppers to skillet and add tomatoes, wine, salt and pepper. Simmer covered until veal is desired doneness, about 15 to 20 minutes. Taste to check for seasonings. Serve over white rice. Serves 4.

Variation: Substitute 2-3 cups left-over veal roast. Do not brown veal. Simmer only until well heated. *Ivanette Dennis*

Variation: Use scallopine and reduce cooking time to 5 minutes.
Lynn Trentham

Veal Foyot

2	pounds veal scallopini	½	cup bread crumbs
½	teaspoon salt	½	cup grated Swiss cheese
¼	teaspoon ground pepper	½	cup dry white wine
1	tablespoon butter	3	tablespoons melted butter
½	cup chopped onion		

Salt and pepper veal pieces. Heat butter in small heavy skillet. Add onions and cook until golden. In a bowl, combine bread crumbs and Swiss cheese. Spread 1 tablespoon cooked onions on one side of each piece of veal. Cover with crumb and cheese mixture. Press mixture with flat side of a knife to make it stick to veal. Sprinkle remaining onions in oven-proof dish (large enough to hold all veal pieces.) Place veal in dish without overlapping. Add wine and cover veal with melted butter. Bake uncovered for 30 minutes at 350⁰, basting occasionally with juices from pan. Serves 4. *Valerie McMahan*

☆   ☆   ☆

Veal Daube

1	(4-5 pound) veal rump or shoulder roast	¼	teaspoon allspice
3	tablespoons bacon drippings, divided	¼	teaspoon thyme
		¼	teaspoon sage
⅛	teaspoon dried red pepper flakes	2	bay leaves, crushed
		¼	cup flour
1	clove garlic, minced	1	onion, minced
1	teaspoon salt	4	carrots, sliced
⅛	teaspoon black pepper	2	turnips, diced
⅛	teaspoon mace	1	bell pepper, diced
⅛	teaspoon ground cloves	1	cup boiling water

Mix 1 tablespoon bacon drippings with red pepper and garlic and rub into roast. Combine salt, pepper, mace, cloves and allspice and sprinkle the roast with this mixture. Then rub into the roast a mixture of thyme, sage, bay leaves and flour. Brown the roast in 2 tablespoons bacon drippings. Remove roast and brown prepared vegetables in drippings. Add the roast and boiling water. Cover and simmer until tender about 2 to 2½ hours. Serve with natural gravy or thicken with flour if desired. Serves 8.

Use leftovers in veal and bell peppers. (see index)   *Ivanette Dennis*

Marinated Leg of Lamb

1	(5-6 pound) leg of lamb	½	cup finely chopped parsley
2	teaspoons seasoned salt	¼	cup wine vinegar
1	clove garlic, minced	¼	cup olive or salad oil
1	cup coarsely chopped onion		

Dry leg of lamb with paper towel. Rub well with seasoned salt and place in large bowl. Combine garlic, onion, parsley, vinegar and oil; pour over leg of lamb. Let sit at least 2 hours, turning occasionally. Place in roasting pan, reserving marinade for basting. Roast in 325° oven, basting frequently. Allow 30 minutes roasting time per pound for medium done; 18 minutes for "pinky" rare. Leg of lamb may be marinated overnight in refrigerator. If this is done, let stand ½ hour at room temperature before roasting. Serves 8.   *Lynn Trentham*

☆   ☆   ☆

Shish Kebabs

MARINADE:

1	cup Viva or Italian dressing
1	clove garlic, minced
2-3	tablespoons wine vinegar
1½	pounds lean lamb cut in cubes

½	teaspoon oregano, crumbled
3-4	sprigs Italian parsley

VEGETABLES:

Cherry tomatoes
Boiling-size onions

Bell peppers
Mushrooms

MARINADE: Combine dressing, garlic, wine vinegar, oregano and Italian parsley. Add lamb and marinate 6 to 8 hours or overnight.

VEGETABLES: Bell pepper chunks and onions need to be parboiled separately until amost done.

Thread lamb alternately with desired vegetables on skewers and broil over charcoal or in a broiler about 16 minutes for medium or until lamb is desired doneness. May baste with marinade. Serves 4-6.

Judy Duncan

Lamb Shanks

Lamb shanks
1   package Lipton Onion
      Soup Mix

Place lamb shanks on big squares of aluminum foil. Sprinkle shanks with ½ package of soup mix. (Be sure soup mix is blended) Securely wrap shanks, place on cookie sheet and bake in 325⁰ oven for 2 hours or until very tender.   *Peggy Thorburn*

☆   ☆   ☆

Far East Leg of Lamb

Leg of lamb (no more than
6 pounds)
½ cup yogurt
2   tablespoons grated fresh
ginger
3   cloves garlic, crushed
1½ teaspoons salt
¼   teaspoon black pepper

Juice of 1 lime or ½ lemon
1   tablespoon ground
coriander
¼   teaspoon cayenne pepper
½   teaspoon ground cloves
½   teaspoon cinnamon
½   teaspoon ground
cardamon

Make several gashes in lamb. Mix yogurt with fresh ginger, garlic, salt, pepper and lime or lemon juice. Spread over lamb. Marinate 2 hours or longer. Mix coriander, cayenne pepper, cloves, cinnamon and cardamon and heat over moderate heat. Cool and sprinkle over lamb.

Roast at 325⁰ for 2½ hours or until roast is medium rare. Add water ½ cup at a time if juices evaporate. Remove roast to serving platter. Add small amount of water to pan if needed, cover and simmer over high heat for 2 minutes. Scrape sides and bottom of pan, and pour juices over roast. Serves 6-8.   *Ruth Dirks*

Joan Bennett's Leg of Lamb

1   (6-8 pound) leg of spring
lamb
1   clove garlic, crushed
2   teaspoons dried ginger
1   onion, grated
Freshly ground pepper

2   teaspoons Lawry's
seasoned salt
1   teaspoon paprika
2   tablespoons olive oil
Juice of 1 lemon

Mix garlic, ginger, onion, pepper, seasoned salt, paprika, olive oil and lemon juice together until they form a paste. Spread paste all over lamb and let it stay at room temperature for 2 hours or more. Preheat oven to 350⁰. Place lamb in open roasting pan and cook for 15 minutes per pound. Lamb will be rare. Roast 30 minutes per pound for medium, 18 minutes per pound for "pink". For well done lamb roast at 325⁰ for 2½ hours for a 4½-5 pound leg. Best with fresh green beans, new potatoes and green salad. You may serve with a sauce of ½ cup mint jelly melted with 2 tablespoons butter. Serves 6 to 8. Use leftovers in Lamb with White Wine (see index).   *Ivanette Dennis*

☆   ☆   ☆

Lamb with White Wine

Delicious Leftovers!

¼ cup flour	½ stick butter
1 teaspoon salt	2 cups diced cooked lamb
Pepper to taste	¼ teaspoon marjoram,
½ cup milk	optional
1 cup beef bouillon	½ cup dry white wine
¼ pound fresh mushrooms, sliced or 1 (4½ ounce) jar mushrooms	

Mix flour with salt and pepper. Reserve. Combine milk and bouillon. Reserve. Sauté mushrooms in butter. As soon as the mushrooms begin to brown, sprinkle with seasoned flour and stir. Add milk mixture. Cook, stirring constantly, until thickened. Add lamb, marjoram and wine. Cover and simmer 5 minutes or until hot. Serve on hot spinach noodles. Serves 4.   *Ivanette Dennis*

Asparagus Egg Casserole

3 cans (16 ounces each) asparagus tips	⅛-¼ teaspoon freshly grated nutmeg
6 tablespoons butter	½ cup heavy cream
6 tablespoons flour	12 hard-cooked eggs
2 cups milk	1 (2 ounce) jar chopped
¼ cup asparagus liquid	pimiento
¾ teaspoon salt	Buttered bread crumbs
¼ teaspoon white pepper	Parmesan cheese

Drain asparagus, reserve juice. Make white sauce (see index) with butter, flour, milk and asparagus liquid. Cook until thickened. Season with salt, pepper and nutmeg. Add cream. Heat. Cover bottom of 9x13 glass dish with asparagus. Top with sliced eggs. Add pimientos. Pour sauce over top. Sprinkle with buttered bread crumbs and parmesan cheese. Bake at 350⁰ until hot and bubbly, about 20 minutes. Serves 8.

Hazel Wise

☆   ☆   ☆

Asparagus and Pea Casserole

3	cups saltine cracker crumbs	1	(15½ ounce) can asparagus
2	sticks margarine, melted	1	(15½ ounce) can green peas
1	stick butter		
6	tablespoons flour	2	(4 ounces each) cans sliced mushrooms
3	cups milk		
¼	pound Old English cheese, grated		

Combine crumbs and melted margarine. Reserve. Make a white sauce of butter, flour and milk, (see index). Add grated cheese and reserve. Drain vegetables and layer asparagus, peas and mushrooms in a buttered 8x11 baking casserole. Pour sauce over all. Top with crumb mixture. Bake at 450⁰ for 10 to 15 minutes. Serves 8.   *Joyce Jenkins*

Ham Hock and Red Beans

New Orleans Special

Hot peppers to taste		1	tablespoon chili powder
1	bell pepper, chopped	2	tablespoons salt
2	onions, chopped	1	teaspoon pepper
Ham hock		2	garlic cloves, minced
2	pounds red pinto beans		

Combine all ingredients. Boil in enough water to cover for several hours. Add water as needed. Good served with spoonful of cooked rice. Serves 10-12.

I have used this recipe many times for large groups at backyard parties with barbecue or hamburgers. It's also good with baked ham.

Frances Falkner

Orange Beets

12	beets	2	tablespoons cornstarch
2	tablespoons butter	2	cups orange juice
¼	cup lemon juice	Dash of salt	
¼	cup sugar		

Cook, peel and slice beets. Combine butter, lemon juice, sugar, cornstarch, orange juice and salt and cook over medium heat until slightly thick. Pour sauce over hot, sliced beets. Serves 6.   *Nancy Brown*

☆   ☆   ☆

Beets Bengali

2	(1 pound each) cans whole beets	2	ribs celery, chopped
2	cups white vingegar	2	tablespoons chopped preserved ginger
2	tablespoons sugar	2	tablespoons lemon juice
1	onion, sliced	1	teaspoon dry mustard
8	water chestnuts, drained and chopped	1	cup mayonnaise
		1	teaspoon curry powder

Drain beets. Add vinegar, sugar and onion. Bring to boil, lower heat and simmer 5 minutes. Cool; then refrigerate until chilled. Drain beets. Discard liquid. Cut out center; then scrape with spoon to make hollow. Chop beet centers and combine with water chestnuts, celery, ginger, lemon juice, mustard, mayonnaise and curry powder. Stuff beets.

Variation: Also good with plain canned beets. Omit pickling.

Novella Bailey

Broccoli Pecan Casserole

2	(10 ounces each) packages frozen chopped broccoli	1	onion, chopped or 1½ teaspoons instant onion flakes
1	(10¾ ounce) can cream of mushroom soup	¼	cup melted butter
1	cup mayonnaise	2	cups bread crumbs
¾	cup chopped pecans	1	cup grated sharp cheese
2	eggs, well beaten		

Cook broccoli according to package directions and drain. Stir in soup, mayonnaise and pecans. Add eggs and onions; mix well. Pour into a greased 8 x 13 casserole. Toss bread crumbs with melted butter and sprinkle buttered crumbs over top of casserole. Bake at 350⁰ for 20 minutes. Add cheese and bake 10 minutes longer. Serves 8.

Marge Grogg

☆   ☆   ☆

Wild Rice Broccoli Bake

1	(6 ounce) package long grain & wild rice	3	tablespoons flour
1	cup sliced celery	¼	teasoon salt
2	(10 ounces each) packages frozen broccoli spears, cooked and drained	2	cups milk
		1	cube chicken bouillon
3	tablespoons butter or margarine	1	cup Parmesan cheese, divided
		1	tablespoon lemon juice

Cook rice according to package directions. Stir in celery. Pour into shallow 2 quart casserole. Arrange broccoli spears on top. In separate pan, melt butter and stir in flour and salt. Add milk and bouillon cube, cooking and stirring constantly until smooth and thickened. Add ¼ cup of cheese and lemon juice. Pour over broccoli. Sprinkle with remaining cheese. Bake at 375⁰ until hot and bubbly, about 20 minutes. Serves 6-10. Freezes well.   *Adele Hutton*

Broccoli and Carrots Almondine

1	pound broccoli, trimmed	3	tablespoons lemon juice
1	pound carrots, pared and sliced diagonally	3	tablespoons minced parsley
Dash of salt		¼	teaspoon pepper
½	cup slivered almonds	¼	teaspoon salt
3	tablespoons cooking oil	1½	teaspoons basil, crumbled
3	tablespoons margarine		

Place broccoli and carrots in large skillet, add water to depth of ½ inch. Sprinkle with salt. Cover tightly and boil gently for 6 minutes. Drain remaining water, cover and keep vegetables warm. Roast almonds in oil in large saucepan, stirring over medium high heat. When almonds turn light gold, remove from pan and reserve. Combine margarine, lemon juice, parsley, pepper, salt and basil. Heat, stirring until margarine is melted. Pour over vegetables in skillet and toss well. Sprinkle with almonds in serving dish. Serves 4-6.   *Darlene Nossaman*

☆   ☆   ☆

Broccoli Supreme

1	egg, slightly beaten		Dash of pepper
1	(10 ounce) package frozen broccoli, partially thawed		Pimientos, if desired
		3	tablespoons butter
1	cup cream style corn	1	cup Pepperidge Farm Herb Stuffing Mix
1	tablespoon grated onion		
¼	teaspoon salt		

Combine egg, broccoli, corn, onion, salt and pepper. Add pimientos if desired. Melt butter and toss with stuffing mix. Stir ¾ into vegetables. Put into a greased 1½-2 quart casserole. Sprinkle with remaining stuffing crumbs. Bake at 350⁰ for 35 to 40 minutes. Freezes well. Serves 4-6.

Mary Childress Jones

Party Broccoli

1	onion, chopped	1	teaspoon M.S.G.
1	stick of butter	1	(8 ounce) can mushrooms, drained
4	(10 ounces each) packages frozen broccoli spears	½	cup bread crumbs made from Pepperidge Farm Stuffing Mix
1	cup cream of mushroom soup		
1½	(6 ounces each) rolls garlic cheese		

Sauté onions in butter. Cook broccoli according to package directions. Drain. Melt cheese in mushroom soup. Add M.S.G. mushrooms and onions. Alternate layers of broccoli spears and sauce in a lightly buttered 8x10 casserole. Sprinkle bread crumbs over the top and bake at 300⁰ until bubbly, about 20 minutes. Serves 12-14.   *Eloise McIntosh*

☆   ☆   ☆

Broccoli au Gratin

May Be Made Ahead

2	cups milk	1	teaspoon salt
4	tablespoons flour	½	teaspoon pepper
1	(16 ounce) package cream cheese, softened	2½	pounds broccoli
		4	tablespoons bread crumbs
1	ounce Roquefort cheese, at room temperature	½	stick butter

Heat milk. Blend in flour, cream cheese, Roquefort, salt, pepper and stir over low heat until smooth. Cook broccoli until barely tender. Drain and place in 3 quart casserole and pour cheese sauce over broccoli. This much may be prepared the day before. Bake 350° oven for 50 minutes. Top with bread crumbs, dot with butter and return to oven for 10 minutes. Serves 4-6   *Louise Propps*

Almond Broccoli Casserole

½	stick butter	1	(8 ounce) can sliced water chestnuts
2	(10 ounces each) packages frozen chopped broccoli, thawed	1	(4½ ounce) jar sliced mushrooms
1	(10¾ ounce) can cream of mushroom soup	1	(6 ounce) roll Nippy sharp cheese
1	(3 ounce) package slivered almonds		

Melt butter and sauté broccoli until tender about 20 minutes. Add all other ingredients. Pour into buttered 2½ quart casserole and bake at 350° until hot, about 25 minutes. Serves 6-8.   *Ute Schnetzinger*

☆   ☆   ☆

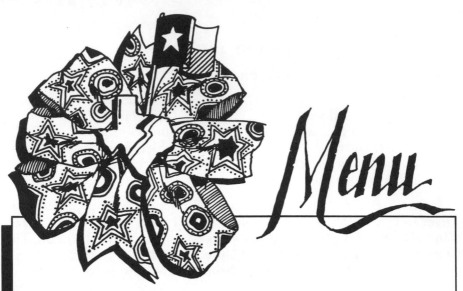

Menu

BREADS TO WARM THE HEART

Inside-Out Cinnamon Rolls

Beautiful Bread

Hot Cross Buns

My Neighbor's Coffee Cake

AWARD WINNING PICKLES

Mama Jones Peach Pickles

Pickled Okra

RWC Pickles

HOMEMADE PRESERVES AND JELLIES

Strawberry Preserves

Fig Preserves

Wine Jelly

Jalapeño Jelly

Texas Grown Produce

Farmers' Market

Fragrant breads, old-fashioned pickles, jams, jellies and farm-fresh vegetables stir up nostalgia. Food memories linger long and Texans treasure their fond recollections of days when meals and snacks were homemade and often homegrown.

Ranchers and cowboys might remember the aroma of chuck wagon sourdough biscuits. The average, older Texan more likely reminisces about hot buttermilk biscuits topped with cane syrup or blackberry jelly. He remembers blackeyed peas and cornbread at the noonday meal he called dinner.

Texas cooks still make wonderful breads, but no longer depend on their backyard gardens or the farmer who went door-to-door with a wagon load of fresh fruits and vegetables. They go to a local farmers' market.

A Saturday morning trip downtown to the City of Dallas Farmers' Market is a symphony of foreign languages. Visitors wear Indian saris, Vietnamese pajamas or blue jeans and boots.

Look for the sheds selling homegrown Texas produce. Its grapefruit, oranges, peaches, watermelons, cantaloupes, tomatoes, peanuts, pecans and onions are the tastiest found anywhere. This year around market brings many seasonal delights.

Photography
Donna Rogers

Escalloped Cabbage

1	head cabbage, chopped	3	hard-cooked eggs, chopped
1	onion, chopped		
2	tablespoons flour	1	(2 ounce) jar chopped pimientos
2	tablespoons melted margarine		
1	cup whole milk	1	bell pepper, chopped
1	cup grated sharp Cheddar cheese		Buttered bread crumbs

Cook cabbage and onion until barely tender. Put in greased casserole. Make white sauce (see index) with flour, margarine and milk. Mix cheese, chopped eggs, pimientos and bell pepper with white sauce and pour over cabbage. Cover with crumbs if desired. Bake at 350° for 30 minutes. You may cook cabbage and onion and make white sauce in a microwave. Serves 6-8. *Ivanette Dennis*

Zesty Carrots

1	(16 ounce) can diced carrots	Pepper to taste
½	cup mayonnaise	½ cup buttered bread crumbs or crushed crackers
2	tablespoons grated onion	
2	tablespoons horseradish	Butter, as desired
1	teaspoon salt	Dash of paprika

Drain and spread carrots in bottom of a baking dish. Mix mayonnaise, onion, horseradish, salt, pepper and spread over top of carrots. Sprinkle with crushed crackers or bread crumbs. Dot with butter. Garnish with a peppering of paprika. Bake until carrots are heated well and crumbs are slightly browned. Serves 4-6. *Eloise McIntosh*

Microwave Tangy Cauliflower

1	head cauliflower	½ cup mayonnaise
½	tablespoon minced onion	1 teaspoon dry mustard
½	cup shredded Cheddar cheese	

Place cauliflower in covered casserole or browning bag. Microwave 7 to 8 minutes on FULL POWER or until just tender. Mix mayonnaise, onion and mustard together. Spread mayonnaise mixture over cauliflower. Sprinkle with cheese. Microwave 1 minute at FULL POWER to melt cheese. Serves 6. *Charleye Conrey*

☆　　☆　　☆

Cauliflower Mayonnaise

1 head cauliflower
Salt to taste
¾ cup mayonnaise
2 hard-cooked eggs
1 teaspoon vinegar
1 tablespoon olive oil
½ clove garlic, minced
1 teaspoon Worcestershire

¼ cup finely chopped celery heart
1 tablespoon finely minced onion
Pepper to taste
Tabasco to taste
Lemon juice (optional)

Remove outer leaves of cauliflower. Place head in kettle and add one inch of water. Sprinkle with salt, cover tightly and simmer until cauliflower is tender but still firm. Drain well and keep warm. Preheat oven to 400⁰. Place mayonnaise in a mixing bowl. Put eggs through a sieve and add to the mayonnaise. Blend vinegar, oil and garlic and beat with a fork; add to mayonnaise mixture. Add Worcestershire, celery, onion, salt and pepper. Add Tabasco and, if desired, a little lemon juice. Place cauliflower head in a baking dish and spoon mayonnaise mixture over it. Bake 5 minutes and serve immediately. Serves 4-6. *Lois Williams*

Celery Casserole

Great for Pot Luck!

2 stalks celery
2 (10¾ ounces each) cans cream of celery soup
1 (8 ounce) can sliced water chestnuts

¼ cup toasted slivered almonds

DRESSING:
1 stick margarine
½ cup water

4-6 ounces Pepperidge Farm Herb Stuffing Mix

Cut celery in small pieces. Simmer in water 5 minutes. Drain. Add soup, sliced water chestnuts and toasted almonds to celery. Reserve.

DRESSING: Mix margarine, water and herb stuffing. Layer dressing and celery mixture in 9x13 inch buttered casserole. Bake at 300⁰ for 1 hour. Serves 8. *Pat Cutler*

Variation: Add 1 chopped onion and cook with celery.

☆   ☆   ☆

Fancy Celery Casserole

3 cups diced celery
¼ cup slivered almonds
1 (8 ounce) can sliced water chestnuts, drained
1 (4 ounce) can sliced mushrooms, drained
2 tablespoons butter
2 tablespoons flour

1 cup milk
2 chicken bouillon cubes
¼ teaspoon pepper
⅓ cup grated Parmesan cheese
2 tablespoons buttered breadcrumbs

Place celery in 1½ quart saucepan. Cover with water. Bring to a boil and cook for 5 minutes. Drain and reserve 1 cup cooking water. Place celery in a 1½ quart casserole and add almonds, water chestnuts and mushrooms. Make a white sauce with butter, flour and milk (see index). Heat reserved liquid and dissolve bouillon cubes. Gradually stir into white sauce, stirring constantly until smooth. Add pepper and pour over celery. Sprinkle with cheese and top with bread crumbs. Bake at 350⁰ for 20 minutes. Serves 6.   *Betsy Halford*

Pat's Corn Casserole

1 onion, chopped
¼ cup chopped bell pepper
4 tablespoons margarine
1 (16 ounce) can cream style corn
2 cups milk

1 egg, beaten
½ cup yellow corn meal
1 teaspoon salt
¼ teaspoon red pepper
1 (3 ounce) can French-fried onion rings

Sauté onion and bell pepper in margarine; add corn. Mix milk with egg and add to corn. Add cornmeal, salt and red pepper. Pour into 2½ quart casserole. Bake at 350⁰ for 30 minutes. Cover with onion rings just before serving and brown lightly.   *Tura Bethune*

☆   ☆   ☆

Maque Choux

(Mock Shoe)

¾   cup chopped onion
¾   cup bacon drippings
10 ears fresh corn (cut off the cob) or
4   cups frozen corn, thawed

4   tomatoes, peeled and chopped
⅓   cup minced bell pepper
1   teaspoon salt
1   teaspoon black pepper

Sauté onions in bacon drippings about 5 minutes until tender. Add corn and cook 10 minutes stirring constantly. Add tomatoes and bell pepper and cook 5 minutes or until very soft. Add salt and pepper. May be served as a vegetable or as stuffing in green pepper or tomato. Serves 6.

Louise Propps

Party Green Beans

BEANS:

3   (10 ounces each) packages frozen French style green beans
1   (16 ounce) can bean sprouts, drained
    or
1   pound fresh mushrooms, sliced

2   (8 ounces each) cans water chestnuts, drained
¼   cup Parmesan cheese
¼   cup grated Swiss cheese

CREAM SAUCE:

4   tablespoons butter, divided
2   tablespoons flour
1¼ teaspoons salt
½   teaspoon pepper

Dash of cayenne pepper
½   teaspoon Worcestershire
2   cups light cream
1   cup chopped almonds

BEANS: Cook beans in boiling water for 5 minutes. Drain. Turn into greased shallow 2 quart casserole and alternate layers of beans, sprouts or mushrooms, water chestnuts, and mixed cheese.

CREAM SAUCE: Melt 3 tablespoons butter. Blend in flour, salt, pepper, cayenne pepper and Worcestershire. Add cream. Stir to thicken. Pour over vegetables lifting mixture gently with fork so sauce will penetrate. Do not stir. Melt remaining tablespoon butter in small sauce pan; add almonds. Stir to coat well. Bake at 375⁰ until bubbly, about 20 to 30 minutes. Serves 10-12.

Brenda Chattaway

☆   ☆   ☆

Deviled Green Beans

1 onion, chopped	1 (3 ounce) can tomato sauce
1 clove garlic, minced	
½ bell pepper, chopped	1 cup grated Cheddar cheese
2 whole canned pimientos, chopped	1 (10 ounce) package frozen cut green beans
3 tablespoons butter	
2 teaspoons prepared mustard	

Sauté onion, garlic, bell pepper and pimientos in butter until onions are limp. Stir in mustard, tomato sauce and cheese. Cook frozen beans in a small amount of salted water until just tender. Combine beans with sauce and pour into a greased 1 quart casserole. Bake at 350⁰ for 25 minutes or until cheese is melted. Serves 4.   *Tura Bethune*

Variations on a Green Bean

A Quickie!

1 pound fresh green beans, snapped	¼ teaspoon salt
	Butter, if desired
1½ teaspoons lemon juice	
½ teaspoon Spice Island Bouquet Garni	

Sprinkle green beans with lemon juice and Bouquet Garni. Microwave or steam beans to desired tenderness. Add salt. Dot with butter if desired. Serves 4.

Variation: Melt ½ stick butter with ½ teaspoon Dijon mustard. Add to herbs and salt.

Variation: Omit herbs. Add 6 slices bacon, fried, drained and crumbled, 1 cup slivered toasted almonds, and 2 tablespoons melted butter.
                    The Cookbook Committee

Hint: When using dried herbs, crush the herb in the palm of your hand before adding it to the dish. This releases the flavors of the herb.

☆   ☆   ☆

Green Beans with Zucchini and Bacon

INGREDIENTS:

1	(10 ounce) package frozen cut green beans	2	zucchini, sliced ¼ inch thick
4	slices bacon	¾	teaspoon salt
¼	cup butter or margarine		Dash of pepper
1	onion, minced		

Prepare green beans, but cook only half as long as label directs. Drain. In 12 inch skillet over medium heat fry bacon until crisp. Drain and crumble. Set bacon aside and wipe skillet clean with paper towels. Add butter and onions to skillet. Cook until onions are tender, about 3 minutes. Increase heat to medium high, add zucchini and cook, stirring frequently until tender crisp, about 4 minutes. Stir in bacon, green beans, salt and pepper and cook about 1 minute longer. Serves 6.

Virginia Steenson

Green Bean Bundles

Quick and Easy

3	(15 ounces each) cans whole green beans	8	slices bacon
			Barbeque sauce

Wrap one slice bacon around a serving of green beans. Place in flat greased pan. Pour barbeque sauce over beans. At this point you may refrigerate or bake for 35 to 40 minutes in 350⁰ oven. Serves 8.

Great with Brisket!   *Cookbook Committee*

Sweet and Sour Green Beans

4	slices bacon	2	(1 pound each) cans whole green beans
2	onions, chopped		Sliced almonds
½	cup brown sugar		Chopped pimiento
2	teaspoons vinegar		

Cook bacon and remove from pan. Sauté onion in drippings. Add brown sugar, vinegar and green beans. Crumble bacon into mixture. Simmer 40 minutes. Garnish with almonds and pimiento. Serves 8.

Valerie McMahan

☆   ☆   ☆

Baked Eggplant

1	eggplant	Dash of Worcestershire sauce
¼	cup chopped onion	Salt to taste
2	tablespoons butter	Pepper to taste
3	tablespoons chopped parsley	Butter crackers (not saltines)
1	(10¾ ounce) can cream of mushroom soup	

Cut top off eggplant lengthwise. Scrape out the inside, leaving about ½ inch around sides and bottom of shell. Simmer eggplant pulp in salted water until it is tender. Drain completely and chop. Sauté onion in butter and add parsley. Mix with eggplant and soup; add Worcestershire, salt and pepper. Mix with enough crumbled crackers to make a good stuffing consistency. Pile filling back into eggplant shell. Sprinkle with cracker crumbs and dot with butter. Bake at 375⁰ for 25 to 30 minutes.

Virginia Dennis

Variation: Peel eggplant and combine all ingredients in a casserole.

Eggplant Casserole

3-5	cups chopped eggplant	¼	cup evaporated milk
½	cup chopped onion	Salt to taste	
1	cup chopped celery	Pepper to taste	
1	cup crushed cheese crackers, divided	1 egg	
½	stick butter	Seasoned salt, if desired	

Peel eggplant, chop and parboil until tender. Drain well and mash. Place cooked eggplant in buttered quart casserole. Sauté onion and celery in butter. Add to eggplant along with ¾ cup crushed cheese crackers and mix. Add enough evaporated milk to moisten along with salt, pepper and beaten egg. Top with remaining crushed cracker crumbs. Place casserole in pan of water in 325⁰ oven for one hour uncovered.

Gerry Leftwich

Variation: Add 1 (16 ounce) can stewed tomatoes, drained and ½ teaspoon garlic salt.

☆ ☆ ☆

Herbed Butter

½ stick butter
½ cup minced onion
½ clove garlic, minced
¼ cup celery

½ cup minced parsley
½ teaspoon rosemary
¼ teaspoon basil
¾ teaspoon salt

Sauté onions, garlic and celery in butter until soft. Add parsley, rosemary, basil and salt. Cover and let simmer for 10 minutes. Serve over hot, drained vegetables. Especially good on green beans.   *Patricia Brott*

Martee's Mushroom Flambé

3 tablespoons butter
2 tablespoons olive oil
1 pound large mushrooms, caps only
½ teaspoon salt
½ teaspoon pepper
1 teaspoon tarragon

1 teaspoon chives
1 teaspoon dried parsley
¼ cup dry Sherry
1 teaspoon lemon juice
2 tablespoons brandy
¼ teaspoon sugar

In chafing dish or skillet heat butter and oil; add mushrooms. Sauté 5 to 7 minutes. When almost done season with salt, pepper, tarragon, chives, parsley, Sherry and lemon juice. Cover and simmer over low heat 3 to 4 minutes. Remove cover, heat brandy with sugar and pour over mushrooms and ignite. Serve on toast points or rice. *Tura Bethune*

Baked Mushrooms

1 pound mushrooms, sliced
½ cup diced tomatoes
¼ cup chopped parsley

1 tablespoon Sherry
1 teaspoon salt
⅛ teaspoon pepper

Put mushrooms, tomatoes and parsley on a sheet of aluminum foil large enough to seal tightly. Season with Sherry, salt and pepper. Take long edges of foil and fold over lengthwise two or three times. Repeat with both ends of foil. Bake 20 minutes at 350⁰. May be cooked on charcoal or gas grill, also. Serves 6.

Hint: To microwave, cover a 1 or 1½ quart casserole tightly with Saran Wrap and microwave on FULL POWER about 5 minutes.

Barbara England

☆   ☆   ☆

D'Jo's Mushroom Paprikash

1	pound fresh mushrooms	1	teaspoon flour
2	tablespoons butter or margarine	½	teaspoon salt
1	teaspoon fresh lemon juice	½	teaspoon paprika
2	tablespoons instant minced onion	Dash of cayenne pepper	
		¼	cup of sour cream

Wash and slice mushrooms, including the caps and stems. Sauté in butter and lemon juice 5 or 6 minutes or until tender. Combine onion, flour, salt, paprika and cayenne and add to mushrooms. Stir and cook 1 minute. Add sour cream. Heat, but don't boil. Good with beef fondue or as an accompaniment to any meat. Serves 4.   *Ivanette Dennis*

Walla Walla Onions

7½	cups thinly sliced sweet onions	½	cup uncooked rice
4	tablespoons butter	¾	cup grated Swiss cheese
		⅔	cup half and half

Sauté onions in butter until soft, but not brown. Cook rice in 5 cups salted boiling water for 5 minutes only. Drain, mix onions and rice with cheese. Put in 9 inch square casserole with the half and half. Cover and bake 1 hour at 350⁰. Serves 6-8.   *Pate Stanphill*

Colorful Green Peas

1	(16 ounce) can Le Sueur peas, drained	3	teaspoons sugar
1	(8 ounce) jar whole mushrooms	Salt to taste	
		Pepper to taste	
1	(4 ounce) jar chopped pimientos	3	tablespoons cornstarch
1	stick butter	½	cup half and half
		½	cup Cheez Whiz

Simmer peas, mushrooms, pimientos, butter, sugar, salt and pepper about 30 minutes. Add cornstarch to half and half and blend with vegetables. Add Cheez Whiz and continue stirring over low heat until cheese is melted. Serves 4.   *Eloise McIntosh*

☆   ☆   ☆

Stuffed Onion Cups

Almost Too Pretty to Eat

8	onions, large enough to hollow	½	teaspoon sugar
1	chicken bouillon cube, dissolved	½	teaspoon salt
		¼	cup water for peas
1	cup boiling water	1	lettuce leaf
1	(10 ounce) package frozen green peas	1	tablespoon butter
		1	tablespoon cream
		1	(2 ounce) jar pimientos

Peel onions and place in a single layer in medium size frying pan. Add bouillon, cover and simmer 30 minutes until onions are still firm enough to hold shape. While onions cook, combine peas with sugar, salt and water. Top with lettuce. Cover and simmer 15 minutes. Remove lettuce and drain peas. Stir in butter and cream. Put in blender until smooth. Return to saucepan and keep hot. Lift onions from broth with slotted spoon. Trim tops flat and scoop out centers with teaspoon. Spoon hot puréed peas into onion shells. Top with pimiento. Serves 8.

Lois Williams

Microwave Green Pea Casserole

1	stick butter	2	tablespoons pimiento, chopped
1	cup diced celery	1	(10 ounce) package frozen green peas, partially thawed
2	green onions, minced		
2	tablespoons chopped bell pepper		
⅛	teaspoon garlic powder		Freshly ground pepper
1	(10¾ ounce) can cream of mushroom soup	¾	cup butter salad crackers, crushed
1	(8 ounce) can water chestnuts, sliced and drained		

Melt stick of butter in a 1½ quart baking dish on FULL POWER for 1 minute. Stir in chopped celery, onions and peppers. Cook on FULL POWER 3 minutes. Stir in garlic powder and mushroom soup. Cover casserole with paper towel and heat on FULL POWER for 2 minutes. Add water chestnuts, pimientos, peas and ground pepper. Cover with paper towel and cook for 5 minutes on FULL POWER (stir once during cooking). Stir mixture and sprinkle cracker crumbs over top. Cook uncovered 5 minutes on ½ POWER. Serves 6-8.

☆　　☆　　☆

Peas Royal

3 slices bacon, fried crisp and crumbled
1 (2 ounce) can sliced mushrooms, drained
Juice of ½ fresh lemon
1 tablespoon sugar

2 teaspoons instant minced onion
½ teaspoon salt
1 (10 ounce) package frozen green peas, cooked and drained.

Fry bacon until crisp, drain and crumble. Reserve. Add mushrooms, lemon juice, sugar, onion and salt to bacon drippings. Stir in peas and cook until well heated. Garnish with bacon and serve. Serves 4.

Pat Settle

Herb and Onion Spinach Casserole

3 (10 ounces each) packages frozen chopped spinach
1 envelope Lipton onion soup mix

2 cups sour cream
½ cup herb seasoned stuffing mix
2 tablespoons butter, melted

Cook spinach as directed. Drain very well. Add soup mix and cream; mix. Put into 1½ quart casserole. Top with stuffing mix and dribble with melted butter. Bake until bubbly and completely heated in 350⁰ oven, about 35 minutes. Can be made ahead and refrigerated. Bring to room temperature before baking. Serves 4-6. *Brenda Chattaway*

Spinach and Squash Bake

1½ tablespoons butter
1 (10 ounce) package frozen chopped spinach, thawed
1 (10 ounce package) frozen yellow crookneck squash, thawed
2 eggs, slightly beaten
1 pound small curd cottage cheese

1 tablespoon flour
½ cup American cheese, grated
1 teaspoon salt
½ teaspoon pepper
¼ teaspoon onion powder
¼ teaspoon nutmeg

Grease a 2 quart casserole with butter. Thaw and drain spinach and squash. Add eggs, cottage cheese, flour, cheese, salt, pepper, onion powder and nutmeg. May be done a day before and refrigerated. Bring to room temperature and bake at 325⁰ for 45 minutes. Serves 8.

Vivian Jackson

☆   ☆   ☆

Spinach Cheese Pie

4	frozen patty shells	¼	cup shredded sharp
2	(12 ounces each) packages		Cheddar cheese
	frozen spinach soufflé,	2	tablespoons sliced green
	defrosted		onion
1	(3 ounce) package cream	2	tablespoons grated
	cheese, softened		Parmesan cheese

Thaw patty shells. Roll out on lightly floured surface to fit 10 inch pie plate, sealing edges together. Let rest 5 minutes before placing in pie plate. Flute edges. With spinach, combine cream cheese cut in chunks, shredded Cheddar cheese and green onion. Put mixture into pie shell and top with Parmesan cheese. Bake at 350⁰ for 35 minutes, or until middle is set. Serves 8.

Variation: Use pie crust or phyllo dough instead of patty shells.

Variation: Use 1 (10 ounce) package frozen spinach combined with 6 well-beaten eggs instead of prepared soufflé. Add salt and pepper to taste.
Pat Horton

Spinach Casserole

Make Ahead

2	(10 ounces each) packages	2	dashes of nutmeg
	frozen chopped spinach	2	teaspoons lemon juice
1	cup sour cream		Dash of Tabasco
1	package dry onion soup	½	cup buttered bread crumbs
	mix		

Cook spinach according to directions on package; drain. Blend well with sour cream, soup mix, nutmeg, lemon juice and Tabasco. Pour into buttered, shallow 2 quart casserole. Sprinkle with bread crumbs. Bake at 350⁰ for 20 to 30 minutes until bubbling and crumbs are brown. Should be made a day ahead or early in the day to allow flavors to blend. Serves 4-6. Doubles or triples well for large groups. *Eloise McIntosh*

☆　　☆　　☆

Spinach — Artichoke Casserole

2	(10 ounces each) packages frozen chopped spinach	1	pint sour cream
½	cup finely chopped onion		Salt to taste
1	stick butter		Pepper to taste
1	(16 ounce) can artichokes	½	cup grated Parmesan cheese

Cook spinach as directed on box. Drain. Sauté onion in butter. Mix artichokes and sour cream with spinach, onion, salt and pepper and place in casserole. Stir Parmesan cheese into casserole and also sprinkle some on top. Bake at 350⁰ for 20 to 30 minutes. Serves 6.   *Pat Knott*

Spinach Ricotta Cheese Pie

FILLING:

1	(10 ounce) package frozen chopped spinach	¼	cup finely chopped onion
1	pound Ricotta cheese	2	teaspoons prepared mustard
¼	pound thinly sliced pepperoni	½	teaspoon oregano
¼	pound chopped mushrooms	¼	teaspoon salt
½	cup grated Swiss cheese	⅛	teaspoon pepper
½	cup grated Parmesan cheese	1	egg, slightly beaten
			Dough for double crust 9 inch pie

SAUCE:

1	(15 ounce) can tomato sauce		Dash of pepper
½	teaspoon garlic salt	1	teaspoon Italian herb seasoning.

Thaw spinach, drain and press out as much moisture as possible. Blend with Ricotta cheese, pepperoni, mushrooms, Swiss cheese, Parmesan cheese, onion, mustard, oregano, salt and pepper. Stir in egg. Roll out one half prepared pie pastry. Place bottom crust in a 9 inch pie plate or an 8 inch square casserole. Spread filling in pie, roll out the remainder of pastry and put on filling. Trim and flute the edges, prick top, and bake at 425⁰ for 25 minutes or until crust is brown.

SAUCE: Heat tomato sauce, garlic salt, pepper and Italian seasoning. Pour over pie or serve on the side.   *Vivian Jackson*

☆   ☆   ☆

Creamed Spinach

1   pound fresh spinach or 2
     (10 ounces each) packages
     frozen spinach
¼   cup butter or margarine
1   onion, chopped
1   clove garlic, crushed

½   cup sour cream
Dash of salt
¼   teaspoon pepper
Pinch of nutmeg
Paprika to taste

Remove stems from spinach, wash leaves thoroughly and tear into large pieces. Cook spinach in a small amount of boiling water 5 to 10 minutes or until tender, or cook frozen spinach according to package directions. Drain and place on paper towels and squeeze until barely moist. Melt butter in a large skillet. Sauté onions and garlic until tender. Stir in sour cream, salt, pepper and nutmeg. Add the spinach. Cook over low heat until thoroughly heated. Sprinkle with paprika. Serves 4-6.

Variation: Garnish with 2 hard-cooked chopped eggs.

Ruth Canada and Lynda Corbin

Spinach Rice Casserole

4   (10 ounces each) packages
     frozen chopped spinach
4   eggs, beaten
1   teaspoon salt
1   pound sharp Cheddar
     cheese, grated
1   cup milk
4   cups cooked rice

1   teaspoon Worcestershire
½   teaspoon rosemary
½   teaspoon thyme
½   teaspoon marjoram
1   tablespoon finely chopped
     onion
¼   cup melted butter

Cook spinach for 5 minutes and drain thoroughly. Mix with eggs, salt, cheese, milk, rice, Worcestershire, rosemary, thyme, marjoram and onion. Pour into a greased 2½ quart casserole. Top with melted butter. Bake 30 to 45 minutes at 350°. This may be made the day before and baked before serving. Serves 12.

Sally Kinne

Microwave frozen vegetables in package rather than removing to a separate container. The texture and color will be better, there is less liquid to drain or squeeze.

☆   ☆   ☆

Stouffer's Restaurant Spinach Loaf

6 tablespoons butter,
   divided
1½ cups milk
4½ tablespoons flour
Salt to taste

Pepper to taste
3 cups cooked, chopped,
   drained spinach
3 eggs, beaten slightly

Make a white sauce with 4 tablespoons of butter, milk, flour, salt and pepper (see index). Add spinach and eggs to white sauce along with 2 tablespoons of butter. Place in a buttered mold in pan of hot water. Bake until a knife comes out clean, about 1 hour at 350⁰. Serves 6.

Ruth Becker

Cheddar Squash Bake

2 pounds yellow crooked-
   neck summer squash or
   zucchini
1 cup sour cream
2 eggs, separated
2 tablespoons flour
1½ cups shredded Cheddar
   cheese

4 slices bacon cooked crisp,
   drained and crumbled or
   BacOs
⅓ cup fine dry bread crumbs
1 tablespoon melted butter

Slice squash. Cook covered in a small amount of boiling salted water 15 to 20 minutes or until tender. Drain well. Sprinkle with a small amount of salt. Mix sour cream, egg yolks and flour. Fold in stiffly beaten egg whites. In a 12x7½x2 inch baking dish layer half the squash, half the egg mixture and half the cheese. Sprinkle bacon on top. Repeat layers of squash, egg and cheese. Combine crumbs and butter and sprinkle on top. Bake uncovered in 350⁰ oven for 20 to 25 minutes. Top with additional bacon and parsley if desired. Serves 8-10.   *Ruth Canada*

☆   ☆   ☆

Yellow Squash Casserole

3 pounds yellow squash	1 cup grated Longhorn
Salt to taste	Colby cheese
1 teaspoon sugar	2 cups bread crumbs
1 (16 ounce) carton cottage	½ cup Parmesan cheese
cheese	½ stick melted margarine

Slice, boil and drain squash. Add salt. Mix together sugar, cottage cheese, Longhorn cheese and add to squash. Put in greased 2 quart casserole. Top with bread crumbs and Parmesan cheese. Pour margarine over all. Bake at 400⁰ for 30 minutes. Serves 8. *Elbie Guindon*

Zucchini and Yellow Squash Casserole

2-3 yellow squash, grated	1 tablespoon salt
2-3 zucchini, grated	½ teaspoon white pepper
1 cup Ritz cracker crumbs	½ cup milk
2 eggs, lightly beaten	½ cup sour cream
2 tablespoons grated onion	1 cup grated Cheddar cheese
4 tablespoons chopped bell	
pepper	

Mix squash, zucchini, cracker crumbs, eggs, onion, bell pepper, salt, pepper, milk, sour cream and cheese together. Pour into buttered 2 quart casserole. Bake at 350⁰ for 35 to 45 minutes. Serves 6-8.

Variation: Vary the colors and kinds of squash according to the season. Or add ½-1 cup grated carrot. *Novella Bailey*

Zucchini Sticks

3 zucchini	1 tablespoon milk
Salt to taste	Cracker crumbs, finely
Pepper to taste	crumbled
Flour	3 tablespoons butter or oil
1 egg	Lemon juice

Wash, but do not peel, zucchini; slice off ends. Cut into lengthwise sticks about ½-inch thick. Sprinkle with salt and pepper and roll in flour. Dip in mixture of the slightly beaten egg and milk; roll in crumbs. Fry in hot butter until lightly browned and crisp on all sides, about 5 to 6 minutes. Sprinkle each stick with lemon juice. Serves 6.

Anna Wade Pierson

☆   ☆   ☆

Baked Zucchini

Colorful and Tasty

4	slices bread	3	green onions, cut in 1 inch pieces
1	clove garlic	½	teaspoon salt
4	tomatoes, peeled and quartered or	½	teaspoon pepper
1½	cups canned, drained, chopped tomatoes	½	teaspoon paprika
1	tablespoon salad oil	2	pounds zucchini, thinly sliced

Preheat oven to 400°. Grease 2 quart casserole. In a blender or processor crumb bread and set aside. Put garlic, tomatoes, oil, onions, salt, pepper, and paprika into blender, cover and chop until onions are coarsely chopped. Cover bottom of casserole with ½ of crumbs. Put zucchini into casserole and pour mixture over it. Top with remaining crumbs. Bake uncovered about 50 minutes until zucchini is tender. Serves 8.

Bee Krapf

Variation: Substitute 1 (10 ounce) can Ro-Tel tomatoes for the tomatoes.

Tomatoes Florentine

Serve Warm or Cold

2	(10 ounces each) packages frozen chopped spinach		Salt to taste
½	bell pepper, chopped		Pepper to taste
¼	cup chopped onion	½	cup mayonnaise
2	ribs celery, chopped	1	teaspoon lemon juice
2	hard-cooked eggs, chopped	6-8	tomatoes, hollowed and drained

Cook and drain the spinach. Mix with pepper, onion, celery and eggs. Add salt and pepper. Stir in mayonnaise and lemon juice. Spoon into tomato shells. Allow one tomato per serving.

Variation: Add bouillion or beef base to cooking water for spinach.

Mary Pittman

☆　　☆　　☆

Greenback Tomatoes

2 (10 ounces each) packages
frozen chopped spinach
2 cups Progresso bread
crumbs
6 green onions and tops,
chopped
6 eggs, slightly beaten
½ cup melted butter

¼ cup Parmesan cheese
¼ teaspoon Worcestershire
1 teaspoon salt
½ teaspoon pepper
1 teaspoon thyme
¼ teaspoon Tabasco
12 large thick slices of tomato

Cook spinach and drain well. In large mixing bowl combine crumbs, onions, eggs, butter, Parmesan, Worcestershire, salt, pepper, thyme and Tabasco. Arrange tomato slices in buttered shallow baking dish. Mound spinach mixture on top of each tomato slice. Bake at 350⁰ about 15 minutes. Serves 12.

This is a good vegetable dish for a buffet supper because it is colorful, tasty and arranged in individual servings.

Variation: Great for hors d'oeuvres. You may use it to stuff little cherry tomatoes. Reduce cooking time accordingly. *Happy Wylie*

Microwave Corn Filled Tomatoes

6 large tomatoes
Salt to taste
2 tablespoons butter or
margarine
1 tablespoon chopped onion
2 · tablespoons chopped bell
pepper

1 (16 ounce) can whole
kernel corn, drained
¼ cup potato chips, crushed
Grated Parmesan cheese

Cut tops off tomatoes; hollow out inside. Save tomato pulp for soup. Place tomatoes on glass serving platter. Sprinkle with salt. Combine butter, onion and bell pepper in 4 cup glass measure. Microwave on ⅔ POWER for 4 to 5 minutes or until butter is melted. Stir in corn and crushed potato chips. Spoon crumb mixture into tomatoes. Sprinkle with Parmesan cheese. Microwave on FULL POWER for 6 to 7 minutes or until heated through. Let stand 3 minutes before serving. Serves 6.

☆   ☆   ☆

Alma's Sausage Stuffed Tomatoes

6	stuffing sized tomatoes	1	egg
¾	pound bulk sausage	¼	cup grated Parmesan
½	cup chopped onions		cheese
1	cup bread crumbs		

Remove stem end of tomatoes. Scoop out pulp. Reserve. Turn upside down to drain. Brown sausage and reserve a small amount of drippings. Sauté onion and chopped tomato pulp until onions are tender. Add bread crumbs, sausage, beaten egg and cheese. Fill tomato cups and bake 20 minutes at 325⁰. Sprinkle with more Parmesan cheese. Serves 6.

Tura Bethune

Layered Vegetables

Nice Dish for Company

8	ribs celery, cut in 4 inch lengths	¼	cup water
1	(10½ ounce) can beef bouillon	2	cups frozen tiny onions
		½	pound fresh green beans, French cut
2	tablespoons butter	2	tablespoons brown sugar
6	carrots, cut in quarters lengthwise		Salt to taste
			Pepper to taste

Boil celery in bouillon until just tender. It should be pale green and crunchy. Melt butter in large skillet. Add carrot quarters and water. Cover and simmer until just tender. Add onions and green beans. Bring to quick boil, adding additional ¼ cup water if necessary. Turn down heat and cook 5 minutes. (All vegetables will be crunchy except carrots and onions.) Sprinkle sugar over onions and season all vegetables except celery with salt and pepper to taste. Layer vegetables on flat serving dish in this manner: celery, carrots, onions and green beans. Serves 6-8.

Ruth Dirks

☆   ☆   ☆

Green Vegetable Casserole

1   (10 ounce) package frozen   ½   pint heavy cream,
     lima beans, cooked   whipped
1   (10 ounce) package frozen   ½   cup mayonnaise
     green peas, cooked   2   tablespoons horseradish,
1   (16 ounce) can green   optional
     beans, cooked   1   (3 ounce) can grated
2   bell peppers, cut into   Parmesan cheese
     strips

Drain vegetables. Layer in large casserole with bell peppers. Blend
whipped cream, horseradish and mayonnaise and pour over vegetables.
Sprinkle with cheese. Bake at 350⁰ for 45 minutes or until light brown.
Serves 8.   *Janna Pickering*

Quick Mixed Vegetable Casserole

2   (10 ounces each) packages   ¼   cup chopped pimiento
     frozen mixed vegetables   1   egg, lightly beaten
2   (10½ ounces each) cans   ½   pound Monterey Jack
     cream of celery soup   cheese, sliced
½   cup chopped almonds   2   tomatoes, sliced
½   cup Parmesan cheese   3   hard-cooked eggs,
½   onion, chopped fine   quartered (optional)
1   tablespoon dried or fresh
     dill weed

In medium bowl combine vegetables, soup, almonds, Parmesan cheese,
onion, dill, pimiento and egg. Mix well. Spoon into 1½ quart baking
dish. Arrange cheese slices and tomatoes on top. Bake uncovered in a
350⁰ oven about 30 minutes until cheese is melted and casserole is heated
through. Before serving garnish with quartered eggs. To microwave,
cover and microwave on FULL POWER 8 minutes; then turn and
microwave 5 minutes more on FULL POWER. Serves 8.

Martha Brott

☆   ☆   ☆

Jezabel Sauce

1 (10 ounce) jar apple jelly	1 (5 ounce) jar freshly
1 (18 ounce) jar peach preserves	grated horseradish
1 ounce dry mustard	Freshly ground black pepper

Mix jelly, preserves, mustard, horseradish and pepper and let stand at least half a day. Good with any kind of pork. Keeps forever in refrigerator. Good with eggrolls, too. Makes about 3 cups.

Lynn MacWithey

Variation: Substitute pineapple preserves and currant jelly. Serve with heated cocktail smoked sausages in a chafing dish. May omit dry mustard, and substitute an 8 ounce jar of Dijon mustard.

White Sauce

BUTTER:
Thin — 2 tablespoons
Medium — 3 tablespoons
Heavy — 4 tablespoons

FLOUR:
Thin — 1½-2 tablespoons
Medium — 3 tablespoons
Heavy — 4 tablespoons

SALT:
Thin — ¼ teaspoon
Medium — ¼-½ teaspoon
Heavy — ½ teaspoon

MILK:
Thin — 1 cup
Medium — 1 cup
Heavy — 1 cup

Melt butter and stir in flour and salt. Blend until smooth. Slowly add milk. Stir constantly over low heat, without boiling until desired thickness is obtained. May be made in the microwave. Follow manufacturer's directions.

In this cookbook, correct amounts of sauce ingredients are listed in the recipe.

The Cookbook Committee

☆ ☆ ☆

"H" Sauce

For Horseradish Haters

3	tablespoons butter or margarine	2	tablespoons flour	
2	tablespoons finely chopped onions	1	cup milk	
		⅓	cup horseradish mustard	

Melt butter and sauté onion until tender. Remove from heat, stir in flour; then milk to make a smooth sauce. Add mustard and heat until warm. Serve warm with beef fondue or roast beef. Delicious cold on ham sandwiches.

Variation: For a real horseradish sauce, use ⅓ cup grated horseradish instead of mustard.

Ivanette Dennis

Saucepan Hollandaise

Perfect Everytime

3	egg yolks	¼	cup boiling water
2	tablespoons lemon juice		Salt to taste
1	stick butter		Pepper to taste
			Dash of cayenne pepper

In a small heavy saucepan, combine egg yolks and lemon juice. Blend until smooth, using a wooden spoon or rubber scraper. Add ½ stick butter. Cook over low heat, stirring constantly, until butter is melted. Add remaining butter and continue stirring until melted. Add boiling water, a tablespoon at a time, and blend. Continue cooking and stirring until sauce is thickened. Remove from heat immediately. Season with salt, pepper and cayenne. If sauce is refrigerated, it may be reheated in a heavy saucepan over low heat, stirring constantly. Serves 8.

I've never had a failure with this recipe.

Ruth Becker

☆　　☆　　☆

Remoulade Sauce Eloise

Make Ahead

4   hard-cooked eggs, yolks only
4   cloves garlic, finely chopped
3   tablespoons dark mustard (German)
3   cups mayonnaise (do not substitute)
2   tablespoons paprika
3   tablespoons prepared horseradish

2   tablespoons Worcestershire
Dash of Tabasco
5   tablespoons vinegar (regular or wine)
4   heaping tablespoons finely chopped parsley
9   teaspoons sugar to taste
Salt to taste
Pepper to taste

Sieve egg yolks. Mix with garlic, mustard, mayonnaise, paprika, horseradish, Worcestershire and Tabasco. Blend in vinegar; then add parsley, sugar, salt and pepper. Stir until well-blended. Chill at least 12 hours. Add vinegar if too thick. Serves 12.   *Eloise McIntosh*

Favorite Sauce

For Fish, Steak, Potatoes, Crackers, etc.

1   cup sour cream
4   tablespoons margarine, softened
3   tablespoons crumbled Bleu cheese

2   teaspoons chopped chives
¼   cup sliced ripe olives

Combine sour cream and margarine. Add Bleu cheese, chives and olives. Mix well. Chill at least one hour to blend flavors. Makes about 1½ cups.
Dolores M. Spence

Seafood Sauce

4   tablespoons lemon juice
4   tablespoons vinegar
4   tablespoons prepared mustard
4   tablespoons prepared horseradish
2   teaspoons salt

½   teaspoon black pepper
2   teaspoons paprika
Dash of cayenne
½   cup oil
½   cup finely diced celery
½   cup minced onion

Combine above ingredients, chill and serve as a dip for cold shrimp.

☆   ☆   ☆

Remoulade Sauce

1 cup mayonaise	1 teaspoon paprika
1 tablespoon chopped onion	½ teaspoon salt
1 tablespoon chopped parsley	1 tablespoon vinegar
1 tablespoon chopped celery	½ teaspoon Worcestershire
2 tablespoons Dijon mustard	3-4 drops of Tabasco
1 tablespoon prepared horseradish	

Combine all ingredients and beat until well blended. Refrigerate several hours before serving to allow flavors to develop.   *Tura Bethune*

Velvet Drinking Dessert

1 pint coffee ice cream	1 or 2 jiggers Creme de Cacao
1 or 2 jiggers Cognac	

Put all ingredients into blender and blend 10 seconds. Pour into sherbert glasses. Serves 4.   *Pearl Leino*

Variation: Substitute vanilla ice cream and add 2 ounces Cointreau.
        Jean Zinser

Good dessert with a crisp cookie as well as an after dinner drink.

Scotch Parfait

Must Be Made in Advance

1 cup honey	Toasted slivered almonds
¾ cup Scotch	Maraschino cherries (optional)
2 cups whipping cream	
Grated bitter chocolate (do not substitute)	

Blend honey and Scotch (this takes a little time to incorporate the Scotch into the honey). Whip cream until stiff. Fold honey mixture into cream. Spoon into parfait glasses and freeze overnight. Prior to serving, top with grated chocolate, almonds, and a cherry. If desired you may purchase chocolate dessert cups from a gourmet food shop and spoon the mixture into cups prior to serving.

This needs to be made 24 hours in advance. This does keep well in freezer. Non-Scotch drinkers will love this dessert!
        Goodies from Goodman by Jimmy and Bob

☆   ☆   ☆

Diet Grapefruit with Triple Sec Dessert

½ grapefruit
4-5 Maraschino cherries
1-2 tablespoons Triple Sec or
    other orange flavored
    liqueur

Carefully peel and segment grapefruit. Place segments in pretty serving bowl and add 4-5 halved cherries. Just before serving stir in 1-2 tablespoons Triple Sec or Cointreau. Serves 1.   *Mary Cooprider*

Lemon Ice Milk

Cool and Refreshing

2 quarts milk
4 cups sugar
1 pint half and half

Juice of 5 lemons
1 tablespoon finely grated
  lemon rind

Mix milk, sugar, half and half. Add lemon juice and rind. Freeze according to manufacturer's directions for ice cream freezer.

Linda Juba

Lime Sherbet

Doesn't Require Ice Cream Freezer

1 (3-ounce) package lime
  Jello
1 cup hot water
½ cup sugar
2 cups milk

1 cup half and half
¼ cup lemon juice
1 teaspoon grated lemon
  peel

Dissolve gelatin in hot water. Add sugar, milk, half and half, lemon juice and lemon peel. Mix thoroughly. Put into a 2 quart flat dish and put into freezer. Freeze until firm. Break into chunks with wooden spoon. Turn into chilled bowl and beat until fluffy and smooth. This can also be done in food processor. Return to cold tray and put in freezer.

Cool and refreshing summer treat.   *Linda Juba*

☆   ☆   ☆

Grape Ice Cream

2½-3	cups sugar	½	cup lemon juice
2	cups whipping cream	2	cups grape juice
1	quart half and half		

Combine sugar, whipping cream and half and half in large mixing bowl. Beat 1 minute in electric mixer at medium speed or until sugar dissolves. Add juice and beat well. Pour mixture into 1 gallon freezer can and freeze, according to freezer directions. *Barbara Eveleth*

"Jamocha" Almond Fudge Ice Cream

Homemade

1	quart half and half	1	cup chopped roasted almonds
2-3	tablespoons instant coffee or more to taste		Whole milk
6	eggs	1	(16 ounce) can Hershey's chocolate fudge sauce, well-chilled
1¼	cups sugar		
½	teaspoon salt		
1	tablespoon vanilla		

Scald half and half and add instant coffee. Stir until coffee dissolves. Beat eggs well; add sugar and beat until light and fluffy. Add salt, vanilla and half and half mixture. Pour into ice cream maker cannister, and add whole milk to fill line. Refrigerate overnight. When ready to make ice cream, add almonds to ice cream mixture and freeze in ice cream maker. When machine turns off, remove dasher and add teaspoonsful of fudge sauce and marble through ice cream. Fudge sauce must be cold, or it will melt ice cream too fast. Place in freezer for two hours before serving. Serves 12.

Our family has experimented with this "low calorie" recipe for years, and this is our favorite dessert. *Pat Williams*

☆　　☆　　☆

Strawberry Crêpes

CRÊPES:

¼ cup cold milk
4 eggs, plus 3 egg yolks
1½ cups flour
2 tablespoons sugar

4 tablespoons butter, melted
¾ cup cold water
1 teaspoon salt
4 tablespoons brandy

FILLING:

1 (8 ounce) package cream cheese, softened
½ pint sour cream

3 tablespoons grated orange rind
½ cup sugar

SAUCE:

3 tablespoons butter
3 tablespoons grated orange rind
¾ cup orange juice
½ cup sugar
3 pints fresh strawberries, or 1 (20 ounce) bag frozen strawberries, puréed

1 pint strawberries, sliced, optional
2-3 tablespoons Cointreau or Triple Sec
2 tablespoons brandy

CRÊPES: Place milk, eggs, egg yolks, flour, sugar, melted butter, cold water, salt and brandy in blender and blend well. Refrigerate for a few hours. Cook crêpes in 6 or 7 inch skillet until lightly browned.

FILLING: Mix cream cheese and sour cream, and beat well. Mix orange rind and sugar. Blend with cream cheese mixture until fluffy. Put 2 tablespoons filling in center of each crêpe. Roll and place seam side down in a 9x13 dish.

SAUCE: Place butter, orange rind, orange juice, sugar and strawberries in sauce pan and bring to a boil, stirring until sugar is dissolved. Add Cointreau and brandy, stirring over moderate heat to just boiling. When ready to serve, heat crêpes in 350⁰ oven for 15 minutes, or until heated through. Serve with sauce poured over crêpes. *Ruth Holzschuh*

☆   ☆   ☆

Popsicles

Especially for Children

1	(24 ounce) package Koolaid	1	cup sugar
½	(3 ounce) package Jello	2	cups boiling water
		2	cups cold water

Choose your favorite flavor of Koolaid and Jello. Mix with sugar and boiling water. Dissolve well and then add cold water. Pour into popsicle molds. Neat treat for your children. The Jello keeps this mixture from freezing hard like an ice cube so that these popsicles resemble what you can buy at the store. Much cheaper and makes gobs.

The Cookbook Committee

Hot Fudge Sauce

4	squares (1 ounce each) Baker's chocolate	½	cup white Karo
1	stick margarine	½	teaspoon salt
3	cups sugar	2	teaspoons vanilla
1	(13 ounce) can evaporated milk		

Melt chocolate and margarine in double boiler. Alternately add sugar (¼ cup at a time) and milk until dissolved. Add Karo, salt and vanilla. Keeps beautifully in refrigerator.

Reheat about ½ hour before serving and let sit at room temperature. The sauce will be thick, warm, fudgy and just right as a topping.

The Cookbook Committee

German Chocolate Fondue

9	tablespoons whipping cream	1	(60 grams) bar Tobler Bittersweet
1	(300 grams) bar Toblerone (Tobler Milk Chocolate with honey and almonds)	3	tablespoons rum or Cognac

Heat cream and chocolate together until chocolate is melted. Add rum. You may add more cream if too thick. Use cubed French bread, cherries, bananas, mandarin oranges or anything desired to dip into warm chocolate. Serves 6.

Ute Schnetzinger

☆ ☆ ☆

Cherries Jubilee

2	(16 ounces each) cans Bing Cherries, pitted	½	cup chopped, blanched almonds
1	(10½ ounce) jar currant jelly	12	large vanilla ice cream balls
1	teaspoon cinnamon	1	cup whiskey (96 proof) or Cognac
¼	cup lemon juice		

Drain cherries and pour into shallow casserole. Beat jelly until smooth, stir in cinnamon and lemon juice. Pour over cherries. Sprinkle almonds over all. Heat in 350^0 oven for 10 minutes. Place ice cream balls in serving bowls. Transfer cherries to chafing dish. Pour whiskey or Cognac over cherries and flame. Spoon cherries and flaming sauce over ice cream and serve. *Martha Aldridge*

Bing Cherry Parfait

1	(16 ounce) can Bing Cherries	2	dozen crisp almond macaroons
½	cup Bourbon	1	cup chopped pecans
½	gallon vanilla ice cream		Whipped cream topping

Drain cherries, cut in half and soak in Bourbon for 24 hours. Soften ice cream; add cherries and liquid in which cherries have soaked. Fold in crumbled macaroons and chopped pecans. Mix thoroughly. Fill parfait glasses and place in freezer. Add whipped cream just before serving. *Freddi Thomson*

Sherried Prunes

1½	pounds pitted dried prunes	1	tablespoon vanilla
2	cups Almadens Golden Sherry	1½	cups sugar

Rinse prunes in hot water. In container (a crock if available) mix Sherry and vanilla, add prunes and sugar. Cover and keep at room temperature, stirring every day or so until sugar dissolves. Allow to stand at least a week before serving.

I had the nerve, gall or the audacity to give Helen Corbitt some of these prunes I had fixed. She told me she had a recipe for brandied prunes, but mine was better. So I gave her the recipe. In her next to last cook book, **Helen Corbitt Cooks for Company,** *this recipe appears with me being given credit for it."* *Zoe Thompson*

☆   ☆   ☆

Caramel Cream Pears

6	firm pears, peeled, halved and cored	1/3	cup margarine
1	cup sugar	1	cup heavy cream

Place pears, cut side down, in a 9x13 inch baking pan. Dot with margarine and sprinkle with sugar. Bake at 450°, 45 minutes to 1 hour or until pears are tender and sauce is golden brown. Remove pears. Gradually stir in heavy cream. Return pears to pan and bake at 350° for 10 minutes longer. Serve warm or at room temperature. If desired serve with whipping cream and chopped walnuts. *Phyllis Roberts*

Variation: Add 2 tablespoons Kirsch and 1 teaspoon vanilla to cream.
Betsy Gibson

Baked Peaches

8	peaches	1	stick butter
1	pound brown sugar		Vanilla ice cream

Wash peaches and dry well. Do *not* peel or pit! Place in large, deep baking dish. Dump brown sugar on top of peaches and place butter on top of sugar. It is not necessary to cut up the butter. Bake for about 1½ hours in 350° oven, basting occasionally with juices which will form. Place peaches in serving dishes when you are about to serve your meal, leaving the pan of sauce in the oven. When ready to serve, place small portion of vanilla ice cream on top of each peach and spoon sauce over all. Serves 8. *Ruth Becker*

☆　　☆　　☆

Mother's Bread Pudding

PUDDING:

½   cup white raisins
Rum
Very thinly sliced bread
3   cups milk

⅔   cup sugar
2   eggs, whole
2   egg yolks
1   teaspoon vanilla

SAUCE SABAYON:

½   cup sugar
3   egg yolks

⅔   cup dry white wine
1   tablespoon dark rum

PUDDING: Plump raisins in heated rum. Drain thoroughly. Butter 6 slices bread. Cut off crusts and cut into 4 squares each. Scatter raisins over bottom of 8x10 baking dish and place squares of bread over raisins. Heat milk until film shines on top. Stir in sugar until dissolved. Beat eggs and yolks together well. Slowly add hot milk, beating constantly. Stir in vanilla. Pour mixture over the bread. Place baking dish in roasting pan and fill pan with water to reach ⅔ depth of baking dish. Bake 350⁰ for 40 to 45 minutes or until knife comes out dry.

SAUCE SABAYON: Place sugar and yolks in double boiler and beat with rotary beater until thick and creamy. Stir in wine and rum. Place over simmering water and cook, whipping constantly until sauce thickens and doubles in volume. Do not overcook or it will curdle. Serve warm.

Dottie Pinch

Fudge Pudding

A Tasting Luncheon Favorite

2   tablespoons flour
1   cup sugar
2   eggs, slightly beaten
1   stick butter

2   tablespoons cocoa
1   cup pecans, chopped
1   teaspoon vanilla

Combine flour and sugar. Add gradually to eggs. Stir butter and cocoa in saucepan over low heat until butter is melted. Beat slowly into egg mixture. Mix well. Stir in pecans and vanilla. Pour into shallow 9x9 greased pan and place in larger pan of hot water. Bake at 350⁰ for 30 minutes. May be served warm or cool, with whipped cream or ice cream. Serves 8.

Dorothy Carr

☆   ☆   ☆

Cream Cheese Cups

Tour of Homes Favorite

CHEESE CAKE:

3 (8 ounces each) packages cream cheese	½ teaspoon vanilla
1 cup sugar	5 eggs

TOPPING:

1 cup sour cream	¼ teaspoon vanilla
¼ cup sugar	

CHEESE CAKE: Bring cream cheese to room temperature. Blend with sugar until fluffy. Add vanilla and eggs. Line muffin tins with cupcake papers. Fill ¾ full. Bake for 40 minutes at 300⁰. Remove from oven, cool 10 minutes.

TOPPING: Beat all ingredients. Cover cheesecakes with topping, return to oven for 5 minutes. Makes 25. Refrigerate.

Variation: Line cupcake papers with vanilla wafer crumbs. Add 1½ teaspoons lemon juice or almond extract to cream cheese mixture. Substitute 1 can pie filling (cherry, blueberry, peach, etc.) Cool cheese cups and then spoon on pie filling. Chill. These freeze beautifully.

Pumpkin Cheesecake

Original Recipe

3 (8 ounces each) packages cream cheese	½ teaspoon nutmeg
1½ cups sugar	½ teaspoon ginger
1 cup brown sugar	3 eggs
¼ cup flour	1 (16 ounce) can pumpkin
1 teaspoon cinnamon	Graham cracker crumbs

Blend cheese, both sugars, flour, cinnamon, nutmeg and ginger. Add eggs and beat until fluffy. Mix in pumpkin. Butter a springform pan, lightly coat the bottom of pan with graham cracker crumbs. Pour in batter. Bake for 1½ hours in 350⁰ oven. *Linda Juba*

☆ ☆ ☆

Amaretto Cheesecake

A Very Special Dessert

CRUST:

1½ cups graham cracker crumbs

¼ cup sugar

¼ teaspoon cinnamon

¾ stick unsalted butter or margarine, melted

2 tablespoons crushed toasted almonds

FILLING:

3 (8 ounces each) packages cream cheese, softened

1 cup sugar

4 eggs

⅓ cup Amaretto

¼ teaspoon almond extract

¼ teaspoon vanilla extract

TOPPING:

1½ cups sour cream

2 tablespoons sugar

2 tablespoons Amaretto

¼ cup sliced almonds, toasted

Grated chocolate, optional

Strawberry halves, optional

CRUST: Mix crumbs, sugar, cinnamon, butter and almonds, press firmly on bottom of a lightly greased 9-inch springform pan. Bake 5 minutes in a 225° oven.

FILLING: Beat cream cheese at high speed of an electric mixer until light and fluffy; gradually add 1 cup sugar, beating well. Add eggs one at a time, beating well after each addition. Stir in ⅓ cup Amaretto. Add almond and vanilla extracts; pour mixture into prepared pan. Bake at 375° for 45 to 50 minutes. Do not overcook. Cake will become firm when chilled.

TOPPING: Combine sour cream, 2 tablespoons sugar and 2 tablespoons Amaretto; stir well and spoon over cheesecake. Bake at 500° for 5 minutes. Let cool to room temperature on a wire rack; chill. Garnish with almonds, grated chocolate and strawberry halves. Yield 12 servings.

Danna Almon

☆ ☆ ☆

New York Cheesecake

Exceptional

1	pound cream cheese	½	cup flour
1	pound Ricotta cheese	1	teaspoon vanilla
2	cups sugar	¼	pound soft butter
4	eggs	1	pint sour cream

Put cream cheese, Ricotta cheese, sugar, eggs, flour, vanilla, butter and sour cream in large mixer bowl. Beat at high speed for 20 minutes. Pour into 9 or 10 inch buttered spring form pan. Bake at 350⁰ for 1 hour. Turn off oven and let stand for 2 hours. Will keep 4 weeks in refrigerator. Serves 16. *Lynn Trentham*

Expresso Cheesecake

CRUST:

1½	cups crushed almond macaroons (about 40 cookies)	6	tablespoons melted butter

CHEESECAKE:

4	(8 ounces each) packages cream cheese	⅔	cup sugar
6	semi-sweet chocolate squares, melted	⅓	cup milk
3	eggs	2	teaspoons instant expresso coffee

Mix crushed macaroons and melted butter and press in 9x3 inch springform pan. Beat cream cheese; add chocolate, eggs, sugar, milk and coffee. Pour into pan and bake at 350⁰ for 45 minutes. Cool in pan on wire rack. Remove from pan and refrigerate at least 6 hours. Serves 8-12.

Variation: This can be made without a crust; just dust pan generously with flour. *Martha Clem*

☆ ☆ ☆

No Bake French Cream Cake

Very Rich.

2 cups vanilla wafer crumbs, divided (about ½ pound)
1 stick butter
1 cup powdered sugar
2 eggs, beaten

1 cup whipping cream
½ cup chopped nuts
1 cup drained crushed pineapple

Place 1 cup crumbs in ungreased 8 inch square pan. Thoroughly cream butter and sugar. Add eggs and beat well. Spread carefully over crumbs. Combine cream, nuts and pineapple. Spread over creamed mixture, then sprinkle with remaining crumbs. Let stand 18 to 24 hours in refrigerator. Cut into squares and serve. May top with a scoop of vanilla ice cream. Serves 12-16.   *Thecia Faulkner and Dot McCalpin*

Lemon Fluff

Make Ahead of Time

4 eggs, separated
1 lemon
1 cup sugar, divided
1 (3 ounce) package lemon gelatin

½ cup boiling water
½ pint whipping cream, whipped
8 vanilla wafers, finely crumbled

Beat egg yolks and set aside. Grate the lemon rind, squeeze the juice and add both to egg yolks with ½ cup sugar. Cook over boiling water, stirring constantly until the mixture thickens. Dissolve the lemon gelatin in the boiling water. Cool before adding it to the egg mixture. Blend well and refrigerate until it starts to congeal. Beat the egg whites until frothy and add remaining ½ cup sugar a tablespoon at a time, beating well between additions. Fold carefully into gelatin mixture. Fold in whipped cream and pour into an 8 inch square dish. Sprinkle with vanilla wafer crumbs and refrigerate until congealed. Serves 8.

Eileen MacWithey

☆　　☆　　☆

Chocolate Refrigerator Dessert

Make Ahead

2	cups powdered sugar		1	cup pecans
¼	teaspoon salt		1	teaspoon vanilla
4	tablespoons cocoa		1¾	cups vanilla wafer crumbs, divided
½	cup margarine			
2	eggs, separated			

Sift sugar, measure, sift again with salt and cocoa. Cream margarine. Add sugar, salt and cocoa creaming until light and fluffy. Add unbeaten egg yolks one at a time beating until thoroughly blended. Add pecans and vanilla. Fold in stiffly beaten egg whites. Line 9x13 pan with heavy waxed paper cut to extend over the sides. Spread half of wafer crumbs over bottom of pan. Pour in mixture. Top with remaining crumbs. Chill in refrigerator overnight or several hours. Serve plain or with whipped cream. Serves 15-20.   *Anna Wade Pierson*

Chocolate Creme Gâteau

1	(12 ounce) package chocolate chips		1	cup chopped nuts
4	eggs, separated		1	teaspoon vanilla
Pinch of salt			1	pint whipping cream
¼	cup sugar		1	(10 inch) angel food cake

Melt chocolate chips over low heat. Cool. Beat egg yolks until light and stir into chocolate. Beat egg whites until stiff, add 2 tablespoons sugar gradually. Fold into chocolate mixture. Whip cream until stiff and add salt, remaining sugar, vanilla and nuts. Tear cake into bite-sized pieces. Put ½ of cake in a greased 9x13 glass dish. Pour ½ of chocolate mixture over cake. Repeat. Chill 6 hours or overnight. Top with whipped cream and additional nuts if desired. Serves 12.   *Imp Lightner*

Variation: Melt 1½ cups chocolate chips in 4 tablespoons water. Increase sugar to ½ cup. Omit whipping cream. This version is not as rich and saves a few calories.

☆   ☆   ☆

Pineapple Triffle

1   (3 ounce) package lemon
Jello

½   cup sugar

2   cups boiling water

1   (8 ounce) can crushed
pineapple, drained

½   pint whipping cream

Combine Jello and sugar. Dissolve in boiling water. When it begins to set add pineapple and whipped cream. Pour into a 2 quart dish or individual serving dishes. Chill.

This is my husband's grandmother's recipe which she taught me to make when I was a bride. The "triffle" means a little bit of dessert.

Eileen MacWithey

Virginia Torte

Ice Cream and Crunch

ALMOND LACE COOKIES:

⅔   cup finely chopped
blanched almonds

½   cup sugar

1   tablespoon flour

½   cup butter

2   tablespoons light cream

¾   gallon vanilla ice cream

CHOCOLATE SAUCE:

½   cup butter

4   squares unsweetened
chocolate

1½ cups sugar

½   cup cocoa

1   cup half and half

Pinch of salt

1   teaspoon vanilla

COOKIES: Place almonds, sugar, flour, butter and light cream in a saucepan and bring slowly to a boil, stirring constantly. Drop by teaspoonsful on foil covered cookie sheet. They spread a lot, but it makes no difference if they run together. Bake 6 to 8 minutes at 375⁰. Watch carefully. They should be golden brown. When cool they are easily removed from the foil.

ASSEMBLY: In 9x13 pan place layer of cookies, layer of ice cream, layer of cookies, layer of ice cream and top layer of cookies. Cover and place in freezer. This keeps well in the freezer and can be made up to a week ahead of time.

SAUCE: At serving time melt butter and chocolate. Mix sugar and cocoa. Add sugar mixture, half and half and salt. Bring to boiling point only, stirring constantly. Add vanilla. Cut ice cream mixture into squares and serve with chocolate sauce. Serves 12.

Ruth Holzschuh

☆   ☆   ☆

Pizza Fruit Platter

Beautiful Dessert

1	(18.5 ounce) package yellow cake mix	1	envelope Dream Whip (do not substitute)
¼	cup water		Strawberries
2	eggs		Bananas
¼	cup butter		Seedless green grapes
¼	cup brown sugar		Pineapple
½	cup nuts, chopped		Peaches

Heat oven to 350⁰. Grease and flour two round pizza pans. (I use Pam). Combine cake mix, water, eggs, butter and brown sugar and mix thoroughly. Fold in nuts. Divide batter evenly between the two pans. Bake 15 to 20 minutes. Cool on rack. Freeze one pizza base. The following directions are for one pizza, double if you want to use both. Prepare Dream Whip. Spread over pizza base. Arrange the following fruit in a circular pattern starting with strawberries on outer edge, followed by sliced bananas, seedless green grapes, pineapple tidbits, sliced peaches or nectarines, etc. and finish by putting a whole strawberry in the center. Brush with apricot glaze and refrigerate. This recipe can be made ahead several hours and looks beautiful.

APRICOT GLAZE:

⅓	cup apricot preserves	2	tablespoons water

Heat until preserves are melted. Remove from heat, strain and cool. Brush over top of fruit, making sure to cover bananas well. Serves 12.

Pat Williams

Huguenot Torte

4	eggs	2	cups chopped pecans or walnuts
3	cups sugar		
8	tablespoons flour	2	teaspoons vanilla
½	teaspoon salt	½	pint cream, whipped
5	teaspoons baking powder		Additional chopped nuts
2	cups chopped tart cooking apples		

Beat eggs in electric mixer until frothy and lemon colored. Add sugar, flour, salt, baking powder, apples, nuts and vanilla. Stir. Pour into well-buttered 8x12 inch pan. Bake at 325⁰ for 45 minutes or until crusty and brown. To serve, scoop up with pancake turner, keeping crusty portion on top. Serve with whipped cream and a sprinkling of chopped nuts. Serves 16.

Adele Hutton

☆   ☆   ☆

Date Meringue

A Testing Luncheon Favorite

4	egg whites	1	cup chopped pecans
1	cup sugar	2	tablespoons flour
1	teaspoon baking powder	6	tablespoons cracker
1	teaspoon vanilla		crumbs (saltines or Ritz)
1	(8 ounce) package chopped dates		

Bring egg whites to room temperature and beat until stiff, but not dry. Add sugar gradually while beating. Add baking powder and vanilla. Roll dates and pecans in flour. Fold cracker crumbs, dates and pecans in egg white mixture. Pour mixture into a well greased 9 inch square pan. Bake at 300^0 about 60 minutes or until crusty on top. Serve warm or chilled. Top with whipped cream. This is very easy to make and keeps a long time in the refrigerator, just cover baking pan with foil. Serves 8-12.

Betsy Halford

Chocolate Amaretto Mousse Cake

6	ounces chocolate chips (do not use imitation flavored)	4	egg yolks
18	whole blanched almonds	$\frac{1}{3}$	cup sugar
$\frac{1}{2}$	cup Amaretto	2	cups milk
2	envelopes unflavored gelatin	4	egg whites, stiffly beaten
		2	cups whipping cream, whipped, divided
$\frac{1}{4}$	cup water	2	packages lady fingers, split

Place chocolate in top of double boiler over very hot, but not boiling water. Stir until chocolate melts. Dip bottom half of almonds into chocolate and place on waxed paper. Chill. Gradually stir Amaretto into remaining chocolate. Set aside. In sauce pan combine gelatin and water and dissolve. Stir in egg yolks, sugar and milk. Stir over low heat until mixture thickens slightly and coats a metal spoon. Stir in chocolate. Chill until mixture mounds. Fold in egg whites. Remove one cup of whipped cream for garnish. Fold remaining cream into chocolate mixture. Line bottom and sides of an ungreased 9 inch spring-form pan with split lady fingers. Pour in chocolate mixture. Chill. When ready to serve, remove sides of pan and pipe rosettes of reserved cream around outer edge of cake. Press an almond into each rosette. Chill until ready to serve. Makes 1 nine inch cake. Serves 10. May be made one day ahead.

Lois Williams

☆　　☆　　☆

My Hypocritical Mousse

Gourmet Dessert, But Easy as 1-2-3!

3	tablespoons Carnation hot cocoa mix	Dash of salt
1	teaspoon instant coffee	½ (4 ounce) container of Cool Whip
2	cups milk	Semisweet or sweet chocolate
1	(3¾ ounce) package instant vanilla pudding	for curls

Dissolve cocoa mix and coffee in milk. Make pudding according to package direction using milk in which the cocoa mix and coffee has been dissolved. Let set for about 5 minutes. Fold in Cool Whip. Divide pudding between 4 or 5 sherbet glasses. Top with chocolate curls. Curl chocolate by drawing a vegetable parer across a square or bar of chocolate which is at room temperature.

Variation: Recipe may be doubled; placed in a spring form pan lined with split lady fingers. If lady fingers are dry, sprinkle with Sherry or rum. Allow to set until firm. Turn out on serving plate. Garnish with whipped cream and chocolate curls. Serves 4-5.   *Ruth Dirks*

Frozen Fruit Mousse

20	large marshmallows	1 cup cream, whipped
2	tablespoons lemon juice	
1	(10 ounce) package frozen raspberries or strawberries, thawed	

Melt marshmallows in double boiler. Add lemon juice. Cool slightly and add fruit, fold in whipped cream. Pour into 10x10 freezer dish and freeze. Serves 8.   *Linda Juba*

☆   ☆   ☆

Frozen Almond Chocolate Mousse

Yummy and Rich

⅔	cups almonds, divided	1	(6 ounce) package
½	cup graham cracker		chocolate chips
	crumbs	2	eggs, separated
3	tablespoons melted butter	1	cup whipping cream,
3	tablespoons sugar, divided		divided
1	pint coffee ice cream	3	tablespoons dark rum

Toast almonds in 300° oven for 15 minutes. Chop while warm. Combine ⅓ cup almonds with crumbs, melted butter and 1 tablespoon sugar. Pack in even layer in oiled 9 inch spring form pan. Bake at 350° for 10 minutes. Cool; place in freezer until chilled. Spoon ice cream over crumb crust. Return to freezer. Melt chocolate chips over hot water. Beat egg whites in small bowl to soft peaks. Beat in remaining 2 tablespoons sugar. Beat ½ cup cream. Beat egg yolks; add melted chocolate and rum. Beat well. Fold in egg whites and whipped cream. Set aside 2 tablespoons almonds for topping. Beat remainder into chocolate mixture. Pour over ice cream layer. Sprinkle with almonds. Freeze. At serving time beat remaining ½ cup whipping cream and decorate with almonds. Soften ½ hour before serving. Serves 12. *Patti Henry*

Frozen Grand Marnier Soufflé

1	cup sugar	¼	cup Grand Marnier
⅓	cup water	2	cups heavy cream
2	tablespoons grated orange	1	(10 inch) angel food cake
	rind		cut in 1 inch cubes
6	egg yolks		

Over moderate heat bring to a boil the sugar, water and grated orange rind. Cook the syrup to 220° on a candy thermometer. Beat the egg yolks until thick and lemon colored. Pour the syrup in a stream over the egg yolks and beat until thick. Cool. Beat in the Grand Marnier. Beat the heavy cream until lightly whipped and fold into the egg yolk mixture. Fit a 4 cup soufflé dish with a 6 inch band of wax paper doubled and oiled to form a collar extending 2 inches above the rim and tie with a string. Spoon a 2 inch layer of the custard into the dish and top it with half the cake cubes. Cover the angel food cake cubes with another layer of the custard and add the remaining cake cubes and another layer of the custard on top. Freeze for 6 hours. Serve with whipped cream flavored with Grand Marnier. Serves 6-8. *Kaye Burkhardt*

☆　　☆　　☆

Grand Marnier Soufflé

⅓ cup butter
¾ cup flour
½ teaspoon salt
1½ cups milk
5 eggs, separated
3 additional egg whites

1 cup sugar
2 tablespoons lemon juice
1 teaspoon grated lemon rind
½ cup Grand Marnier

Lightly grease a 2 or 2½ quart soufflé dish, then sprinkle it with granulated sugar to prevent sticking. Cut a strip of foil about 30 inches long and 6 inches wide so it will overlap itself by at least 2 inches when placed around outside of dish. Fold it in half lengthwise, then grease one side with butter and sprinkle with sugar. Tie collar around dish with string, sugared side in, extending collar at least 2 inches above top of dish.

Melt butter over low heat in saucepan, don't let it brown. Remove from heat, add flour and salt, mixing until smooth. Add milk gradually, stirring constantly. Return to heat and cook, stirring constantly until thick and smooth. Remove from heat. Separate eggs. Set egg whites aside. Beat the 5 egg yolks until thick. Add hot cream sauce a small amount at a time, beating constantly until all the sauce has been added and the mixture is a creamy custard. Set aside to cool. If you make the sauce ahead of time, keep it covered and at room temperature. When it is hot weather, refrigerate the sauce until 30 minutes before continuing with the soufflé. Preheat oven to 350⁰. Beat all 8 egg whites until soft peaks form when the beater is lifted gently. Keep all the egg whites returning to the center of the bowl. Add sugar gradually, beating constantly until stiff meringue is formed. Set aside. Gradually beat in lemon juice a few drops at a time to the egg yolk mixture. Stir in lemon rind and Grand Marnier mixing them into the egg mixture well. Add all at once to the egg whites using light strokes to mix. Pour into the soufflé dish and set dish in a pan containing 1 inch of hot water. Bake at 350⁰ for 1 hour and 20 minutes. Remove from oven, cut string to remove collar and serve immediately. Serves 6. *Suzann Deppe*

☆ ☆ ☆

Mexican Kahlua Soufflé

1	tablespoon cornstarch	1	tablespoon unflavored
¼	cup plus 1 tablespoon		gelatin
	water	½	cup Kahlua
1	cup evaporated milk	¼	teaspoon vanilla
3	eggs, separated		Pinch of salt
5	tablespoons sugar, divided		

Mix cornstarch with a little water and add to milk. Cook over low heat, stirring constantly until thickened. Beat egg yolks lightly with 4 tablespoons of the sugar. Soften gelatin in ¼ cup of water. Add yolks and gelatin to milk and cook for 5 minutes, stirring constantly. Allow to cool slightly and add Kahlua and vanilla. Add salt and 1 tablespoon of sugar to egg whites and beat until standing in peaks. Fold into the yolk mixture, pour into soufflé dish and chill until set. Serves 6.

Freddi Thomson

Grasshopper Soufflé

1	cup sugar, divided	1	(8 ounce) package cream
2	envelopes of Knox gelatin		cheese
2	cups water	¼	cup Crème de Menthe
4	eggs, separated	1	cup heavy cream, whipped

Combine ¾ cup sugar and gelatin and gradually add water. Stir over low heat until dissolved. Remove from heat, blend in beaten egg yolks. Return to heat and cook 2 to 3 minutes. Gradually add softened cream cheese and mix until well blended. Stir in Crème de Menthe. Chill until thickened. Beat egg whites until soft peaks form; gradually add remaining ¼ cup sugar. Beat until stiff peaks form. Fold whites and whipping cream into creamed mixture. Wrap a 3 inch collar of aluminum foil around top of 1½ quart soufflé dish. Secure with tape. Pour soufflé mixture into dish and chill until firm. Remove collar before serving. Garnish with berries and cream. Serves 4-6. *Brenda Chattaway*

☆　　☆　　☆

Paskha

Russian Easter Dessert

4	(8 ounces each) packages cream cheese	2	tablespoons Kirsch
2	sticks butter	¾	cup toasted slivered almonds
3	egg yolks	1	cup firm, fresh strawberries, sliced
2	cups powdered sugar		
1	envelope unflavored gelatin, dissolved in 2 tablespoons cold water	1	(6 inch) clay flower pot lined with cheesecloth that has been wrung out in cold water
2	teaspoons vanilla		
1	cup whipping cream		

Beat cheese and butter on low speed until well blended. Add egg yolks one at a time. Gradually beat in sugar. Blend dissolved gelatin into cheese mixture. Blend vanilla, whipping cream and Kirsch and add to cheese mixture. Fold nuts and strawberries carefully into mixture. Spoon mixture into mold and cover with clear plastic wrap. Refrigerate overnight. When ready to serve, unmold onto plate, remove cheesecloth and decorate with gumdrops, candied violets or serve with strawberry sauce. Serves 16.   *Martha Clem*

The Russians use XB (symbol for "Christ is Risen"), forming this with the gumdrops or whatever you decorate with.

Four Layer Lemon Delight

1	cup flour	2	(3¾ ounces each) packages instant lemon pudding
½	cup margarine		
½	cup chopped pecans	1	tablespoon lemon juice
1	(8 ounce) tub plus 1 cup Cool Whip, divided	3	cups minus 1 tablespoon milk
1	cup powdered sugar		
1	(8 ounce) package cream cheese		

Mix flour, margarine and pecans. Pat into a 9x13 inch baking dish and bake 15 minutes at 375°. Cool. Beat 1 cup Cool Whip, powdered sugar and cream cheese until fluffy. Spread on nut-crust. Mix pudding, lemon juice and milk. Spread over the second layer. Top with container of Cool Whip. Refrigerate at least 4 hours.   *Susan MacWithey*

☆   ☆   ☆

Brandied Fruit

Time Consuming, but Worth It!

Dissolve.....................	1	yeast cake in ¼ cup warm water
Add.......................	1	cup pineapple chunks or tidbits, drained
	1	cup sliced peaches
	1	cup red Maraschino cherries
	3	cups sugar

(You may add ½ cup brandy at this point – it is optional – I do not.) Mix and stir often. Keep this mixture in a pretty jar, at least ½ gallon, but do not seal completely. This sets on the cabinet and is a "conversation piece."

Two weeks later add.........	1	cup peaches, drained
	1	cup sugar
Two weeks later add.........	1	cup pineapple chunks or tidbits, drained
	1	cup sugar
Two weeks later add.........	1	cup cherries, drained
	1	cup sugar

Do not let the mixture go below the original 3 cups or it will lose its fermenting power. It may be divided after the last addition listed. Do not refrigerate. Apricot halves, pear halves, and mandarin orange sections may be used in place of peaches, etc. Once the starter is made, and divided you should add a cup of fruit and a cup of sugar about every ten days to two weeks.

The juice serves well when giving a starter to a friend. Use one cup juice and 2 cups fruit. At this time add fruits as in step two in recipe, let set one day, then stir every day until all sugar is dissolved. Continue to stir most every day and add new fruit and sugar each two weeks. Serve over ice cream, cottage cheese and make lots of brandied fruit cakes.

Pearl Stewart

☆　　☆　　☆

Brandied Fruit Cake

2	cups sugar	½	teaspoon salt
¾	cup cooking oil	3	cups Brandied Fruit,
3	eggs, beaten		drained (see p. 301)
3	cups flour	2	cups pecans
1	teaspoon baking soda	2	teaspoons vanilla

Cream sugar, oil and eggs. Add flour, soda and salt. Fold in fruit, pecans and vanilla. Flour and grease a Bundt pan. Pour in cake batter. Bake in preheated oven at 325° for 1 hour and 15 minutes. Test with toothpick.

Variation: For a different flavor to the cake add ½ teaspoon salt; ¼-½ teaspoon cloves, and ¼-½ teaspoon nutmeg.

I have learned the cake may need to cook one hour 15 to 30 minutes, so be sure to check cake before taking from oven. The cake keeps well and freezes beautifully, so do not hesitate to make cake when your brandied fruit is ready.

Pearl Stewart

Apple Blossom Cake

2	cups sugar	1¼	cups oil
3	cups flour	2	eggs
1½	tablespoons baking soda	½	teaspoon cinnamon
1	(16 ounce) can apple pie filling	½	teaspoon nutmeg
		½	teaspoon allspice
1	cup chopped pecans	1	teaspoon vanilla flavoring

Do not use a mixer. Big wooden spoon works best. Mix all of above until moistened. Pour into a greased tube or Bundt pan. Bake at 325° for 1 hour and 20 minutes. Dust with powdered sugar.

Dolores Spence

☆   ☆   ☆

Coconut-Lemon Cake

CAKE:

2	sticks butter		3	cups flour
2	cups sugar		2½	teaspoons baking powder
4	eggs		½	teaspoon salt
2	teaspoons vanilla		1	cup milk

FILLING:

1	cup sugar		½	cup water
3½	tablespoons cornstarch		3	egg yolks
¾	cup fresh orange juice		1	(3½ ounce) can coconut
¼	cup fresh lemon juice			

ICING:

3	egg whites		1½	tablespoons water
¾	cup light corn syrup		⅓	teaspoon vinegar
¾	cup sugar			

CAKE: Preheat oven to 350⁰. Cream butter and sugar. Add eggs and beat well. Add vanilla. Sift flour, baking powder and salt together; add alternately with milk. Bake for 25 to 30 minutes in 3 greased 8 inch round layer pans.

FILLING: Combine sugar and corn starch. Mix orange and lemon juice with water and add slowly. Bring to boiling point and remove from heat. Beat egg yolks and add gradually to hot mixture. Return to heat and boil 2 minutes. Cool. Add coconut. Split each layer into halves and cover with filling.

ICING: Combine egg whites, corn syrup, sugar, water and vinegar in top of a double boiler. Beat constantly over rapidly boiling water until icing stands in peaks. Frost with icing. Sprinkle with coconut.

Millie Fiedorek

Hint: For a perfect pound cake, or any cake, have eggs and butter at room temperature.

☆   ☆   ☆

Orange Cake

CAKE:

1	orange	2	eggs
1	cup raisins	2	cups sifted flour
1	cup sugar	1	teaspoon baking soda
1	cup butter	¾	cup sour milk

ICING:

¼	cup melted margarine	1	(16 ounce) box powdered
2	tablespoons orange juice		sugar
Dash of salt			

CAKE: Grease and flour a 9x13 inch pan. Grind orange and raisins. Reserve 2 tablespoons for icing. Cream sugar and butter; then slowly add eggs and orange-raisin mixture. Dissolve soda in milk. Add this to the mixture alternately with the flour. Bake at 350⁰ for 30 minutes. Serves 15-18.

ICING: Add margarine, 2 tablespoons reserved orange-raisin mix, orange juice and salt to powdered sugar. Mix until smooth.   *Lucy Kuhn*

Holiday Apple Cake

2	cups sugar	1	teaspoon baking soda
2	eggs	3	cups peeled diced raw
1½	cups cooking oil		apples
3	cups flour (sift before measuring)	1	cup chopped pecans
		¾	cup red candied cherries
1	teaspoon cinnamon	¾	cup coconut
½	teaspoon salt	2	teaspoons vanilla

Cream sugar and eggs. Add cooking oil slowly and beat well. Combine flour, cinnamon, salt and soda. Mix well. Add apples, pecans, cherries, coconut and vanilla. Mix well. Pour into tube pan and bake at 325⁰ for 1 hour.   *Pate Stanphill*

Variation: Cherries and coconut may be omitted.

☆   ☆   ☆

Rhubarb Upside Down Cake

1	stick margarine	2	teaspoons baking powder
2	cups sugar, divided	⅓	cup milk
2	eggs	4	cups sliced rhubarb
½	teaspoon vanilla	1	cup minature
1¾	cups flour		marshmallows

Cream margarine until soft; add 1 cup sugar and cream until well blended. Add eggs and vanilla and beat until light and fluffy. Sift flour with baking powder and add to first mixture alternately with milk, beating well between additions until batter is smooth. Place rhubarb which has been cut in ½ inch slices in a heavy oven-proof 10 inch skillet. Sprinkle 1 cup sugar evenly over rhubarb and distribute marshmallows over all. Pour cake batter over this and bake in a preheated oven at 375⁰ until the top springs back when touched lightly with the finger. Turn out on plate 5 minutes after it comes from oven. Serves 8.

Eileen MacWithey

Yum Yum Cake

CAKE:

2	eggs	2	cups flour
2	cups sugar	2½	teaspoons baking powder
2	cups crushed pineapple, undrained		

TOPPING:

1	cup sugar	1	cup coconut
1	stick margarine	1	cup chopped pecans
1	(5½ ounce) can evaporated milk	1	teaspoon vanilla
		½	teaspoon lemon juice

CAKE: Preheat oven to 350⁰. Grease and flour a 13x9x2 inch pan. Beat together eggs and sugar. Stir in crushed pineapple. Add flour and baking powder and mix thoroughly. Bake 25 to 30 minutes. (There isn't supposed to be any shortening in cake.)

TOPPING: Boil sugar, margarine and evaporated milk 3 or 4 minutes. Stir in coconut, pecans, vanilla and lemon juice. Make holes in top of cake with toothpick. Pour over hot cake. Serves 24.   *Chris Norman*

☆   ☆   ☆

Jam-Nut Cake

1	cup butter	1	cup nuts
2	cups sugar	3	cups flour
4	eggs	1	teaspoon nutmeg
1	cup buttermilk	1	teaspoon cloves
1	teaspoon baking soda	1	teaspoon cinnamon
1	cup of raisins		
1	cup jam, strawberry or your favorite flavor		

Cream butter and sugar. Add eggs, one at a time and beat well after each addition. Beat the soda into the buttermilk until it foams. Add to cake and beat well again. Cut the raisins in half and add with the jam and nuts. Beat again. Sift together flour, nutmeg, cloves and cinnamon. Combine thoroughly. Pour into a well greased tube cake pan and bake about 1 hour and 30 minutes in a preheated 275-300° oven.

Tura Bethune

Sausage Cake

3	cups firmly packed brown sugar	3¼	cups sifted flour, divided
1	pound bulk sausage, uncooked	1	teaspoon nutmeg
		3	teaspoons baking powder
1	egg, beaten	2	teaspoons baking soda
¼	cup raisins	¼	teaspoon salt
1	cup chopped pecans	1	cup strong black coffee
		1	teaspoon vanilla

Mix sugar with sausage and egg. Reserve. Mix ¼ cup flour with raisins and pecans. Reserve. Sift remaining flour, nutmeg, baking powder, soda and salt together and add to sausage mixture alternately with coffee. Add vanilla and beat well. Add floured raisins and nuts. Pour into well greased tube pan. Bake at 350° for 1¼ hours. Freezes indefinitely. Great served with eggs. Serves 12-14.

Jean Zinser

☆   ☆   ☆

Hawaiian Banana Cake

CAKE:

1⅞ cups flour
1½ cups sugar
¾ teaspoon salt
1½ teaspoons baking soda

¾ cup margarine
1½ cups banana purée
3 eggs

CREAM CHEESE FROSTING:

½ pound powdered sugar
4 ounces cream cheese

½ stick softened butter
1 tablespoon lemon extract

Mix flour, sugar, salt and soda together. Add margarine and combine as you would in making pie crust. Mash bananas with fork and add to the flour and shortening, along with well beaten eggs. Fold the liquid ingredients into the dry very quickly and do not overmix. Spoon into buttered and floured 11 inch round pan. Put pan down with a thump to remove air holes. Bake in 350⁰ oven for 45 minutes or until it tests done with cake tester. This is a very good cake served without icing. May be dressed up with cream cheese frosting. Mix together until smooth, powdered sugar, cream cheese, butter and lemon extract. Pecans may be added before spreading on cake. *Dorothy Carr*

Pumpkin Pudding Cake

CAKE:

1 (29 ounce) can or 2 (16 ounce) cans pumpkin
½ teaspoon salt
2 teaspoons ginger
2 teaspoons cinnamon

3 eggs, beaten
2 tablespoons molasses
½ cup sugar
1 (14 ounce) can sweetened condensed milk

TOPPING:

½ box white cake mix (or 1 one layer box)
1¼ sticks margarine

Whipped cream or ice cream, optional
1 cup chopped pecans

Preheat oven to 350⁰. Mix pumpkin, salt, ginger, cinnamon, eggs, molasses, sugar and sweetened condensed milk. Put into 9x13 dish.

TOPPING: Crumble dry cake mix over pumpkin mixture; then drizzle with melted margarine and cover with chopped pecans. Bake at 350⁰ for 1 hour. Top with whipped cream or ice cream, if desired. Serves 15-20. *Anna Wade Pierson*

☆   ☆   ☆

Coke Cake

Served at Progressive Dinner

CAKE:

2	cups flour	½	cup buttermilk
2	cups sugar	2	eggs
1	cup pecans	1	teaspoon baking soda
2	sticks margarine or butter	1	teaspoon vanilla
3	heaping tablespoons cocoa	1½	cups miniature
1	cup Coke		marshmallows

ICING:

1	stick margarine or butter	1	cup chopped pecans
3	tablespoons cocoa	1	teaspoon vanilla
6	tablespoons Coke		
½	(16 ounce) box powdered sugar		

CAKE: Combine flour, sugar and nuts in mixing bowl. Heat butter, Coke and cocoa to boiling. Pour over flour and sugar mixture. Mix thoroughly. Add buttermilk, eggs, soda, vanilla and marshmallows. Beat together. Pour into greased 9x13 inch pan. Bake at 350⁰ for 30 minutes.

ICING: Combine butter, cocoa and Coke. Heat to boiling. Pour over powdered sugar. Beat with nuts and vanilla. Spoon over *hot* cake. If icing is too thick heat more Coke and add to filling.   *Ann Daniel*

Long before the Europeans came to the America's, Indians discovered Texas' vast store of oil. The first Texas oil well was drilled in 1866 and the state continues to lead the United States both in oil and natural gas production and in reserve supplies.

☆   ☆   ☆

Double Toffee Cake

Freezes Well

CAKE:

2	cups flour	1	cup water
1	cup sugar	1	(3¾ ounce) package
2	teaspoons baking powder		instant vanilla pudding
¾	cup oil	1	(3¾ ounce) package
4	eggs		instant butterscotch
1	teaspoon salt		pudding
1	teaspoon vanilla		

TOPPING:

1½	cups brown sugar	1	tablespoon cinnamon
1	cup chopped nuts		

Grease and flour Bundt pan. Beat together flour, sugar, baking powder, oil, eggs, salt, vanilla, water and puddings. Set aside. Put ⅓ of the batter in bottom of pan. Mix together topping of brown sugar, nuts and cinnamon. Sprinkle ½ of topping on top of batter. Next cover with ⅓ of batter, other ½ of topping and finish with last ⅓ of batter. Bake at 350⁰ for 40 to 45 minutes. Cool 1 hour in pan before removing. Serves 10-12. *Mary Eileen MacWithey*

Old Kentucky Pound Cake

8	eggs, separated	1	teaspoon vanilla, or lemon
2⅔	cups sugar, divided		or almond extract
1	cup Crisco	3½	cups sifted flour
1	cup butter	½	cup canned milk or cream

Whip egg whites until stiff using ½ cup of the sugar, refrigerate. Cream the rest of the sugar, egg yolks, shortening, butter and flavoring on medium speed for about 10 minutes. On low speed fold in flour and cream alternately. Continue beating for 5 more minutes. Fold egg whites into batter and pour into greased, floured Bundt or 10 inch tube pan. May also use 2 loaf pans. Bake in preheated 325⁰ oven for 1 hour, 45 minutes. *Martha Clem*

☆   ☆   ☆

Old Fashioned Pound Cake

1	cup butter (do not substitute)	½	teaspoon salt
½	cup Crisco	½	teaspoon baking powder
3	cups sugar	1	cup milk
5	eggs	1	teaspoon lemon juice
3	cups flour		Dash of nutmeg (scant ⅛ teaspoon)

Blend together butter and Crisco. Add sugar gradually, creaming well. Add eggs, one at a time. Sift together flour, salt and baking powder. Mix milk, lemon juice and nutmeg and add alternately to the mixture, starting and ending with flour. Put in greased, floured 10 inch tube pan. Bake at 350° for 1 hour 30 minutes. Turn on cooling rack.

Dottie Pinch

Variation: Increase butter to 2 sticks. Omit lemon juice and nutmeg. Add ½ teaspoon vanilla and ½ teaspoon butter flavoring. May need to increase baking to 1 hour and 45 minutes. *Katy Glidewell*

Lucy's Apricot Praline Torte

Absolutely Divine

Poundcake   Apricot preserves

PRALINE POWDER:

¾	cup chopped almonds	2	tablespoons butter
¼	cup sugar		

BUTTERCREAM:

1	stick unsalted butter (do not substitute)	2-3	tablespoons cream or milk
2½	cups powdered sugar	½	cup praline powder
		1	teaspoon vanilla

PRALINE POWDER: Melt butter and sugar until sugar starts to carmelize. Watch carefully. *Do not let scorch.* Add almonds. Remove from heat. Pour onto greased platter. When cooled crush in food processor or blender.

BUTTERCREAM: Cream butter and sugar. Add cream or milk. Fold in praline powder and vanilla. Cut your favorite pound cake into three layers. Spread a layer of heated apricot preserves; then buttercream. Add another layer of cake, preserves, and buttercream. Place top layer on cake and dust lightly with powdered sugar. May be prepared ahead and freezes well.

Linda Juba

☆   ☆   ☆

Rich Cream Cheese Pound Cake
with English Lemon Sauce

A Tour of Homes Recipe

CAKE:

¾ cup butter
2 (3 ounces each) packages cream cheese
1½ cups sugar
1 teaspoon vanilla

4 eggs
1¾ cups flour
½ teaspoon baking powder
¼ teaspoon salt
Powdered sugar

SAUCE:

4 eggs, beaten
2 cups sugar
½ cup butter

1 tablespoon shredded lemon peel
½ cup lemon juice

CAKE: Bring butter, cream cheese and eggs to room temperature. Grease and flour fluted tube pan. Set aside. In a large bowl beat butter and cream cheese until creamy. Gradually add sugar beating at medium speed 4 to 5 minutes. Add vanilla and eggs, one at a time, beat 1 minute after each addition. Combine flour, baking powder and salt. Gradually add to cream cheese mixture. Beat at low speed. Turn batter into pan. Bake 55 minutes at 325⁰. Cool 10 minutes. Remove from pan. Cool completely. Sprinkle powdered sugar on top. Serves 10-12.

SAUCE: Combine eggs, sugar, butter, lemon peel and lemon juice in medium sauce pan. Cook over medium heat stirring constantly until mixture is thick and bubbly, about 10 minutes. Chill and serve with Cream Cheese Pound Cake. Makes 2⅔ cups. *Danna Almon*

To make sweetened condensed milk mix ⅔ cup sugar and 1 cup powdered milk. Add 3 tablespoons melted butter and ½ cup boiling water. Mix until smooth. Refrigerate. Makes 1½ cups.

☆   ☆   ☆

Black Forest Cherry Torte

CAKE:

1   stick butter or margarine
1½ cups sugar
5   eggs
2¼ cups sifted flour

½   cup baking cocoa mixed with a little water
1   teaspoon baking powder

FILLING:

Kirschwasser (cherry brandy)
1½ (10 ounces each) jars seedless raspberry jelly
2   (16 ounces each) cans pitted sour cherries
½   pint heavy cream, whipped

1   ounce German sweet chocolate
1   (3 ounce) package vanilla pudding
1   stick unsalted sweet butter

Preheat oven to 350⁰. Cream butter and sugar until light and fluffy. Add the eggs and flour alternately, and blend thoroughly. Beat in the cocoa. Add the baking powder and mix well. Pour batter into 9 inch spring form pan. Bake approximately 1 hour. Allow cake to cool. When cool, you may fill and assemble the cake.

Prepare the vanilla pudding according to package directions. Add butter after the pudding has cooled somewhat, and stir until mixture cools further. Set aside.

Slice cooled cake in three layers. Sprinkle the layers with Kirschwasser. Spread some raspberry jelly over the top of each layer.

Drain cherries and spread a few cherries on top of the first layer. Put about ½ of the vanilla pudding mixture on top of the cherries. Place second layer on top of first layer. Place cherries and pudding mixture on top of second layer as before. Place third layer on top of cake.

Spread whipped cream on top and sides of cake. Decorate the top of the cake with the remaining cherries. Grate the chocolate over top of cake. Refrigerate until serving time. Makes 12-15 servings.

Cake may be baked the night before and assembled during the day you wish to serve it.

Add cocoa to the second half of pudding if you wish. Serves 8.

Lois Williams

☆   ☆   ☆

Chocolate Chip Date Pudding Cake

1	(8 ounce) package dates	1	stick butter
1	teaspoon baking soda	1	cup sugar
1½	cups hot water	2	eggs, slightly beaten
2	tablespoons cocoa	1	(6 ounce) package
1	teaspoon vanilla		chocolate chips
¾	cup flour	½	cup nuts

Mix dates, soda and hot water. Let stand until cool. Cream butter with sugar, add eggs, cocoa and vanilla. Add date mixture and flour alternately to the butter mixture. Pour into 9x13 pan and sprinkle with chocolate chips and nuts. Bake 40 minutes at 350⁰.

Mary Childress Jones

Devil's Food Cake

Old Fashioned Goodness

1¾	cups sugar	½	cup cocoa
½	cup shortening	2	cups sifted flour
1	teaspoon salt	1½	teaspoons baking soda
1	teaspoon vanilla	1½	cups buttermilk
2	eggs		

Cream sugar with shortening until light and fluffy. Add salt and vanilla; beat in eggs. Sift together cocoa and flour. Dissolve soda in buttermilk. Add flour to creamed mixture alternately with buttermilk. Bake in 2 greased and floured 9-inch cake pans at 350⁰ for 30 minutes. Let cake stand 5 minutes before removing from pan; then turn out on wire rack to cool.

Linda Juba

Frosting for Devil's Food Cake

2	(1 ounce each) squares baking chocolate	3-4	tablespoons cold coffee
1	stick margarine	1	teaspoon vanilla
3½	cups powdered sugar	1	cup pecan halves

Melt chocolate; cool. Cream margarine with powdered sugar, add melted chocolate, coffee and vanilla. Mix until light and fluffy. Place pecan halves between layers on frosting as well as garnishing top of cake.

Linda Juba

Fudge Nut Upside Down Cake

3	tablespoons butter or margarine	3	tablespoons cocoa
3	tablespoons brown sugar	1	cup sifted flour
1	cup chopped pecans	1	teaspoon baking powder
2	tablespoons Crisco		Dash of salt
1	cup white sugar	¾	cup milk
1	egg, separated	1	teaspoon vanilla

Melt butter and stir in brown sugar and pecans. Put in bottom of a greased 9-inch round cake pan. Cream Crisco and sugar. Add unbeaten egg yolk. Sift together cocoa, flour, baking powder and salt. Add alternately with a mixture of milk and vanilla. Beat egg white until stiff. Fold in egg white. Pour on top of sugar and pecan mixture. Bake 30 minutes at 350°. Turn out on cake plate while hot. Serve with whipped cream.

Eloise McIntosh

Cream Cheese Chocolate Chip Cupcakes

FILLING:

1	(8 ounce) package cream cheese	1⅛	teaspoons salt, divided
1	egg	1	(6 ounce) package chocolate chips
⅓	cup sugar		

CAKE:

1½	cups flour	1	cup water
¼	cup cocoa	⅓	cup Wesson oil
1	teaspoon baking soda	1	teaspoon vanilla
1	cup sugar	1	teaspoon vinegar

TOPPING:

Sugar	Chopped nuts

Combine cream cheese, egg, ⅓ cup sugar, ⅛ teaspoon salt and chocolate chips and beat well. Set aside. Sift together flour, cocoa, 1 teaspoon salt, 1 cup sugar and baking soda. Add water, oil, vanilla and vinegar and beat well. Fill paper baking cups ⅓ full. Put 1 heaping teaspoon cream cheese filling mixture on top. Top with sugar and chopped nuts. Bake at 350° for 30 to 40 minutes. Makes 22-24 large cupcakes.

Irene Howland

☆   ☆   ☆

Karen's German Chocolate Cupcakes

Sinfully Rich!!

1	(4 ounce) package German Chocolate	1¾	cups sugar
2	sticks butter (do not substitute)	4	eggs, beaten
		1	teaspoon vanilla
2	cups flour	1½	cups pecans, chopped

Preheat oven to 300°. Melt chocolate and butter. Cool. Dump flour and sugar in bowl. Add eggs, chocolate mixture, vanilla and nuts; stir gently. Grease and flour muffin pans (do not use cupcake liners). Fill pans ½ full. Bake for 30 minutes. Turn cupcakes out on rack to cool when done.   *Linda Juba*

Louisiana Chocolate Pound Cake

CAKE:

2	sticks margarine	3	cups flour
½	cup shortening	½	teaspoon salt
3	cups sugar	1	cup milk
5	eggs	2	teaspoons vanilla
½	cup cocoa	1	teaspoon butter flavoring
½	teaspoon baking powder	1	cup pecan halves

ICING:

1	cup sugar	¼	cup water
3	tablespoons cocoa	1	teaspoon vanilla

CAKE: Cream margarine, shortening and sugar. Add eggs one at a time, beating well after each. Sift cocoa, baking powder, flour and salt. Add to mixture alternately with milk. Start and end with dry ingredients, beating well. Grease and flour tube pan. Pour batter into pan and press pecans on top covering entire cake. Bake at 325° for 1 hour 15 minutes to 1 hour 30 minutes, or until cake tests done. Do not overbake. Serves 10-12.

ICING: Boil sugar, cocoa, water and vanilla for 1 minute. Punch holes in cake with ice pick and pour boiled mixture over hot cake. Cool completely before removing from pan.   *Pat Bailey*

☆   ☆   ☆

Cranberry Holiday Cakelets

¾ cup flour
½ teaspoon salt
½ teaspoon baking powder
2 cups fresh cranberries
1 (8 ounce) package chopped pitted dates

3½ cups pecans
2 eggs
¾ cup sugar
1 teaspoon lemon extract

Sift flour, salt and baking powder together. Combine cranberries, dates and pecans with flour mixture in large bowl. Toss until evenly coated. Beat eggs, sugar and extract together until fluffy; add to flour mixture and mix thoroughly to coat fruit and nuts. Preheat oven to 300°, fill muffin tins or fluted paper liners ⅔ full. Bake 45 to 50 minutes. Cool in pan 15 minutes, remove and cool thoroughly. May be wrapped and stored in refrigerator for 3 weeks or frozen up to six months. Makes 12.

Gail McAda

Cajun Cake

CAKE:
2 sticks margarine
4 eggs
1½ cups flour
2 cups sugar
½ cup cocoa

1 cup coconut
1 cup black walnuts, finely chopped
1 (6½ ounce) jar marshmallow creme

ICING:
1 stick margarine
1 tablespoon vanilla
1 (16 ounce) box powdered sugar

½ cup cocoa
½ cup milk

CAKE: Mix margarine, eggs, flour, sugar, cocoa, coconut and walnuts in large bowl. Pour into well-greased and floured 13x9x2 inch pan. Bake at 350° for 20 to 25 minutes. Remove from oven and spread with marshmallow creme. Let cool; then ice.

ICING: Blend all ingredients with a mixer. Spread on cake.

Sue Johnson

☆　　☆　　☆

Old Fashioned Osgood Pie

2	cups sugar	1	teaspoon cloves
1	stick butter	1	teaspoon cinnamon
2	tablespoons white vinegar	1	cup pecans
4	eggs, separated	1	cup chopped dates

Mix sugar, butter, vinegar, egg yolks, cloves, cinnamon, pecans and dates. Add 4 slightly beaten (5 seconds or so) egg whites. Bake at 350⁰ for 35 minutes or until set. Makes 1 large deep dish pie. If egg whites are beaten too long the top crust of the pie will crack and break.

Jeanne Housely

Bourbon Pie

CRUST:

2	cups chocolate snaps crumbs	1	stick butter or margarine

FILLING:

21	large marshmallows	½	pint whipping cream
1	cup evaporated milk	3	tablespoons Bourbon

CRUST: Mix crumbs and melted margarine. Pat in 9 inch pie pan. Bake at 325⁰ for 8 to 9 minutes or microwave 1½ minutes on FULL POWER, turning once. Cool.

FILLING: Melt marshmallows in undiluted milk, but do not boil or microwave 3 minutes on ¾ POWER. Chill. Whip cream and fold in marshmallow mixture. Add Bourbon. Pour into pie crust and refrigerate 4 hours or overnight. Top with whipping cream, if desired and garnish with chocolate curls. Serves 8.

Betty Stripling

Pineapple No-Cook Pie

1	cup powdered sugar	1	(6 ounce) can crushed pineapple, drained
1	(8 ounce) package cream cheese	1	cup chopped pecans
1	(3 ounce) container whipped topping	1	(9 inch) graham cracker crust

Cream sugar and cream cheese together. Fold in topping, pineapple and nuts. Put in graham cracker crust and chill.

Paula King

☆   ☆   ☆

No-Fail Tender Flaky Pie Crust

2	cups flour	⅓	cup tap water (not iced)
1	teaspoon salt		(May need up to 2
⅔	cup lard or ¾ cup		teaspoonsful more in a dry
	vegetable shortening		climate)

Mix flour and salt in a 3 quart mixing bowl. With a wire pastry blender, cut in half of the fat very fine until it looks like corn meal. (This causes the pastry to be very tender); cut in remaining fat to size of very large peas (this causes pastry to be flaky). With a spoon or clothes sprinkler, add the measured water a tablespoonful at a time, tossing flour and water together as evenly as possible. Continue until all flour has been dampened and will barely hold together when pressed. (Too much water causes pastry to be less tender; too little causes it to be crumbly.) Shape gently into a firm ball; cover well and let rest 10 minutes. (This makes it easier to roll out so less handling is required.)

Flour canvas pastry cloth and stockinette-covered rolling pin as directed by manufacturer. (The less flour taken up by the pastry and the less handling of the dough, the more tender the crust.) Divide the pastry into two portions. (For double crust pie, the bottom crust should be slightly larger than the top.) Shape each portion into a firm ball. Place one ball on prepared pastry cloth, press down gently to flatten and roll out from the center in all directions with a light even pressure. This should result in an evenly shaped round piece of pastry. (Avoid rolling back and forth.) Determine thickness by your preference, but the circle of dough should be large enough so that it does not have to be stretched when fitted into the pan. Roll pastry onto the rolling pin to position it in the pie pan. (Or fold pastry in quarters, placing center point in center of pie pan and unfold.)

For one crust pie: Flute edge; cut off excess dough with a knife run around edge of pan. Prick bottom of crust liberally with tines of fork (to allow air entrapped under pastry to escape when heated and prevent bubbles) and bake on center rack of oven preheated to 425° until lightly browned, about 15 minutes. Place baked pie shell on cake rack to cool. Fill with cooked filling according to your recipe. (When baking filling in the pie shell as for custard, pumpkin and pecan pie, do not prick crust.)

For double crust pie: Position pastry for lower crust in pie pan as directed above. Do not prick. Roll out smaller piece of dough. Cut a design or gashes near center of pastry to serve as vents for steam to escape during baking. Fill lower crust according to your recipe. Moisten edge of lower crust with water; place top crust over filling; press to seal edges (to prevent leakage.) Crimp edges and bake as recipe directs.

Mary Cummins

☆　　☆　　☆

Party Pastry Triangles

1 cup flour	¼ cup butter
½ teaspoon salt	¼ cup hot water
1 tablespoon baking powder	1 tablespoon lemon juice
¼ cup vegetable shortening	1 egg yolk, beaten

Sift flour, salt and baking powder. Cut shortening into dry ingredients until shortening is in pea size lumps. Melt butter in hot water. Cool to room temperature. Add lemon juice and egg yolk. Add liquid to dry ingredients. Chill several hours. Roll ⅓ inch thick. Cut into triangles and prick with fork. Bake on ungreased sheet at 375⁰ until lightly browned. May be frozen baked or unbaked.

This resembles puff pastry. *Virginia Matzen*

Meringue

3 egg whites	3 rounded tablespoons sugar
⅛ teaspoon salt	1 teaspoon vanilla
¼ teaspoon baking powder	

Beat egg whites, salt, and baking powder until it forms stiff peaks. Gradually fold in sugar and vanilla. Put on cream pie. Spread meringue against edges of crust to prevent shrinking. Bake at 350⁰ until lightly browned, about 12 to 15 minutes. *Anna Wade Pierson*

Three Generation Sour Cream Raisin Pie

1 cup sugar	1 cup sour cream
½ teaspoon cinnamon	⅛ teaspoon salt
½ teaspoon ground cloves	2 tablespoons vinegar
2 eggs, beaten	Pastry for double crust (9 inch)
1 cup seedless raisins	pie

Mix sugar, cinnamon and cloves together well. Add to beaten eggs. Add raisins, sour cream, salt and vinegar. Mix well. Pour into pastry lined deep 9 inch pie pan. Moisten edges; add upper crust. Bake at 350⁰ until crust is golden brown, about 45 minutes. *Emma Lawton*
Mary Cummins
Eileen MacWithey

☆　　☆　　☆

TAIL GATE PICNIC
Texas Style

Driskill Hotel Cheese Soup

Gazpacho Dip   Salted Chips

Clark Gable's Pork Tenderloin

M. E.'s Crunchy Asparagus

Sour Cream Macaroni

Green Salad *featuring* Avocado Dressing

Herbed Bread Thins

Hot Dog Bun Bread Sticks

Strawberry Crêpes

Texas Stadium

Oh, your dream is to dine
On the fifty-yard line!
Texas Stadium is your—
Fantaisie du jour.

Roger Staubach is there.
Tom Landry takes a chair,
Dandy Don and Bob Lilly...
Oh, you know you're being silly...

Enjoy your fantasy. In Texas, the sky's the limit on dreaming. Who knows? Neiman Marcus may one day have a fantasy tailgate dinner in its famous Christmas catalog. Sports fans in Texas indulge their fancies at tailgate parties at Texas Stadium and numerous other sports arenas.

The Metroplex has four major league sports franchises. In addition to the Dallas Cowboys, the Texas Rangers play baseball, the Dallas Mavericks shoot basketballs and the Dallas Sidekicks score soccer goals. Amateur athletics, for individuals or teams, are big events from the college level to little league.

Texans take their sports as seriously as their food and love combining their favorites. From elaborate meals in posh suites to nachos and hot dogs in the stands, they munch while they watch.

The Cowboys won their first world championship in 1971, the first year they played in the new Texas Stadium. The opening event in the 63,855 seat stadium was a Billy Graham Crusade and it has housed many diverse events. Surely, it isn't too farfetched to fantasize a private dinner at the stadium under a star studded sky.

Indeed, champagne and candlelight...
You wish you may, you wish you might!

Recipes from **THE TEXAS EXPERIENCE**
prepared by

Chef René Peeters
Compliments of
The Grand Kempinski Hotel
Addison

Photography
Mike Flahive

Kentucky Pie

1	stick of margarine	1	cup chocolate chips (may reduce to ¾ cup)
1	cup sugar		
½	cup flour	1	cup nuts, chopped
1	teaspoon vanilla	¼-½	cup Bourbon
2	eggs, beaten	1	(9 inch) unbaked pie shell

Melt stick of margarine. Add sugar, flour, vanilla, eggs, chocolate chips, nuts and Bourbon. Pour into unbaked pie shell. Bake at 350⁰ for 30 minutes. Cook until toothpick or cake tester inserted in center of pie comes out clean. May be served with whipped cream.

Virginia Dennis

Red Raspberry Pie

Pretty for Valentine's or Christmas

RED FILLING:

2	(3 ounces each) packages red raspberry Jello	2	tablespoons lemon juice
2½	cups boiling water	2	packages frozen red raspberries (do not thaw)
½	cup sugar		

WHITE FILLING:

2	(8 ounces each) packages cream cheese	½	teaspoon salt
2	cups powdered sugar	2	packages Dream Whip
		¼	teaspoon vanilla

CRUST:

1	stick plus 2 tablespoons margarine	1	cup sifted flour
		1	tablespoon sugar

RED FILLING: Dissolve Jello in hot water. Add sugar, lemon juice and frozen raspberries. Stir gently, but well. Chill until partially set.

CRUST: Cut margarine and sugar into the flour. Press into 13x9 inch pan and bake 20 minutes at 350⁰. Cool.

WHITE FILLING: Cream sugar, cream cheese, salt, vanilla and ¼ of the whipped Dream Whip mix. Mix well. Fold in the remainder of the whipped Dream Whip. Spread mixture on cooled crust. Chill until cold. Top with Red Filling. Chill until serving time. This is a rich dessert so serves 12 amply. Cuts well.

Dottie Pinch

☆　　☆　　☆

Refrigerator Banana Split

CRUST:
1   stick melted margarine
2   cups crushed graham
     crackers

FILLING:
2   sticks cold margarine, do   1   teaspoon butter flavoring
     not soften   1   (16 ounce) box powdered
2   eggs   sugar
1   teaspoon vanilla

TOPPING:
4   bananas   Nuts
1   (15¼ ounce) can crushed   Maraschino cherries
     pineapple, drained
1   (8 ounce) carton Cool
     Whip

CRUST: Mix margarine and crumbs and press into 9x13 inch pan.

FILLING: Beat margarine, eggs, vanilla and sugar in electric mixer for
10 to 15 minutes. Spread on crust and chill.

TOPPING: Cover dessert with bananas sliced lengthwise in thin strips.
Sprinkle with crushed pineapple. Spread Cool Whip over pineapple layer.
Garnish with nuts and cherries. Serves 12.   *Marjo Jeanes*

Ruth Root's Chocolate Strata Pie

2   egg whites   2   egg yolks, slightly beaten
½   teaspoon vinegar   ¼   cup water
½   teaspoon cinnamon,   1   (6 ounce) package
     divided   chocolate chips
¼   teaspoon salt   1   cup cream, whipped
¾   cup sugar, divided   1   (9 inch) baked pie shell

Beat egg whites with vinegar, ¼ teaspoon cinnamon and salt. Add ½
cup sugar. Gradually beat until meringue stands in glossy peaks. Spread
on bottom and sides of pie shell. Bake at 350° for 15 to 18 minutes. Cool.
Add egg yolks to water and melted chocolate. Spread 3 tablespoons over
cooled meringue. Chill remainder. Combine ¼ cup sugar, ¼ teaspoon
cinnamon with the whipped cream. Spread half of mixture over chocolate
layer in pie shell. Combine remainder of whipped cream with chilled
chocolate mixture and spread over whipped cream layer. Chill 4 hours
prior to serving.   *Paula King*

☆   ☆   ☆

Lemon Cloud Pie

CRUST:
1	cup sifted flour	1	teaspoon grated lemon rind
½	teaspoon salt		
⅓	cup shortening	1	teaspoon lemon juice
1	egg, slightly beaten		

FILLING:
¾	cup sugar	1	cup water
¼	cup cornstarch	½	cup lemon juice
1	teaspoon grated lemon rind	1	(3 ounce) package cream cheese, softened
2	slightly beaten egg yolks		

TOPPING:
2	egg whites	¼	cup sugar

CRUST: Sift flour and salt. Cut in shortening until size of small peas. Combine egg, lemon rind and lemon juice; stir with flour mixture. Form into ball and roll out crust as usual. Few drops of water may be added if too dry. Bake 12 to 15 minutes at 400⁰.

FILLING: Combine sugar, cornstarch, grated lemon rind, egg yolks, water and lemon juice. Cook over medium heat, stirring constantly until thick. While hot add cream cheese. Blend thoroughly with beater. Scoop out into mixing bowl and cool thoroughly.

TOPPING: Beat 2 egg whites until stiff. Add ¼ cup sugar. Beat. Fold into cooled lemon filling; mix thoroughly. Pour into cooled crusts and refrigerate. Garnish with whipped cream and Angel Flake coconut if desired. Serves 6-8.

Sharon Odell

> Add sliced bananas to an egg white and beat until stiff. The bananas will disappear, leaving a delicious substitute for whipped cream.

☆   ☆   ☆

Mother's Pumpkin Pie

This recipe is at least 75 years old.

2	cups cooked pumpkin	½	teaspoon ginger
2	tablespoons melted butter	½	teaspoon allspice
1	cup sugar	1½	cups milk
½	cup dark corn syrup	2	eggs
½	teaspoon salt	1	unbaked 10-12 inch pie
½	teaspoon cinnamon		shell or 2 unbaked 8 inch
¼	teaspoon cloves		pie shells
½	teaspoon nutmeg		

Mix pumpkin, butter, sugar, syrup, salt, cinnamon, cloves, nutmeg, ginger, allspice and milk. Beat eggs well and add to mixture. Pour into pie shell. Preheat oven to 425⁰. Bake 10 minutes. Lower oven to 350⁰. Bake 50 minutes.

Mother's Note: This makes two pies if you use large cups.
Jean Zinser

Easy Peach Pie

2	(16 ounces each) cans freestone peaches	1	tablespoon lemon
½	cup sugar	¼	teaspoon nutmeg
2	tablespoons flour	½	teaspoon almond extract (optional)
Dash of salt		1	(9 inch) unbaked pie shell
2	tablespoons butter		

Drain ⅓ cup syrup from peaches into a pan. Add sugar, flour, salt. Cook until bubbly. Add butter, lemon, nutmeg and almond extract. Arrange peaches in pie shell. Pour sauce over peaches. Bake 40 to 45 minutes at 400⁰.
Valerie McMahan

Peach Pie

½	cup butter	3-4	peaches
½	cup flour	1	cup cream
1	cup sugar	1	(9 inch) unbaked pie shell

Mix butter, flour and sugar. Sprinkle half of mixture into 9 inch pie pan lined with pastry. Slice peaches into shell. Sprinkle remaining crumb mixture over peaches. Pour cream over all. Bake at 350⁰ for 45 minutes to 1 hour or until filling is set. Serves 6.
Eileen MacWithey

☆   ☆   ☆

Peach Sour Cream Pie

1 cup sour cream	2 tablespoons flour, divided
¾ cup brown sugar, firmly packed	2½ cups fresh sliced peaches
Pinch of salt	1 (9 inch) unbaked pastry shell
2 egg yolks	

Blend sour cream, brown sugar and salt. Whisk in well beaten egg yolks. Sprinkle 1 tablespoon flour on unbaked pie shell. Arrange peaches on pie shell and sprinkle with tablespoon flour. Pour sour cream mixture over all. Bake at 425⁰ for 10 minutes; reduce heat to 350⁰ and continue baking for about 40 minutes. Serves 6-8.   *Dot McCalpin*

Heavenly Calorie Pie

2   (8 ounces each) frozen
    Graham Cracker crusts

LAYER 1—Blend:

1 (12 ounce) container Cool Whip	1 (14 ounce) can Eagle Brand Milk
1 (8 ounce) package cream cheese	Divide into 4 equal parts

LAYER 2—Blend:

1 (3½ ounce) package sliced almonds	1 stick butter, melted
2 cups coconut	Divide into 4 equal parts

LAYER 3:

1 (8 ounce) jar butterscoth sundae topping.	Divide into 2 equal parts.

For each pie shell make layers in the following order.

Layer of number 1
Layer of number 3
Layer of number 2
Layer of number 1

Top with layer of number 2. Freeze. Very rich. Serves 12-16.

Helen O'Reilly

☆   ☆   ☆

Coconut Cream Pie

PIE FILLING:

6	tablespoons margarine	3	eggs, separated
⅔	cup flour	1	cup coconut
3	cups milk	1	teaspoon vanilla
½-⅔	cup sugar (depends on	1	baked pie shell
	sweetness desired)		

MERINGUE:

3	egg whites	⅓	cup sugar
¾	teaspoon cream of tartar	½	teaspoon almond extract

PIE FILLING: Use a 10-11 inch Teflon skillet. Melt margarine over low heat. Stir in flour and stir with rubber spatula. Cook 4 to 5 minutes. Meanwhile, heat milk to hot, but not quite boiling.

COCONUT CREAM PIE: May use microwave. Pour hot milk into roux. Cook over low heat until thick and creamy and add sugar. Cook 2 to 3 minutes longer. Beat egg yolks and add to milk. Cook 5 minutes longer. Add coconut and vanilla. Pour into prepared pie shell.

MERINGUE: Beat egg whites until frothy with cream of tartar. Add sugar gradually until stiff peaks form. Add extract. Spread meringue to edges of pie crust to seal. Bake at 400⁰ until lightly browned. *Ruth Quance*

Creme de Menthe Pie

Must be made 4 hours in advance

24	Oreo cookies	1	(7 ounce) jar marshmallow
¼	cup melted butter		creme
1	pint whipping cream	¼	cup Creme de Menthe

Place cookies in two large Baggies and crush with rolling pin, or crush in food processor or blender. Mix cookies with butter and press into 9x13 baking dish. Put aside a handful of crumbs to sprinkle on top. Whip cream and set aside. Whip marshmallow creme and Creme de Menthe together. Fold into whipping cream. Pour over crust. Cover with plastic wrap and freeze. Cut into squares to serve. Remove from freezer five minutes before serving. Can be made a week in advance. Serves 14-16. *Pat Cutler*

Frozen P-Nut Butter Pie

⅓ cup white Karo syrup
⅓ cup smooth peanut butter
2 cups Rice Krispies

1-2 pints coffee ice cream
Semi-sweet chocolate, shaved

Mix Karo and peanut butter well. Add Rice Krispies and mix well with wooden spoon. Press out in 9 inch pie plate to make pie shell. Spread ice cream in shell. Shave semi-sweet chocolate over top. Keep in freezer. Use within a day or two. You may freeze shell; then fill with ice cream at serving time. Serves 6-8. *Josephine Sears*

Variation: Substitute Pralines and Cream ice cream and drizzle with butterscotch topping before freezing. At serving time, add more topping and garnish with whipped cream and toasted almonds.

Lemon Custard Ice Cream Pie

CRUST:
1 cup flour
6 tablespoons softened
    margarine

¼ cup powdered sugar

FILLING:
2 eggs, beaten
¾ cup sugar
2 tablespoons flour
3 tablespoons lemon juice

1 teaspoon lemon rind
1 quart lemon custard ice
    cream

TOPPING:
1 cup whipping cream
2 tablespoons sugar

1 teaspoon vanilla

CRUST: Make shortbread crust by blending flour, margarine and sugar. Press mixture into bottom and sides of 9 inch greased pie pan. Bake at 350⁰ for 15 minutes. (325⁰ for glass pan).

FILLING: Mix eggs, sugar, flour, lemon juice and lemon rind. Pour over hot crust and bake 20 minutes longer. Remove from oven and cool completely. Fill crust with 1 quart lemon custard ice cream slightly softened. Freeze.

TOPPING: Beat whipping cream, sugar and vanilla until stiff peaks form. Swirl whipped cream over top of pie. Freeze at least 3 hours. Remove from freezer about 10 minutes before serving. *Zoe Thompson*

☆   ☆   ☆

Chocolate Almond Ice Cream Pie

2	cups chocolate wafer crumbs	1	cup toasted slivered almonds
⅓	cup butter, melted		Fudge sauce (see index)
½	gallon vanilla ice cream, softened	1	cup heavy cream, whipped
¼	cup Swiss Chocolate Almond liqueur		

Combine chocolate wafer crumbs with butter and press into 9 inch pie pan. Bake at 350⁰ for 8 minutes. Cool. Blend softened ice cream with liqueur. Fill pie shell and freeze for at least 2 hours. Pour ½ cup fudge sauce over pie. Refreeze. To serve top with whipped cream, additional fudge sauce and toasted almonds.   *Lynn Trentham*

Lemon Meringue Pie

Rates an A+

FILLING:

5	tablespoons cornstarch	3	egg yolks
1	tablespoon flour	2	tablespoons butter
2½	cups water	5	tablespoons lemon juice
1	cup sugar	1	(9 inch) baked pastry shell
¼	teaspoon salt		

MERINGUE:

3	egg whites	4	tablespoons sugar

FILLING: Mix cornstarch and flour in heavy enameled pan. Blend in sugar and salt. Add water and when well blended stir constantly over low heat until thick and clear. Gradually pour hot mixture over slightly beaten egg yolks, stirring constantly. Return to heat and cook 2 minutes. Remove from heat. Add butter and lemon juice. Mix well. Cool. Pour into pie shell. Cover with meringue.

MERINGUE: Beat egg whites to peaks, gradually beat in sugar. Pile on pie; seal edges. Bake at 325⁰ for 15 minutes.   *Marge Veerman*

☆   ☆   ☆

Date Sticks

1½ cups flour, divided	2 teaspoons baking powder
1 (8 ounce) package pitted dates, chopped	1 cup chopped nuts
	1 teaspoon vanilla
1½ cups sugar	4 eggs

Use ¼ cup flour to dredge dates. Sift 1¼ cups flour with sugar and baking powder. Add eggs and vanilla and beat until mixed. Fold in nuts and dates. Pour into a greased 8x8 inch pan and bake at 275⁰ for 40 to 50 minutes. Cool. Cut into rectangular bars, roll in powdered sugar and serve. *From a 1923 Texas Cookbook*

Dream Bars

CRUST:

1 stick butter, softened	1 cup flour

FILLING:

½ cup coconut	½ teaspoon baking powder
1½ cups brown sugar	½ teaspoon salt
¾ cup chopped nuts	2 eggs
2 tablespoons flour	1 teaspoon vanilla

FROSTING:

1½ cups powdered sugar	2 tablespoons orange juice
2 tablespoons softened butter	1 tablespoon lemon juice

CRUST: Lightly coat 9x9 inch pan with Pam. Cream butter and flour together until smooth. Spread in pan and bake 12 to 13 minutes at 350⁰.

FILLING: Mix coconut, brown sugar, nuts, flour, baking powder, salt, eggs and vanilla together. Spread on baked crust and bake 25 minutes at 325⁰. Cool.

FROSTING: Cream powdered sugar with butter, orange juice and lemon juice. Spread on cool bars. Makes 16 bars. *Vicky Nayes*

☆　　☆　　☆

Creme de Cacao Balls

No Baking

2½ cups (18-24) Oreo cookies
1 cup chopped pecans
1 cup powdered sugar
⅓ cup Creme de Cacao
2 tablespoons dark corn syrup

Crush cookies. If blender is used, put 6-8 cookies in blender at a time. May use rolling pin or food processor to crush if desired. Blend cookies, pecans, powdered sugar, Creme de Cacao and syrup together. Form into 1 inch balls and roll in powdered sugar. Refrigerate. Balls will absorb sugar. Before serving roll ball again in powdered sugar. Makes approximately 100 balls. *Patti Henry*

Sin City Bars

Delicious Both Ways

1 (18.5 ounce) box German Chocolate cake mix
¾ cup butter, melted
1 (14 ounce) package Kraft caramels
¼ cup milk
1 (12 ounce) package chocolate chips
1 cup finely chopped pecans

Mix cake mix with butter and spread in 9x13 inch pan. Bake 350⁰ for 10 minutes. Melt caramels in milk. Pour over cooled crust. Sprinkle chocolate chips and pecans over melted caramels. Bake at 350⁰ for 5 to 10 minutes until chocolate melts. Cool before cutting. Serve plain or with Cool Whip or ice cream. Bars freeze well. *Hat Madsen*

Variation: Increase milk to ⅔ cup. Melt caramels with ⅓ cup milk. Combine cake mix, melted margarine, remaining milk and pecans. Press ½ of cake mixture into 13x9 inch pan and bake 6 minutes at 325⁰. Take out of oven and immediately sprinkle chocolate chips on top. Then pour melted caramel mixture over top. Press remaining cake mixture on top. Bake 15 to 19 minutes at 325⁰. *Elizabeth Gross*

☆　☆　☆

Hershey Cookie Bars

2	cups flour	1	egg
1	cup brown sugar	1	cup butter
½	teaspoon vanilla	1	(8 ounce) Hershey bar

Mix flour, brown sugar, vanilla, egg and butter and pat on cookie sheet. Bake 25 to 30 minutes at 350⁰. Break Hershey bar in chunks and sprinkle on top of mixture. Put back in oven and melt. Cut while warm. Rewarm if necessary to cut. Easy to overcook.

Variation: Cover with 1 cup finely ground nuts before cutting into squares.   *Gail McAda*

Orange or Lemon Slices

DOUGH:

2	cups flour	1	egg
½	teaspoon baking powder	½	teaspoon vanilla
⅓	cup sugar		
1	stick plus 1 tablespoon butter		

FILLING:

5	ounces ground almonds	Juice of 1 orange or 1 lemon
¾	cup sugar	1 egg yolk, beaten

Grated rind of 2 oranges
   or lemons

ICING:
1   egg white
Enough powdered sugar to
   make spreadable icing

DOUGH: Combine flour, baking powder and sugar. Knead in butter; add egg and vanilla and knead into dough. Allow to rest 30 minutes.

FILLING: Mix all ingredients thoroughly.

ASSEMBLY: Divide dough into two portions. Roll out into 2 thin rectangles. Spread one rectangle with filling. Top with 2nd rectangle. Prick dough. Bake at 350⁰ for about 30 minutes or until done. Cool.

ICING: Combine ingredients and spread on top. Cut into slices.
                                                    Kyra Effren

☆   ☆   ☆

Raspberry Kuchen

2	sticks margarine	4	cups flour
1	cup sugar	1	teaspoon salt
3	eggs, beaten, plus milk to make 1 cup	2	teaspoons baking powder
		1	pound raspberry jam

Cream margarine and sugar together. Beat eggs and milk together. Sift flour, salt and baking powder together. Mix all ingredients; roll out half the dough. Place on greased 10x15 inch cookie sheet or jelly roll pan. Dough is soft, so can be rolled in pan. Cover with raspberry jam. Roll remaining dough; cut in ½-inch strips and make lattice top. Bake at 375⁰ about 25 minutes. Makes 25 small squares.

Anna Wade Pierson

Meringue Topped Brownies

BROWNIES:

½	cup Crisco	⅔	cup flour
¾	cup sugar	⅓	cup cocoa
1	egg	½	teaspoon baking powder
1	egg yolk	½	teaspoon salt
1½	teaspoons vanilla	½	cup chopped pecans

MERINGUE:

2	egg whites	¼	cup sugar
¼	teaspoon cream of tartar	¼	cup finely chopped pecans

BROWNIES: Preheat oven to 350⁰. Cream shortening and sugar. Add eggs and beat well. Add vanilla, flour, cocoa, baking powder, salt and pecans. Pour into greased 8x8 pan. Top with meringue.

MERINGUE: Beat egg whites with cream of tartar until foamy. Add sugar gradually. Beat until stiff. Add pecans. Spread over brownie mixture. Bake for 20 minutes. Do not overbake. Cool; cut into bars.

Millie Fiedorek

☆　　☆　　☆

Apricot Squares

⅔ cup dried apricots
½ cup butter or margarine
¼ cup white sugar
1⅓ cups flour, sifted and
    divided
½ teaspoon baking powder

¼ teaspoon salt
1 cup brown sugar, lightly
    packed
2 eggs, well beaten
½ teaspoon vanilla
Powdered sugar

Boil apricots 10 minutes. Drain, cool and chop. Mix butter or margarine, white sugar and 1 cup flour until crumbly. Spread into a buttered 8x8x2 inch pan. Bake at 350⁰ for 25 minutes. Sift remaining flour, baking powder and salt. Beat brown sugar and eggs. Stir in flour mixture, vanilla and apricots. Spread over baked layer. Bake an additional 30 minutes at 350⁰. Cool in pan. Cut in squares. Let stand at least 8 hours. Roll in powdered sugar before serving.   *Lynne Karp*

German Cream Cheese Brownies

4 ounces German Sweet
    Chocolate
5 tablespoons butter,
    divided
1 (3 ounce) package cream
    cheese
1 cup sugar, divided
3 eggs

½ cup plus 1 tablespoon
    flour, divided
1½ teaspoons vanilla, divided
½ teaspoon baking powder
¼ teaspoon salt
½ cup chopped nuts
¼ teaspoon almond extract

Melt chocolate and 3 tablespoons butter over low heat and set aside to cool. Cream remaining butter with cream cheese until smooth. Add ¼ cup sugar. Beat until fluffy; blend in 1 egg, 1 tablespoon flour and ½ teaspoon vanilla. Reserve. Beat 2 eggs until thick and add remaining ¾ cup sugar, beating until thickened. Add baking powder, salt and remaining ½ cup of flour. Blend in cooled chocolate mixture, nuts, almond extract and 1 teaspoon vanilla. Set aside 1 cup of this chocolate batter. Spread remaining chocolate batter in a greased 9 inch square pan. Top with cheese mixture. Drop cup of chocolate batter from spoon onto cheese mixture, swirl to marble. Bake at 350⁰ for 35 to 40 minutes. Refrigerate if storing. Makes 20 brownies.   *Charlotte Clark*

☆   ☆   ☆

Chocolate Fudge Brownies

BROWNIES:

2	(3 ounces each) packages cream cheese	2	eggs
5	tablespoons butter or margarine	2	tablespoons flour
		¾	teaspoon vanilla
⅓	cup sugar	1	package Duncan Hines Brownie Mix, Family Size

FROSTING:

3	tablespoons butter or margarine	1½	cups powdered sugar
2	tablespoons cocoa	2	tablespoons milk
		1	teaspoon vanilla

BROWNIES: Soften the cream cheese and butter; beat together. Add the sugar, eggs, flour and vanilla; beat until smooth and set aside. Prepare the CAKE-LIKE brownie batter as directed on the package. Pour half the brownie batter into a greased 13x9 inch cake pan; pour all the cream cheese mixture over the brownie layer. Spoon the remaining brownie batter in spots over the top. Swirl the two mixtures together with a knife of spatula. Bake at 350° for 35-40 minutes. Cool and frost with recipe below.

FROSTING: Melt butter or margarine in a medium saucepan. Stir in cocoa until dissolved; add powdered sugar, milk and vanilla; add more milk if necessary to make a soft spreading consistency. Frost brownies; let set until firm.
Marjo Jeanes

Becky's Brownie Mix

Tour of Homes Recipe

4	cups flour	2½	cups cocoa
2	cups shortening	4	teaspoons baking powder
6	cups sugar	3	teaspoons salt

Cut shortening into flour. Add sugar, cocoa, baking powder and salt. Store in canister.

BROWNIES:

2	cups brownie mix	1	teaspoon vanilla
2	eggs, well beaten		

Combine brownie mix, eggs and vanilla. Pour in greased pan and bake at 350⁰ for 20 minutes.

Great for Christmas gifts!

☆   ☆   ☆

Hermits

Delicious Spice Bar

¾	cup shortening	1	teaspoon salt
1½	cups sugar	1	teaspoon cinnamon
¼	cup molasses	1	teaspoon ginger
2	tablespoons water	½	teaspoon cloves
2	eggs, beaten	1	cup raisins
3	cups flour	½	cup nuts, chopped
1	teaspoon baking soda	1	egg yolk, beaten

Cream shortening and sugar. Add molasses, water, and eggs. Sift flour, soda, salt, cinnamon, ginger and add to molasses mixture. Add raisins and nuts. Spread dough on ungreased cookie sheet. Glaze with beaten egg yolk. Bake at 350⁰ for 20 minutes. Cut into squares.   *Linda Juba*

Kit's Lemon Butter Cookies

2	sticks butter or margarine		Juice and rind of 1 lemon
1	cup sugar	2	cups flour

Cream butter and sugar. Add lemon rind and juice. Blend in flour. Drop by teaspoons onto ungreased cookie sheet. Bake at 350⁰ for 12 to 15 minutes. Makes 3 dozen cookies.   *Linda Juba*

Lace Cookies

1	cup sugar	1	egg, beaten
1	cup quick oatmeal	1	teaspoon vanilla
3	tablespoons flour	1	stick margarine, melted and cooled
¼	teaspoon salt		

Mix sugar, oatmeal, flour and salt. Add egg, vanilla and slightly cooled margarine. Refrigerate, covered, 4 hours or overnight. Drop by ½ teaspoons onto unbuttered heavy foil on a cookie sheet. Cookies spread to about 3 inches in diameter. Bake at 325⁰ for 12 minutes or slightly longer. Allow to cool on foil before removing.   *Mary Cummins*

☆   ☆   ☆

Butternut Chiffons

A Special Treat!

2	sticks butter or margarine	2	cups flour
1	(3¾ ounce) package chocolate pudding	½	cup chopped nuts
		3	crushed Heath Bars or ½
¼	cup powdered sugar		(7.8 ounce) package of
1	teaspoon vanilla		Bits of Brickle

Soften butter. Add pudding, sugar and vanilla. Beat well. Add flour, nuts and candy. Chill. Form into balls size of walnuts. Bake at 325⁰ for 12 to 15 minutes. Cool 10 minutes and roll in powdered sugar. Keep in covered container. Makes 2½-3 dozen balls.   *Virginia Matzen*

Pink Iceberg Cookies

Beautiful and Delicious!

½	cup butter	1	egg yolk
½	cup plus 2 tablespoons sugar	1	cup sifted flour
		½	teaspoon baking powder

TOPPING:

1	cup ground nuts	3	tablespoons raspberry jam

ICING:

3	tablespoons lemon juice		Red food coloring
2	cups sifted powdered sugar		

Cream butter, sugar and egg yolk until light and fluffy. Add flour and baking powder. Beat until blended. Chill. Turn out on waxed paper; press into 4 balls. Roll ¼ inch thick. Cut into rounds about ¾ inch in diameter. (Can use spice jar top as cutter.) Bake on ungreased cookie sheets about 10 minutes at 350⁰ until delicately browned. Cool. Cookies may be frozen at this stage, but not after topping has been put on. Makes 5 dozen small cookies.

TOPPING: Mix ground nuts and raspberry jam. Place small mounds of mixture on each cookie.

ICING: Mix lemon juice and powdered sugar until it is spreading consistency. Tint delicate pink and drizzle over topping.   *Sharon Odell*

☆   ☆   ☆

Glazed Apple Cookies

Oh-So Good!

COOKIES:

½ cup margarine	½ teaspoon ground cloves
1⅓ cup brown sugar	¼ teaspoon nutmeg
1 egg	¼ cup apple juice or milk
2 cups flour	1 cup chopped nuts
1 teaspoon baking soda	1 cup raisins
½ teaspoon salt	1 cup chopped raw apple, unpared
1 teaspoon cinnamon	

GLAZE:

1 tablespoon margarine	2½ tablespoons apple juice or milk
1½ cups powdered sugar	
⅛ teaspoon salt	¼ teaspoon vanilla

COOKIES: Thoroughly cream margarine and sugar. Add egg and beat well. Sift together flour, soda, salt, cinnamon, cloves, nutmeg; add to the creamed mixture alternately with liquid. Stir in nuts and raisins, fold in apple. Drop from spoon on greased cookie sheets. Bake at 400° for 10 to 12 minutes. Remove cookies from pan at once and cool on cake rack. Cookies are very tender while warm. Makes 24 five inch cookies.

GLAZE: Cream margarine and sugar, add salt. Stir in liquid and add vanilla. Glaze while cookies are hot. *Maggie Pearce*

Microwave Sand Dollars

1 cup butter or margarine	2 cups sifted flour
½ cup powdered sugar	2 cups finely chopped pecans
½ teaspoon salt	
2 teaspoons vanilla	

Cream butter and sugar. Add salt, vanilla, flour and pecans and mix well. Chill dough for 2 hours. Roll scant tablespoons of dough in hand, shaping into balls. Place 12 balls on ungreased microwave cookie sheet and cook on ½ POWER for 5 to 6 minutes. When almost cool, roll in powdered sugar.

☆ ☆ ☆

Cheesecake Dream Cookies

⅓ cup light brown sugar, firmly packed
1 cup unsifted flour
½ cup chopped walnuts
5 tablespoons butter, melted
1 (8 ounce) package cream cheese, softened

¼ cup sugar
1 egg
2 tablespoons milk
1 tablespoon lemon juice
1 teaspoon vanilla

Preheat oven to 350⁰. Grease an 8 inch square pan. In small bowl mix sugar, flour and walnuts. Stir in melted butter until well combined. Reserve ⅓ cup crumbs. Pat remaining batter gently into pan. Bake 12 to 15 minutes. Meanwhile in small electric mixer bowl at medium speed beat cream cheese and sugar until smooth. Beat in egg, milk, lemon juice and vanilla. Pour over crust; sprinkle in remaining crumbs. Bake 25 minutes longer until set. Cool on wire rack. When cool cut into 2 inch squares. Cut each square diagonally in half. Makes 32 cookies. (About 85 calories per cookie).   *Dottie Pinch*

Praline Kisses

1 egg white
1 cup brown sugar

2 cups chopped pecans

Beat egg white until stiff. Gradually beat in brown sugar. Remove beaters. Fold in pecans and stir until well coated. Drop from teaspoon onto greased cookie sheet. Bake at 350⁰ for 8 to 10 minutes. Should barely turn from white to light brown. Makes 2½-3 dozen cookies.
Anna Wade Pierson

French Macaroons

1 egg white
¼ pound almond paste
6-7 tablespoons extra-fine fruit sugar

Candied cherries

Beat egg whites slightly and add to almond paste. Mix until well blended. Add sugar gradually. Place in pastry bag and force through large star tube onto oiled cookie sheet. Decorate by placing a small piece of candied cherry in center of each. Bake at 325⁰ about 12 minutes or until light brown. Remove from cookie sheet while still hot. While still hot brush with syrup made by boiling equal parts of sugar and water together until liquid is clear. Makes 30 macaroons.   *Melissa MacWithey*

☆   ☆   ☆

Yugoslavian Jelly Cookies

DOUGH:

1	cup sweet butter	2½	cups flour
½	cup sugar	1	cup tart jelly, such as
1	egg yolk		blackberry
½	teaspoon salt		

MERINGUE:

4	egg whites	¾	cup finely ground walnuts
1	cup sugar	1	cup chopped walnuts

DOUGH: Cream the butter and sugar; add egg yolk, salt and flour. Make a 1½ inch foil collar to go around the cookie sheet as if you were making a soufflé. Pat the cookie dough onto the cookie sheet. Spread with jelly.

MERINGUE: Beat egg whites, adding sugar gradually until stiff peaks form. Fold in ground walnuts. Swirl over jelly. Sprinkle with chopped walnuts. Bake at 350⁰ for 40 minutes.   *Paula King*

Melting Moments

COOKIE:

⅔	cup cornstarch	⅓	cup powdered sugar
1	cup sifted flour		
1	cup butter, (do not substitute)		

ICING:

¼	cup soft butter	2	tablespoons grated lemon rind
2	cups powdered sugar		
2	tablespoons lemon juice		

COOKIES: Sift cornstarch and flour together; combine with butter and powdered sugar. Drop from a teaspoon on greased cookie sheet and bake at 350⁰ about 15 minutes. Do not brown.

ICING: Cream butter and sugar with lemon juice and lemon rind. Frost after cookies have cooled slightly. These cookies freeze well.*Pat Knott*

☆   ☆   ☆

Meringue Coconut Macaroons

3	egg whites	1	cup coconut
1	cup sugar	1	cup nuts, chopped
2	cups Post Toasties		

Whip egg whites until firm. Gradually add sugar and beat in. Add Post Toasties, coconut and nuts and mix well. Drop from spoon onto greased cookie sheet and bake for 15 minutes at 350° or until light brown. Makes 36 cookies.   *Edna Sherrill*

Grandma O's Ginger Crisp Cookies

¾	cup shortening	2½	teaspoons baking powder
1	cup sugar	1	teaspoon cinnamon
¼	cup Grandma's molasses	¼	teaspoon salt
1	egg	½	teaspoon ginger
2¼	cups sifted flour	⅛	teaspoon ground cloves
¼	teaspoon soda		

Cream together shortening and sugar until light and fluffy. Add molasses and egg and mix well. Mix flour, soda, baking powder, cinnamon, salt, ginger and cloves. Sift in dry ingredients and mix thoroughly. Chill in refrigerator 2 hours. Form into 1¼ inch balls. Roll in granulated sugar. Bake 2 inches apart on greased cookie sheet at 375° for 10 to 12 minutes. About 4 dozen cookies.   *Irma O'Malley*

Chocolate Haystacks

No Baking Required!

1	(6 ounce) package chocolate chips	½	cup peanut butter
1	(6 ounce) package butterscotch chips	1	cup chopped pecans
		2	(1½ ounces each) cans potato sticks

Melt chocolate chips, butterscotch chips, and peanut butter. Stir in pecans and potato sticks. Drop from teaspoon onto wax paper. Refrigerate. Makes 4½-5 dozen cookies.   *Anna Wade Pierson*

☆   ☆   ☆

Chocolate Cheese Drop Cookies

Super Yummy

1½   cups sugar
½   cup margarine
½   cup vegetable shortening
1   (3 ounce) package cream
     cheese
1   egg, beaten
2   tablespoons milk
1   teaspoon vanilla

½   teaspoon salt
2   squares (1 ounce each)
     unsweetened chocolate
2½   cups flour
1½   teaspoons baking powder
½   cup chopped pecans
Pecan halves

Cream sugar, margarine, shortening and cream cheese. Add beaten egg, milk, vanilla and salt and mix well. Melt chocolate over hot water; stir into batter. Sift together flour, baking powder; add a little at a time, mixing well. Stir in chopped nuts. Drop from teaspoon onto greased baking sheet. Place half of a shelled pecan on top of each. Bake at 350⁰ for 12 minutes. Makes 6 dozen.   *Linda Richardson*

Mrs. Williams's Icebox Cookies

3   sticks butter or margarine
2   cups sugar
2   eggs
1   teaspoon vanilla

4   cups flour, sifted
½   teaspoon salt
1   cup nuts, chopped

Cream butter and sugar. Beat eggs with vanilla and add to creamed mixture. Add flour, salt and nuts. Form into logs, about 2 inches in diameter. Roll in plastic wrap or aluminum foil. Chill or freeze until firm. Slice thinly. Bake on ungreased cookie sheet 350⁰ for 8 to 12 minutes.

An English lady shared this recipe with my cousin and it is the best icebox cookie recipe I've ever had.   *Linda Juba*

☆   ☆   ☆

Drop Brownies

1	stick butter or margarine	1	cup sifted flour
1	cup granulated sugar	½	teaspoon baking powder
2	eggs, beaten	¾	teaspoon salt
1½	teaspoons vanilla	1 or 1½ cups broken pecans	
2	(1 ounce each) squares unsweetened chocolate, melted		

Cream butter and sugar. Add eggs, vanilla, melted chocolate and blend well. Sift flour, baking powder and salt together and stir into creamed mixture. Add nuts. Drop by ½ teaspoonsful on lightly greased cookie sheet. Bake at 350⁰ for 10 minutes. Makes 4-5 dozen.

Darlene Nossaman

Fruit Cake Cookies

Easy

1	pound dates	4	eggs
¾	pound candied cherries	1	teaspoon cinnamon
¾	pound candied pineapple	1	teaspoon nutmeg
½	pound seedless raisins	1	teaspoon allspice
1	cup Bourbon	3½	cups sifted flour
½	cup butter	3	teaspoons baking soda in 3 tablespoons milk
1	cup sugar		
½	cup brown sugar	1-1½ pound pecans	

Cut up dates, cherries and pineapple. Add raisins and soak overnight in Bourbon. Cream butter and sugar. Add eggs and beat well. Sift cinnamon, nutmeg and allspice with flour. Alternately add flour mixture with liquid and soda mixture. Fold in fruits and nuts. Drop by teaspoonsful on greased cookie sheet. Bake at 300⁰ for 15 minutes. Makes a huge batch of cookies. Store in air tight container to keep soft and fresh.

Thecia Faulkner

☆   ☆   ☆

Sugar Cookies

1	cup sugar	1	teaspoon vanilla
1	cup powdered sugar	1	teaspoon cream of tartar
1	cup butter or margarine	1	teaspoon baking soda
1	cup vegetable oil	4	cups flour
2	eggs		

Cream sugar, powdered sugar, butter and vegetable oil. Add eggs and vanilla. Beat and add cream of tartar, soda and flour which have been sifted together. Form into balls and place on ungreased cookie sheet. Flatten with a glass that is dipped each time into granulated sugar. Bake at 350° for 10 to 12 minutes. Yields 9 dozen.   *Eloise McIntosh*

Old Fashioned Tea Cookies

Remember Grandma's?

1	pound margarine	5	cups flour
2	cups sugar	2	teaspoons vanilla
2	eggs, beaten		

Cream margarine and sugar. Add eggs. Add flour, a small amount at a time, with vanilla. Dough should be stiff. Form into 3 or 4 log rolls and refrigerate or freeze. Slice and bake at 350° on greased cookie sheet for 8 to 10 minutes. Edges will be brown. Sprinkle tops with sugar before or after baking.   *Dolores M. Spence*

Grab a Goober Cookie

½	cup peanut butter	1	egg
½	cup shortening	¾	teaspoon baking soda
½	cup white sugar	2	teaspoons baking powder
½	cup brown sugar	1¼	cup flour

Cream peanut butter with shortening, white sugar and brown sugar. Add egg. Add soda and baking powder to flour and sift. Add gradually to other mixture. Form into balls and press both ways with tines of a fork. Put on greased sheet and bake 8 to 10 minutes at 350°. *Betsy Gibson*

☆　　☆　　☆

Dish Pan Cookies

No Bake Goodies

1	cup sugar	2	cups peanut butter
1	cup white Karo syrup	6	cups Sugar Frosted Flakes

Mix sugar and syrup and boil one minutes. Add peanut butter and Sugar Frosted Flakes. Drop by teaspoons onto wax paper. Makes 5-6 dozen cookies.   *Barbara England*

Salted Peanut Cookies

Great

1	cup shortening	1	teaspoon baking soda
1	cup white sugar	1	teaspoon baking powder
1	cup brown sugar	3	cups oatmeal
2	eggs, beaten	1	teaspoon vanilla
1½	cups flour	1	cup salted peanuts

Cream shortening and sugars. Add beaten eggs. Mix well. Sift flour, soda and baking powder together. Add to creamed mixture. Add oatmeal, vanilla and peanuts. Mix well. Drop by teaspoonsful on greased cookie sheet. Bake 12 minutes at 350⁰. About 7 dozen cookies.   *Marjo Jeanes*

Oatmeal-Date-Nut Cookies

Daddy's Favorite

1	cup butter	1	teaspoon baking soda
1½	cups brown sugar	1	teaspoon vanilla
2	eggs	½	cup coconut
2	cups flour, divided	½	cup walnuts
1	pound chopped dates	1	cup rolled oats

Cream butter and sugar. Add eggs and beat well. Use ½ cup flour to dredge dates. Reserve. Add remaining flour, soda and vanilla. Fold in coconut, dates, nuts and oats. Drop by teaspoonsful on greased cookie sheet. Bake 10 to 12 minutes at 350⁰. Makes 5 to 6 dozen. These keep very well. They are better a day or two after baking.   *Ivanette Dennis*

☆   ☆   ☆

Date Cookies

1	cup margarine	1	teaspoon vanilla
1	cup brown sugar	1½	cups flour
1	cup white sugar	½	teaspoon salt
3	eggs	1	teaspoon cloves
2	(8 ounces each) packages	1	teaspoon baking soda
	chopped dates	2	teaspoons cinnamon
1	cup chopped nuts	1	teaspoon nutmeg

Grated rind of 1 orange

Mix margarine, brown sugar, white sugar, eggs, dates, nuts, orange rind and vanilla in large bowl. Sift together flour, salt, cloves, soda, cinnamon and nutmeg and add slowly. Mix well. Drop dough about the size of a walnut onto greased cookie sheet. Bake at 350⁰ for 7 to 8 minutes. Do not bake too long. Let sit a few minutes before removing from sheet. Dough may be frozen. Makes 6-7 dozen cookies.   *Mary Rode*

Meltaways

1	cup butter	¼	cup melted butter
1	cup cottage cheese	¾	cup sugar
2	cups flour	1	tablespoon cinnamon

Blend the butter, cottage cheese and flour together and chill for 30 minutes. Divide dough into three parts and roll out in a circle. Mix melted butter, sugar and cinnamon together and spread on dough. Cut dough in small pie-shaped pieces and roll from wide end to center. Bake at 400⁰ for 20 minutes on ungreased cookie sheet. Ice with thin powdered sugar icing. Makes about 30 little pastries.   *Marge Alesch*

Orange Pecans

3	cups sugar	1	tablespoon grated orange
1	cup water		rind
⅓	cup orange juice	4	cups pecan halves

Cook sugar, water and orange juice to soft ball stage. Let cool. Stir until creamy. Add orange rind and pecans. Drop on buttered cookie sheet.
           Mary Bonfoey

☆   ☆   ☆

Swedish Nuts

1	pound pecan halves	¼	teaspoon salt
2	egg whites, stiffly beaten	1	stick butter
1	cup sugar		

Toast pecans until light brown about 30 minutes in 300⁰ oven. Make meringue with egg whites, sugar and salt. Fold in pecans. Melt butter in 9x13 pan, spread nut mixture over butter. Return to oven for 30 minutes or until butter is absorbed. Stir often.   *Doris Trcka*

Variation: Add ½-1 teaspoons cinnamon.

Variation: Substitute ¾ cup brown sugar for white sugar.

Apricot Balls

1	pound dried apricots	Grated rind of 1 orange
1	cup sugar	Juice of 1 lemon
Juice of two oranges		1 cup nuts

Chop apricots. Add sugar, orange juice, orange rind and lemon juice. Cook 10 minutes. Add nuts. Cool. Form into bite-size balls, roll in powdered sugar.   *Maurine Montgomery*

Variation:

1	pound dried apricots	2	tablespoons water
1	whole orange	2	cups pecans
2	cups sugar		

Grind apricots. Chop up whole orange. Add apricot and orange mixture. Bring sugar and water to a boil. Add apricot-orange mixture and pecans. Cook about 7 minutes, stirring constantly. Cool. Roll into balls. Dip in granulated sugar.

☆   ☆   ☆

Almond Roca

1	pound butter	1	teaspoon baking soda
2	cups sugar	6	ounces chocolate chips or
1	cup water		milk chocolate bar
1	teaspoon salt		
3	cups chopped almonds, divided		

Bring butter, sugar, water and salt to a soft ball (240°). Add 2 cups chopped almonds. Boil to soft crack stage (290°). Add soda, remove from heat, and pour into greased pans. Spread into a layer ¼ inch thick. Cover with chocolate chips or grated milk chocolate bar. When melted, spread evenly over top. Chop remaining almonds finely. Sprinkle over candy. When cooled and chocolate has set, break into pieces. Makes about 1 pound. *Eileen MacWithey*

English Toffee

½	cup whole unblanched almonds	3	ounces semi-sweet chocolate
2	cups butter or margarine	5	ounces milk chocolate
2½	cups sugar		

Spread almonds in a shallow baking pan. Bake in a 350° oven until lightly browned, about 10 to 12 minutes. Chop finely while warm; cool. Lightly butter a shallow-rimmed 10x15 inch baking pan and set aside. Combine butter and sugar in a heavy 4 quart pan. Cook over medium heat until mixture boils, stirring hard with a wooden spoon to blend butter and sugar. Then cover with a tight-fitting lid and cook for 3 minutes. Remove pan lid and continue cooking, stirring frequently as mixture thickens until temperature reaches 290° on a candy thermometer (about 6 minutes). Pour into buttered pan and set on a flat surface to cool, about 30 minutes at room temperature. Put both the chocolates in the top of a double boiler and melt over hot water, stirring until smooth. Spread the chocolate over the toffee in the pan and sprinkle at once with the almonds. Cool or refrigerate until chocolate sets. Turn out of pan and break into irregular pieces. Pack in shallow containers and refrigerate until needed. Yield: 2¼ pounds. *Carolyn Stanphill*

☆ ☆ ☆

French Chocolate Balls

2 (6 ounces each) packages
semi-sweet chocolate
pieces
¾ cup sweetened condensed
milk

½ teaspoon almond extract
⅛ teaspoon salt
2 teaspoons cocoa
2 teaspoons instant coffee
2 tablespoons sugar

Melt chocolate over hot water. Stir in condensed milk, almond extract and salt. Pour into wax-paper-lined 8-inch square pan. Chill 30 minutes or until firm enough to hold. Shape into small balls and roll in mixture of cocoa, coffee and sugar.   *Joan Pesce*

Forever Amber Confections

1 (14 ounce) package orange
slice candy
1 cup flaked coconut

1½ cups chopped nuts
1 (14 ounce) can Eagle
Brand milk

Chop orange slices. Mix with other ingredients and bake in a 9x13 baking pan for 25 minutes at 300⁰. Cool. Make into balls and roll in powdered sugar or coconut.   *Pearl Stewart*

Buttermilk Fudge

6 cups sugar
3 cups buttermilk
1 stick butter
1 tablespoon vanilla

1 (12 ounce) package
chocolate chips
2 cups chopped nut meats

Combine sugar and buttermilk in a very large pan; cook, stirring constantly, on medium heat to soft ball stage (235⁰). Remove from heat and add butter, vanilla and chocolate chips. Beat until slightly hardened, adding nuts a few at a time. Pour into 11x14 inch buttered pan.
Charleye Conrey

☆   ☆   ☆

Penuche Fudge

2 cups white sugar
2 cups firmly packed brown sugar
3 tablespoons white corn syrup
1½ cups whipping cream

Dash of salt
2 tablespoons butter
1 teaspoon vanilla
1-1½ cups chopped pecans

Butter sides of heavy pan. Combine white sugar, brown sugar, syrup, cream and salt. Boil to a 234⁰-235⁰ soft ball stage. Remove from stove and add butter. Cool. Add vanilla and pecans. Beat until fudge starts to turn light in color. Drop by teaspoons onto wax paper or pour into greased 9x13 pan.   *Marge Veerman*

Fannie May Fudge

1 cup whole milk
4 cups sugar
1 teaspoon vanilla
2 sticks butter, do not substitute
25 large marshmallows, cut up

13 ounces milk chocolate, cut up
1 (12 ounce) package semi-sweet chocolate chips
2 ounces unsweetened chocolate, cut up
1 cup nuts, optional

Mix milk, sugar, vanilla and butter together. Boil this mixture for 2 minutes. Turn off heat; add cut up marshmallows and stir until melted. Add chocolates, one kind at a time. Stir rapidly until melted. Add nuts now, if desired. Put into two 9x13 pans or one 12x16 jelly roll cake pan, greased with butter. Wait until fudge is set before cutting.
Kay Wunderlich

Old Fashioned Cracker Jack

6-7 quarts popped corn and peanuts
2 cups packed brown sugar
2 sticks margarine, melted

½ cup light syrup
1 teaspoon salt
1 teaspoon vanilla
1 teaspoon baking soda

Pour popcorn and peanuts in a large well-greased roaster pan. Boil brown sugar, margarine, syrup and salt for 5 minutes. Add vanilla and soda. Stir mixture into popcorn and peanuts. Bake 1 hour at 250⁰ stirring every 15 minutes. Pour onto counter and separate with hands. Store in air tight container.   *Marge Grogg*

☆   ☆   ☆

Buckeyes

2	pounds creamy peanut butter, room temperature	3	pounds powdered sugar
1	pound butter, room temperature	2	(12 ounces each) packages chocolate chips
		½	bar paraffin

Mix peanut butter and butter together with powdered sugar until smooth texture develops. Form small balls the size of "buckeyes" (or large, shooting type marbles). Refrigerate balls. Next, melt slowly the chocolate chips and paraffin together in the top of a double boiler or heavy saucepan. Using a toothpick, dip cold "buckeyes" into chocolate until ⅔ covered. Let dry on waxed paper. The golden-brown tip bulges out over the chocolate skirt and looks just like a chocolate dipped nut. If you touch up the toothpick hole, no one will be the wiser until the first bite. Makes 166 candies.   *Carolyn Stanphill*

Peanut Butter Drops

1	cup sugar	1	teaspoon vanilla
1	cup white Karo syrup	4	cups Special K cereal
1	(16 ounce) jar crunchy peanut butter		

Mix sugar and Karo and bring to a boil. Add peanut butter and mix well. Remove from stove and add vanilla. Mix well and add cereal, stirring carefully. Drop by teaspoons on waxed paper and cool. Makes about 4 dozen candies.

This is the favorite after-school treat at my house.   *Sharon Odell*

Homemade "Reese" Candy

1	cup crunchy peanut butter	1	cup Graham cracker crumbs
2	sticks butter, melted		
1	(16 ounce) box powdered sugar	1	(12 ounce) package chocolate chips

Mix peanut butter, butter, powdered sugar and graham cracker crumbs. Spread in a jelly roll pan. Melt chocolate chips and spread on top. Chill and cut into squares.   *Carole Price*

☆　　☆　　☆

INDEX

A

ALCOHOLIC BEVERAGES

NOTES

NOTES

Richardson Woman's Club
P.O. Box 831963
Richardson, Texas 75083-1963

Please send _____ copies of THE TEXAS EXPERIENCE.
Retail price $16.50 each
Postage & handling   2.50 each
Texas gift wrap   1.50 each
(Texas residents   Make checks payable to
add tax)   1.36 each   THE TEXAS EXPERIENCE

Total per Book $ _____   Total enclosed $ _____

Please Mail To:

NAME _____

ADDRESS _____

CITY _____ STATE _____ ZIP _____

- -

Richardson Woman's Club
P.O. Box 831963
Richardson, Texas 75083-1963

Please send _____ copies of THE TEXAS EXPERIENCE.
Retail price $16.50 each
Postage & handling   2.50 each
Texas gift wrap   1.50 each
(Texas residents   Make checks payable to
add tax)   1.36 each   THE TEXAS EXPERIENCE

Total per Book $ _____   Total enclosed $ _____

Please Mail To:

NAME _____

ADDRESS _____

CITY _____ STATE _____ ZIP _____

- -

Richardson Woman's Club
P.O. Box 831963
Richardson, Texas 75083-1963

Please send _____ copies of THE TEXAS EXPERIENCE.
Retail price $16.50 each
Postage & handling   2.50 each
Texas gift wrap   1.50 each
(Texas residents   Make checks payable to
add tax)   1.36 each   THE TEXAS EXPERIENCE

Total per Book $ _____   Total enclosed $ _____

Please Mail To:

NAME _____

ADDRESS _____

CITY _____ STATE _____ ZIP _____

Please list names and addresses of your favorite stores where you would like to see THE TEXAS EXPERIENCE sold.

. . . .

. . . .

. . . .

. . . .

Please list names and addresses of your favorite stores where you would like to see THE TEXAS EXPERIENCE sold.

. . . .

. . . .

. . . .

. . . .

Please list names and addresses of your favorite stores where you would like to see THE TEXAS EXPERIENCE sold.

. . . .

. . . .

. . . .

. . . .